OUTSIDE VERDICT

AN OLD KIRK IN A NEW SCOTLAND

HARRY REID

SAINT ANDREW PRESS
EDINBURGH

This book is dedicated to Andrew McLellan
– fine man, fine minister, fine friend

First published in 2002 by
SAINT ANDREW PRESS
121 George Street
Edinburgh EH2 4YN

ISBN 0 7152 0799 7

The author wishes to record his grateful thanks for assistance from the Baird Trust during the preparation of this book.

The authorial views expressed in this book are those of Harry Reid alone. The opinions expressed by the author and his interviewees do not represent the official views of the Church of Scotland, which can be laid down only by the General Assembly.

The extract on p. 74 from John Buchan, *The Thirty-nine Steps*, is printed by permission of A. P. Watt Ltd on behalf of The Lord Tweedsmuir and Jean, Lady Tweedsmuir; the extract from *The Lion in the North* by John Prebble published by Secker & Warburg. Used by permission of The Random House Group Limited.

While every effort has been made to verify the accuracy of previously published quotations and to obtain permissions where appropriate, the publisher will be pleased to rectify any omissions for future editions of this book.

British Library Cataloguing in Publication Data

A catalogue record for this book is available from the British Library.

Typeset by Waverley Typesetters, Galashiels
Printed in Great Britain by Creative Print & Design, Wales

OUTSIDE VERDICT

CONTENTS

❖

FOREWORD

❖

This book looks at the situation, state and prospects of Scotland's national church. Respectively, I regard these as dire, confused and hopeful.

Andrew McLellan commissioned this book when he was Moderator of the General Assembly. In his opening sermon at St Giles Cathedral, Andrew said: 'Forty years ago, the churches in Canada did a brave thing. They invited an unbelieving journalist called Pierre Berton to take a long look at them from the outside and then write a book. His book was a terrible condemnation of complacency; and, while I remember little else of it, the title is with me yet: *The Comfortable Pew*. Oh Church of Scotland, have you the courage to do the same: to invite some shrewd analyst to put your dreams, your aspirations, your very life to exacting examination? However valuable it is to examine ourselves, we might learn a great deal more from listening to the honest assessment of those who look at us with fresh eyes. I would be so pleased if such a project could somehow be born in my year of office.'

I have to confess that I was unaware of this sermon, preached in May 2000, until three months later, when Andrew contacted me to ask if I was prepared to be his 'shrewd analyst'. He knew that I had just intimated my desire to stand down as editor of *The Herald*, although I had agreed to stay in office until my successor was appointed and ready to take over. This invitation led me to have several discussions with Andrew and with Finlay Macdonald, the Principal Clerk to the General Assembly. I immediately expressed enthusiasm for the project, which I thought was eminently worth-while; but I was not sure if I could undertake it. There were many reasons for my hesitancy; but, right from the beginning of our conversations, I said that the writer of the proposed book would require to deploy a seemingly contradictory mixture of humility and arrogance, in equal measure.

Humility, because an outsider examining the Church of Scotland would be quite wrong to approach it with anything other than humility. It has its faults, of course, but it is a church in which literally hundreds of thousands of good people are working very hard for completely unselfish ends, and only a poltroon could be unimpressed by such (albeit unfashionable) dedication and decency.

On the other hand, arrogance was also required because the proposed book would be worthless if it did not point out weaknesses and offer conclusions, some of them no doubt controversial and even offensive. Humility was necessary, but timidity would be ruinous – hence the arrogance. Indeed, arrogance might be putting it mildly; there is something almost insolent at the heart of this project, where an individual without any religious qualifications comes along and tells a venerable church just where it is going wrong.

Anyway, I was struck by the sheer reasonableness of Andrew and Finlay throughout our discussions. I was also struck by the bravery of the proposition: here was a church commissioning a subjective report that might well tell it all sorts of things it did not want to hear. So, eventually, I decided to accept. And, almost at once, I understood how prescient I had been in laying down the watchwords of arrogance and humility.

The wife of a friend, a committed Kirk member but by no means one of the *unco guid*, attacked me verbally in a Glasgow pub. My wife and I were having a pleasant evening with two former colleagues and their wives when this lady suddenly said to me: 'What on earth gives you the right to pontificate about the Church of Scotland? When did you last darken a church door? You're not even a member, for goodness' sake. Just who exactly do you think you are?'

I tried to deflect this onslaught by suggesting that neither the word 'pontificate' nor the word 'darken' seemed altogether appropriate in this particular context, but this ill-judged attempt at levity just made things worse. The tension was eventually defused, but the incident was salutary; it made me all the more determined to tread carefully as I set out on my journey.

Then I was confronted by another problem – time. Andrew, quite understandably, wanted the book to be produced as quickly as possible; but personal and work commitments meant that I was finally able to embark on the project full-time only at the end of July 2001. (I had, however, been able to spend the entire week of the 2001 General Assembly observing its proceedings closely, and Chapter 1 describes my somewhat mixed impressions.)

Because of the timescale that had been agreed with the Head of Publishing at Saint Andrew Press, the text had to be completed by January 2002. Thus, during the second half of 2001, I was working very intensively – almost too intensively – researching the background, interviewing many different people and at the same time writing the text. And so, if this book should seem disjointed or repetitious at any point, please forgive me; in extenuation, I can only say that the timetable was exigent. Not that this is a complaint; the experience of living the Church of Scotland, night and day, for six months was both invigorating and rewarding.

I found many things wrong with the Church of Scotland, and I have tried to describe these failings as I saw them, honestly and fairly; but I did not meet a single bad or unpleasant person connected with the Kirk. I don't think I could have written a sentence like that if I had been investigating, say, the Scottish legal profession or the Scottish medical profession or Scottish journalism.

I was particularly impressed by, and sympathetic to, the clergy, although I had been told that the current crop of Kirk ministers are intellectually weaker and generally less impressive than their predecessors. That may be so, but I found the ministers to be dedicated and pleasant people, if sometimes weary and embattled. I was received with kindness, patience and candour. I never encountered a Slope or a Chadband. Charlatans and bigots, cranks and rascals may exist within the ministry; but if they do, I was fortunate enough to avoid them. At the same time, I think that the ministry requires far more back-up than it is currently receiving, and this is developed as one of my main themes. The Kirk is running out of ministers, and I explore how more may be recruited; but meanwhile, those who are in the field desperately need support.

A little personal history might be useful. I was born in Glasgow into a churchgoing family, and I was baptised at Netherlee. When I was four, my family moved to Aberdeen, where my parents joined Beechgrove. Stuart McWilliam was the minister. My father was an elder, and became the church treasurer; my mother was active in the Guild. (She is now nearer 90 than 80. Every time I see her, she teases me about this project; she finds the idea of me writing a book about the Church of Scotland enormously funny.)

At Beechgrove, I had to attend Sunday school, which I didn't particularly enjoy. I certainly didn't learn much. I was happier when I was a little older and could sit through the entire morning service, for then I could hear the sermon. I'm afraid there was an element in this of the sermon as entertainment. I can't remember anything of what was said, but I do recall being at once comforted and shaken by the rigour of the preaching.

Stuart McWilliam was a superb preacher; he was also well connected within the Church and could invite up superstars from the south, such as George MacLeod, Prof. James Stewart (one of his predecessors) and Prof. Murdo Ewen Macdonald. They, and others, came to Beechgrove as guest preachers. The 1950s were fat and easy times for the Kirk; these men were assured and confident in their oratorical sweep. Beechgrove was a big church. The membership forty years ago was more than 1,500 – now it is less than 700. The church was usually packed, as I recall.

Then I went off to boarding school in Edinburgh, and I slowly began to lose interest in the Kirk, if not in religion. Chapel on Sunday evenings was enjoyable, particularly when there was a visiting preacher. Campbell MacLean from Cramond came occasionally, and we took to his irreverent and anti-establishment style. I don't know how he went down in Cramond, but he could certainly appeal to adolescent boys in whom anger and rebellion were stirring. Back in Aberdeen, I attended the Beechgrove youth fellowship from time to time, but this was purely for social reasons. I told my parents that I did not want to join the Kirk; they were disappointed, but they never made an issue of it.

I went to university in England and lost all connection with the Kirk, though I did go to the odd (in more senses than one) Anglican service. At this time, I became seriously interested in religious history; I was reading history, and I became fascinated by the Reformation and to a lesser extent the Counter-Reformation. I became intrigued by men like Luther, Cranmer, Knox and Loyola (though not Calvin) – hugely different figures, but all in their own ways titans.

Slowly, I learned about the Scottish Reformation, which was a revolution as well as a reformation – later and less bloody, but more far-sighted than reformations elsewhere. It was the greatest time in Scotland's history; but, even so, it was ultimately a missed opportunity, and it was to some extent wrecked by the aristocracy who did not like Knox's radical social ideas. Burns' phrase of much later, 'a parcel of rogues', springs to mind.

Then I went to Newcastle-upon-Tyne for nine months to learn how to be a journalist. I never once went to church there. I returned to Scotland and started my career; I went to church in Edinburgh once or twice, but subsequently any residual churchgoing habits were finally shed. Yet, whenever I had any influence in Scottish journalism, I tried to take religion seriously. This became less and less easy over the years, as religion in general, and the Kirk in particular, were moving off the news agenda.

I never joined a church and I hardly ever attended worship; but I did regard myself as a Christian and I have been willing, publicly, to bear witness, if that is the right phrase. I did some occasional book-reviewing, and this kept alive my interest in the Reformation period. One book in particular lingers in my mind: Heiko Oberman, *Luther: Man between God and Devil*, trans. Eileen Walliser-Schwarzbart (Yale University Press, 1989). This is a magnificent, if difficult, biography of Luther. (It is interesting that more books have been written about Martin Luther than about anybody else other than Jesus Christ.)

I also arranged for newspaper serialisations of books such as Stewart Lamont's biography of Knox and Ron Ferguson's biography of George MacLeod. I gutted, to use the trade term, both books for *The Herald* – chores that were among my more pleasant journalistic duties. Indeed, *The Herald* went to town on George MacLeod; when

Ron's biography came out, we organised a symposium on the great man, which created much interest.

And finally, I started Ron's column in *The Herald*, a column which I know has become a weekly treat for many Christians, and others, throughout Scotland.

Very many people have been kind, helpful and supportive to me in the preparation of this book. There is a long list of acknowledgements at the back – yet it is nothing like long enough. Ideally, I would have wished to talk to far more people. Nonetheless, this book is almost wholly based on my observations and conversations during an intensive period of research in the last few months of 2001, and to a lesser extent on my experiences during a journalistic career of thirty-two years in Edinburgh and Glasgow. The exception is Chapter 12, where I attempt some less detailed and more far-reaching reflections on religion in general rather than in Scotland specifically.

Here, I want specifically to thank the Faculty of Divinity at the University of Edinburgh, who generously elected me as a visiting fellow so that I could have their general support and, in particular, the use of the splendid library of New College as I wrote this book. I am happy to attest to the constant and at times almost excessive intellectual stimulation I have received from members of the faculty. The individuals at New College who have helped me most are listed at the end.

Three people have been especially supportive through the life of this project. Finlay Macdonald has the responsibility, more than anyone else, of keeping the Kirk show on the road. He has a lot to put up with, and he handles it all with steady good sense and gentle humour; over the last few months, he has had to put up with me too. I was about a third of the way through this book when I learned that he was to be the next Moderator of the General Assembly (the 2002 Assembly willing, of course). I was delighted, and I have tried not to add overmuch to his many burdens as his life has become even busier. I have found his astute and knowledgeable counsel invaluable. He has helped me enormously, but he has never tried to influence me or control me, even when he clearly found some of my ideas peculiar. The Kirk is exceptionally lucky to have such a sage and decent man at its helm.

Ann Crawford, Head of Publishing at Saint Andrew Press, has nursed this project with zeal, common sense and consummate professionalism. She cares deeply about the books she publishes, which alas is not always true in the world of publishing, even religious publishing. She is an exemplary publisher. More than any other individual, she has nurtured this book. I owe her a great deal, and I thank her in particular for her support, her diligence and her patience.

Finally, there is Andrew McLellan, whose book this is and to whom it is dedicated. He is responsible for it, as I have explained; but he is not responsible for its opinions, or indeed for any faults, errors or misjudgements. These are mine alone. He can, however, take credit for whatever merit it may have. He will, I know, disagree with some, perhaps with much, of it – and, over the many occasions when we have discussed my findings and my ideas, he has been scrupulous in his forbearance. He has always been kind. He is a very clever man, but he wears his scholarship and his knowledge lightly. He has guided me wisely, but he has never sought to take over the project he instigated, or even to influence me overmuch. He is, simply, a good man and a good friend. We both hope that this book may in some way help the Kirk to grapple with its many problems. I also hope that it may help to provide something lasting from his moderatorship. In any event, I am profoundly grateful to him.

HARRY REID
February 2002

GUIDE TO TERMS
AND MAJOR REFERENCES

———————— ❖❖ ————————

This is a somewhat opinionated guide, in alphabetical order, to various basic terms and designations used in the Church of Scotland (an arcane and complex organisation) and also to some 'shorthand' references I use in the course of the book.

'121'. Shorthand for 121 George Street, Edinburgh, the Kirk's grandiose administrative headquarters, home to most of its boards and committees, which report annually to the General Assembly. '121' is disliked by many who do not work there and even by some who do work there; it is often regarded as the repository of a byzantine bureaucracy. Various important figures work (very hard) there, including the Principal Clerk to the General Assembly, the Depute Clerk, the General Treasurer, the Solicitor of the Church, and the Clerk to the General Trustees. I say 'important'; but these senior servants of the Kirk have little, if any, managerial sway over the various boards and committees, which are accountable to the Assembly rather than to any executive figure.

Beadle. An excellent old Scots word meaning 'church officer'.

Cathedrals. The Church of Scotland uses some magnificent *pre-Reformation* cathedrals. These are subjective matters; but, in my opinion, the two most beautiful and awe-inspiring are St Machar's in Old Aberdeen and the bigger St Magnus in Kirkwall. The latter is arguably the finest building in all Scotland.

There are other Church of Scotland cathedrals at Brechin, Dornoch, Dunblane, Dunkeld, Edinburgh, Glasgow and Iona. Technically, the church of St Brendan at Birnie near Elgin, and the church of St Moluog on the isle of Lismore, are also cathedrals. Despite the fact that most of them are splendid buildings, I sense that, to this day, some people in the Church of Scotland are uneasy with their cathedrals, because cathedrals are supposed to be where bishops have their thrones.

Charge. Often used as shorthand for a parish. But, these days, one charge (and one minister) can cover several parishes.

Elders. Not a word I like; but we are stuck with it for the time being. Elders are ordained, for life. Some are elected by kirk sessions, others by entire congregations. They have a key role in the running of kirk sessions. They cannot take the sacraments of baptism and communion; but, in many other ways, they can support the minister and sustain the life of the congregation. They are involved in both the rule of the church and in spiritual and pastoral care.

There have been female elders since 1966, and some observers think that, in the long term, female elders will have a more powerful and progressive influence on the Kirk than female ministers. One of the big differences between a Presbyterian and an Episcopalian system is that Episcopalians see no place for elders in the governance of the church. (The other major difference is that Episcopalians have bishops – not a breed liked by traditional Presbyterians.)

General Assembly. The Kirk's supreme ruling body. It meets in Edinburgh, for a week each May. It is chaired by the Moderator of the General Assembly, who is usually elected for one year only. (There is no reason why a moderator cannot be re-elected.) The moderator is generally a male minister, although again there is no reason why the post shouldn't be held by a woman and/or an elder. It has become a matter of some notoriety in recent years that no women or elders have been elected, although nominations have included both.

The Assembly's home is a capacious if austere hall near Edinburgh Castle, designed by Edinburgh's greatest architect, David Bryce, in the middle of the nineteenth century. This hall was appropriated (not forcefully, but by agreement) by the new Scottish Parliament while its own premises were taking shape down the hill at Holyrood. This means that the Assembly has had to seek other venues. In 2001, it was held at the Usher Hall, Edinburgh.

The Assembly has about 800 members, known as commissioners. Most of them change each year; but some, for example former moderators, can attend annually. The membership is divided almost equally between ministers and elders. As a decision-making body, it is cumbersome and not wholly democratic. Reforming it is one of the most difficult and challenging tasks facing the Kirk.

Iona Community. Founded in 1938. It is, according to the late Cardinal Tom Winning, the nearest thing the Kirk has to a religious order. But it is ecumenical. Although it is based on the island of Iona, much of its work is done in Glasgow. It has a publishing imprint, Wild Goose Publications. Leaders have included its founder, the charismatic George MacLeod, and Ron Ferguson. The Rev. Norman Shanks has maintained its essentially left-wing profile. The Rev. Kathy Galloway takes over as leader on 31 July 2002.

Kirk. Used with a capital K, the word is shorthand for the Church of Scotland, which is a reformed church of the Presbyterian persuasion. With a small k, it means an individual church building or congregation.

Kirk session. The lowest court of the church; it rules the congregation. It meets in private and consists of the minister, who acts as its moderator, and elders. Some parishes also have congregational boards to deal with finance and administration, to allow the session to concentrate on spiritual and pastoral matters.

Knox, John. The one titanic figure of genuinely international status that the Kirk has produced; but it was the other way round: he produced the Kirk. He is someone the Kirk should learn to celebrate.

Levison, Mary (née Lusk). The list of women who have significantly influenced the Kirk is sadly exiguous (see Chapter 7); but that may change as a result of the efforts of this exceptional figure, who can take almost all the credit for the Kirk's decision to start ordaining female ministers in 1968 (and female elders two years earlier). She herself was not ordained as a minister until 1978.

Life & Work. The monthly national magazine of the Kirk. It has been invigorated by the spirited and notably independent editing of Rosemary Goring, who revived the authority it previously enjoyed during the distinguished editorship of Bob Kernohan between 1972 and 1990. It is highly profitable; but, unfortunately, it is not available in newsagents or bookstalls. The Kirk has been commendably responsible in eschewing the temptation to use it as a propaganda sheet.

Lord High Commissioner. The monarch's representative at the General Assembly. He or she listens to a very small proportion of the Assembly's actual deliberations, but arrives for the formal opening amid much pomp and ceremony. The LHC is emphatically not a member of the Assembly, but an invited guest. The LHC may not be a Roman Catholic (RC Emancipation Act, 1829). There seems little, if any, pragmatic meaning in the office; the monarch can hardly be effectively briefed about the proceedings of the Assembly by someone who is not present for most of them. Indeed, it seems to me that the Assembly is paid dubious respect by someone, however high, who listens to about ten minutes of a debate and then, conspicuously, leaves.

Manse. The minister's house, almost always tied. There is an enormous variety of shapes, sizes and situations. Manses tend to be unpopular with those who use them, the ministers and their families. In effect, 'manse' is the Scottish word for 'vicarage'.

Ministers. The clergy of the Kirk. As a reformed church, the Kirk presumably in theory believes in the priesthood of all believers; but does it believe in the *ministry* of all believers? Ministers, like elders, are ordained. They have various specific tasks. Conduct of worship locally is almost entirely devolved to the parish minister. Since 1968 (well ahead of the Church of England), the Kirk has ordained female ministers; but there are still, surprisingly and perhaps shamefully, few of them (a little over 150 serving in charges).

Moderators. It is not just the Assembly that has its moderator (chairman); so does each presbytery. Individual ministers act as moderators of their kirk sessions.

New College. The imposing building (by William Playfair) that accommodates the Faculty of Divinity of the University of Edinburgh. It is situated on a splendid site near the top of the Mound, high above Princes Street Gardens. In its impressive quadrangle is the famous statue of John Knox by John Hutchison, under which the Moderator of the General Assembly greeted the Pope in 1982.

The college is, and has been for some time, the intellectual pulse of the Kirk. But the college is emphatically not an adjunct of the Church of Scotland; it is multi-faith and ecumenical, with students and staff from more than thirty countries. The current Principal of New College is a Church of Scotland minister, while the Dean isn't; he is an American ecclesiastical historian. The college library is usually recognised as the best divinity and theological library in the United Kingdom.

Presbytery. An intermediary court between the supreme General Assembly and the local parish. The Kirk has forty-nine presbyteries, encompassing a huge variety, both numerically and territorially. Glasgow is the biggest, covering 153 charges. There is also a grand-sounding 'Presbytery of Europe', no less. There are ongoing proposals to cut the number of presbyteries drastically down to twelve or ten or even as few as seven superpresbyteries; but the fear is that this would just create a second tier of bureaucracy, replicating rather than replacing much of what goes on at 121. The Kirk used to have synods, but it abolished them in 1992. Presbyteries meet in public, generally once a month, and usually in the same venue, although one or two of them are peripatetic in a limited way. As with the Assembly, presbyteries have ministers and elders in more or less equal numbers.

Reformation. The momentous movement for theological and moral reform in the Western Christian church in the sixteenth century that led to the establishment of Protestant churches, particularly in Germany, Scandinavia, the Netherlands and Britain. Its defining figure was Martin Luther, who unfortunately did not have too much of a direct influence on the founding of the Kirk. Having said that, the stirrings of reform up and down the east coast of Scotland from the 1520s to the 1540s were inspired by the work of pioneering Lutheran theologians and preachers.

The greatest of these was the noble and numinous Patrick Hamilton, who was Scotland's first Protestant martyr and by far the nearest thing Protestant Scotland has had to a saint. Men such as Hamilton and George Wishart, another martyr, blazed the trail (in more ways than one) for John Knox (a much less saintly and much more rumbustious figure than Hamilton) and Andrew Melville, the two founding fathers of Scotland's national church.

It is a church that remains to this day a child of the Reformation, and that must always be remembered in any discussion of its situation and its prospects. It is Presbyterian in organisation and (essentially) Calvinist in theology, although its theology has probably been loosened more than its structure.

Saint Andrew Press. The publishing house of the Kirk. Founded in 1954, it is responsible for an impressively eclectic range of books (including this one). It publishes what I call the 'Big Red Book', the Kirk's excellent annual *Year Book*. The Press's most famous author is the late William Barclay CBE, the much-loved Biblical scholar whose New Testament commentaries have been phenomenal international bestsellers. They have been updated and were launched as the *New Daily Study Bible* series (at a ceremony in the Royal Concert Hall, Glasgow) by Saint Andrew Press in November 2001.

Without Walls. My shorthand for the Report of the Special Commission anent Review and Reform in the Church, to give it its full if hardly inspirational title. The fifteen-strong commission was appointed in 1999. It was convened by the Rev. Peter Neilson, associate minister of St Cuthbert's, Edinburgh, with the Rev. Iain Cunningham, minister of Kirkton, Carluke, as vice-convener. Its report, entitled *A Church Without Walls*, was an extended blueprint for renewal, which was to a large extent accepted by the General Assembly of 2001. Some in the Kirk thought that the proposals were very nebulous; others were convinced that they offered the only realistic hope of revival.

THE TWENTY-ONE
PROPOSALS

Although this book is about a church in crisis, I have tried to be positive rather than critical. Specific proposals are scattered through the book; most of them are fleshed out in some detail. No doubt, some of these proposals will be regarded as impractical, and others will be derided as ludicrous. No matter; they are offered in a spirit of goodwill, by someone who is genuinely concerned for the Kirk's future. The Kirk can sometimes react to fresh ideas or proposals with excessive caution or, worse, with world-weary lassitude. But it is not change that is the enemy. Fear of change is the real enemy, lurking with its snares just about everywhere. Luckily, there are also within the Kirk plenty of radical, forward-looking folk who are ready to embrace change. All strength to them.

I am absolutely convinced that the ideas and recommendations proposed in this book would, if adopted, help the Kirk towards significant renewal and revival. That is the great end. It might be useful to outline the *principal* proposals and recommendations here. Most of them are mine, and mine alone; but, in the course of my researches, other people would sometimes put forward ideas of their own, and these I have discussed in the text. These are also presented here, with the instigator's name mentioned (in parentheses). Credit, or blame, where it is due.

Proposal One. The Kirk should lead the way in a great revival of Easter as *the* Christian festival. If this involves a slight downgrading of Christmas, fair enough. The Kirk should organise mass rallies or services at Easter time, preferably outdoors, and deploy the talents of its great preachers (and it still has some world-class preachers) in an exciting, all-Scotland, evangelical enterprise. These Easter celebrations would be positive and joyous occasions; the Kirk could organise mass choirs to take part, and could use the talents of its most creative music-makers. And these could also be ecumenical events, with other churches being encouraged to join in; but the key thing would be that the Kirk would be leading the way.

Two. The office of Lord High Commissioner should be abolished forthwith. It is anachronistic, serves no useful practical purpose, and sends out all the wrong signals.

Three. All manses should be sold within a period of three to five years. I understand that there would be significant administrative, legal and tax difficulties to be overcome; but the prize would be enormous – several hundred million pounds of 'new money'. The interest on this vast sum could be used to pay each minister in the field a very generous annual property supplement, to be added to the stipend. There would still be interest left over to employ a large number of (much-needed) youth development workers, and to spend on some imaginative Christian artistic and creative projects.

I have found that many ministers and their families do not like their manses and would rather live somewhere else.

Four. All ministers and all elders should wear at all times a badge or emblem signifying clearly to the world that they are just that – ministers and elders. These are ordained people, which means that they are, or should be, different from the rest of us. Otherwise, why ordain them? This is not something to be afraid of. If it puts people off, they are probably not suitable for the ministry or eldership anyway.

I accept that the dog collar has become something of a joke, an 'I. M. Jolly'-type symbol. The emblems I have in mind would not be showy, but would be easily identifiable. There could be a nationwide competition to come up with the appropriate designs (possibly based on the cross, or the burning bush, or the holy rude) – one for the ministers, one for the elders. This would create much national interest and would also help to forge links with Scotland's artistic and creative community, which the Kirk has somewhat ignored.

Five. A principal official media spokesperson should be appointed as soon as possible. This would be a minister, who would serve at a very senior level and have access to all the committee and board reports and correspondence which cross the desks of the principal clerk and the depute clerk. Indeed, I would see this spokesperson as working directly alongside the principal clerk and the depute clerk.

Some, if not many, ministers understand and are very good with the media, and I can think of at least two who might shortly be available for this task; and this is an urgent matter. One beneficial consequence of this appointment is that it would free up others in the Kirk to speak out to the media on the clear understanding that they were not officially speaking for the Kirk.

The Kirk should also consider introducing a weekly press conference, with an open agenda. The media might not take much interest at first; but I guarantee that, within a few weeks, this would be a fixture in the diaries of the country's news editors.

Furthermore, there should be the parallel establishment of an ecumenical Scottish Churches' media office. This would act as a discipline for the various Scottish churches and denominations to find what they could agree on – they might be surprised – and would give the wider Scottish public a high-profile example of practical ecumenism in action. (Father Ken Nugent)

Six. The Church of Scotland should begin to develop outreach initiatives in difficult and even dangerous areas *at home* as opposed to abroad. Outreach is most urgently needed here, in Scotland, now. An example would be the creation of small, trained units which could be deployed in the pubs and streets of Glasgow and its environs in the aftermath of Celtic and Rangers ('Old Firm') matches, to try to explain that religion (and indeed football) should not be about sectarian hatred. This is exactly where Christian mission is most needed. Many Scots are unaware of the violent and sometimes murderous mayhem which attends these matches. The Kirk has a direct interest in sorting this out, as some of the perpetrators mistakenly believe themselves to be the foot soldiers of Protestantism.

On this theme, the Kirk should dissociate itself in every way possible from Rangers Football Club. Nobody should be able to make any direct or explicit connections between the two institutions (and they are both institutions).

At the same time, the Kirk should realise that a lot of its potential adherents in working-class Protestant neighbourhoods have been in effect unchurched; the Kirk needs to take some initiatives on behalf of these people, to show that it is punching its weight for them in civic Scotland and in the corridors of political power (see Dr Graham Walker, in Chapter 6).

Seven. The Church of Scotland should persuade the British–Irish Council to set up a major investigation into relations between Protestants and Catholics in both Scotland and Northern Ireland, and indeed in Ireland too. The Kirk should take a lead in setting the agenda for such a high-level investigation. (Dr Graham Walker)

Eight. The Kirk should commission some challenging and inspirational works of public Christian art to remind people that we remain, just about, a Christian country. I have particularly in mind really large public statuary. There are plenty of superb and innovative sculptors around in the new Scotland, and the Kirk should become an enthusiastic patron of modern Christian art. And if anybody tells me that this kind of thing is inimical to the Kirk's traditions, they should have a look at the artwork inside some of its most celebrated Victorian churches. Also, I would point out that the Kirk is quite happy to make use of some splendid pre-Reformation cathedrals.

Nine. The Kirk should develop special creative centres of excellence, including teams of its best ministers, possibly based at some of its finest churches and cathedrals. (Ron Ferguson)

Ten. The nature of the eldership should be radically reviewed. Elders should no longer be expected to serve for life, but for a period of, say, ten years. Elders should also be granted sabbaticals. Despite the unfortunate name, elders should be younger. The Kirk should consider paying elders a mini-stipend. Where is the money to come from? Back to proposal three.

Eleven. (And possibly most controversially.) The constitution of the General Assembly should be overhauled forthwith. At present, the Kirk's supreme body is cumbersome and not effectively democratic. It should be peripatetic. (This would directly benefit the wider Scotland as well as the Kirk.)

It should meet perhaps two or three times a year, over weekends, so that younger elders would find it easier to attend. Any obscure legal and administrative matters could be dealt with at biennial business assemblies. (Lynne Robertson)

To make the governance of the Kirk more democratic, plebiscites of all the ministers and elders should be held from time to time. (This would create enormous national media interest.) Even better: when the Kirk has worked out how many members it *really* has, there could be plebiscites of the entire membership. The Kirk is already more democratic than most churches, and in some ways its democratic structures have militated against efficiency. But, on balance, I think it should be prepared to embrace more democracy.

Conveners of the various boards and committees should be grilled, forensically and in public, by small, select committees of Assembly commissioners. (Very Rev. John Cairns)

Twelve. Although it is in some respects too introverted, the Kirk seems ignorant of itself – always a problem for any organisation, religious or secular. It should commission detailed research to find out exactly how many members it has, and what they want from the Kirk. It should also investigate, in depth, situations where there are congregations side by side, with one growing and the other declining. (Colin McClatchie)

This work would not necessarily be to give the people what they want, which is a denial of leadership, but rather to give the Kirk some detailed knowledge and understanding of its own members – something it appears to lack at the moment.

Thirteen. All members should be vigorously encouraged to tithe, that is, to give 10 per cent of their income to the Kirk (Donald Ross). This would be less urgent if proposal three were implemented; but, if tithing were *combined* with a sale of the manses, the Kirk's money worries would be over for ever. And tithing has more than pragmatic benefits; it is a means of emphasising spiritual as well as financial commitment.

Fourteen. 'Super Sundays' should be organised, when everybody going to church on a specific Sunday should be vigorously encouraged to return the following week with at least one relative or friend who had not been to church for some time. This effort could be backed by local advertising and marketing campaigns. (Alasdair Gibbons)

Having sampled a lot of Kirk worship all over Scotland over a period of a few months, I think many newcomers and returnees might be pleasantly surprised. And, apart from anything else, it is invigorating to worship in a full church – as I did twice, in Glasgow and Inverness.

Fifteen. A smaller point, but important nonetheless. Congregations should remember that it can be difficult for potential visitors to find out where a church is or when public worship is taking place. Churches of other persuasions seem to make much more of an effort to communicate this basic information. In this context, the lost sheep is more important than the regular attender. Locally, kirks should use all available information conduits much more effectively.

Sixteen. Most of the above points are more or less specific. This recommendation is vaguer, but very important. The ministers in the field – that is, in the parishes and in the chaplaincies – must be succoured and encouraged by everyone in the Kirk. They hold the key to revival. At present, too many of them are embattled, overworked and weary. They also complain, with justification, of isolation. The eldership, in particular, must learn to help their ministers more.

As for ministerial recruitment, congregations should do more. Most congregations must surely contain at least one or two potential ministers, possibly many more. These people should be encouraged by congregations to put themselves forward for the regular enquirers' conferences. Everyone in the Kirk should be encouraged to think and act on ministerial recruitment and retention – week in, week out – for it is the most immediate problem. The nature of the ministry will change in time; of course it will. But, at present, what has to be addressed is the desperate shortfall of ministers.

Seventeen. Slowly but surely, the Kirk should disengage from Edinburgh. Within five or six years, 121 George Street should be sold and the (smaller) headquarters operation should move to a more central and appropriate location, say Stirling or Perth, where comparatively cheap office accommodation could be rented on the outskirts of town.

Eighteen. Trained and *young* youth workers should be appointed to work with every larger congregation. In time, youth workers may become almost as important as the ministers.

Nineteen. Another more vague proposal. The Kirk should rediscover its past. Some of that past is shameful; the most obvious example is the anti-Irish racist campaign of the 1920s and 1930s, and the Kirk must not hide from the bad it has done. But much of its past is glorious, and it would help to renew confidence in its mission if people inside and outside the Church of Scotland became more aware of its immense contribution to the making of Scotland, a country which has, to its credit, done rather more good than bad in the world. The Kirk should emphatically not be afraid of its roots in the Reformation period, and it should learn to celebrate saintly figures like Patrick Hamilton and titanic figures like John Knox. Any organisation that is frightened of the past is frightened of the future.

Twenty. The number and size of the various central boards and committees should be pruned drastically. Many people I spoke to thought this should happen, sooner rather than later; but the first person to propose it directly to me was Prof. Steve Bruce, so I shall append his name at the end of this paragraph. There is an important psychological issue here: the Kirk has lost the ability to pare its central structures. As its membership declines, its centralised bureaucracy increases. This tendency must be reversed at once. (Steve Bruce)

Twenty-one. More pruning. To be fair to the Kirk, it has been cutting back on its overseas activities; but it needs to act more vigorously to shed non-priority operations. I have in mind, for example, its ministries in places like Bermuda, the Costa del Sol and Guernsey. To maintain these ministries when there are well over 150 vacant charges in Scotland is frivolous.

I'd like to add, as a kind of grateful afterthought to all this, that it says much for the Kirk that it allows its own publishing house to bring out a book that is proposing radical and difficult change, *as advocated by an outsider*. Whatever the Kirk does and does not do in the future, I wish it well. And a final thought: throughout his life, George MacLeod asserted that the Church of Scotland's best days were ahead of it. I agree.

INTRODUCTION

❖

Is the Church of Scotland in crisis? Of course it is. It is haemorrhaging members; it has lost 700,000 in the past forty years, and the loss is accelerating. In 1957, it had more than 1,300,000 members. Now it has barely 600,000. Even more worrying is the loss of ministers, the men and women who are the lifeblood of the Kirk. There has been an acute shortage for quite some time, and another 200 of them are due to retire soon, while qualified candidates for the ministry are coming forward at fewer than twenty a year.

Meanwhile, the Kirk is seriously overchurched; it has nearly 1,000 redundant buildings, many of them actual churches. Yet to close and sell a superfluous church can be a traumatic and deeply painful experience for loyal members who have loved that building. Such an action can test their commitment to the utmost.

And this failing organisation has an ever more bloated bureaucracy, with no fewer than twenty-seven centralised boards and departments and committees presiding over the decline. You can sit in the entrance lobby of 121 George Street in Edinburgh, the grandiose granite edifice that is the Kirk's headquarters, and watch committee men and women going in, and going out, in their very considerable numbers.

Now there is a new body, a Stalinist-sounding Central Co-ordinating Committee, to try to make sense of this profusion of panels and boards and teams. As the membership falls, the committees grow. You do not have to be Brain of Britain to work out that eventually, if these trends continue, there will be more committees than there are ministers; one day, indeed, there could be more committees than there are members.

There: that is the case for the crisis, as it were. But there is another story. My old friend Ron Ferguson, in the course of three protracted conversations I had with him in the cathedral manse of St Magnus, Orkney, told me repeatedly that I must not become 'hypnotised' by numbers and by the statistics of decline, or matters of structure and organisation. These were all ultimately irrelevant, he said; and he talked movingly of the creativity within the Kirk, and the potential which was as yet unleashed, and other such things.

But let me return to the negatives. The Kirk has lost confidence; it is failing to recruit enthusiastic new and young members; it is clearly irrelevant to many Scots, partly because it is not punching its (still considerable) weight, as one prominent layman told me, partly because of the uncertainty of its spiritual response to an aggressively secular, selfish and hedonistic society. Does it go with the tide or defy it? (There are dangers here of a serious split, if not an actual schism.) It does not know if it is, or wants to be, a national church any more; it speaks with many voices. It is almost too democratic. Its ministers, who should be its elite troops fighting the good fight, are often beleaguered and fatigued; its elders (unfortunate word), who should be its shock troops, are often felt to be unsupportive, sometimes to the point of being invisible.

To balance this once again, let me look at other positives. The Kirk is generous: its members may be fewer, but those who are left are giving more and more money. It is not scared to go into the bad places where so many others don't go, to succour the dispossessed and the bereft and the despised – the very people, as Andrew McLellan has so eloquently said, who will lead us to Jesus Christ. It still has great, if diffuse, intellectual energy. It has the huge benefit of the service of many seriously good people. It can still provide worship at which visitors are received warmly and the Word of God is preached powerfully and well. It is still respected, or, at worst, treated with indifference, in the wider Scotland; it is not hated or loathed, except by a tiny minority of aberrant bigots and mischief-makers. (Perhaps, perversely, you could argue that that is one of its problems – the Kirk has maybe been at its best, certainly at its strongest, when it has had overt enemies.)

And yet it seems to lack the will to gather and harness its significant remaining strengths, and to tell the Scottish nation about them, and to cohere as a honed and godly organisation. It does not seem proud, or even particularly aware, of its (for the most part) great and noble past, and of the good it has done in Scotland and beyond. It seems generally ignorant of John Knox, its founding father, a titan of a man who is still, more than 400 years on, internationally acclaimed, yet who has here within Scotland so often been traduced, absurdly, as a killjoy and a knave, or even worse.

The Kirk still has hundreds of thousands of members, in a small country of 5,000,000 people; and, of these members, more than 40,000 are ordained elders, who should surely be special people, chosen to give spiritual as well as social leadership. It is almost miraculous that the Kirk is *not* more influential in today's Scotland.

At times, during the intensive few months of research that I undertook in the preparation of this book, I became depressed. In purely secular terms, the Kirk should be the second most significant institution in our country, after our new Parliament – and that is a very new Parliament in an old country, a country that the Kirk has helped to nurture and develop for well over 400 years. And yet I was conscious of searching for something that wasn't there. Many of the parts were fine; but where was the whole? I, like so many of my fellow countrymen, could not find the Kirk; it was lost. I could find bits of it, good bits; but the Kirk itself seemed to have well-nigh disappeared.

So, there is much to worry about. But I think there is also ground for hope – enormous hope. In this book, if not in this Introduction, I make various proposals for renewal, proposals that if implemented might help to arrest the Kirk's decline. Some of these may be regarded as frivolous or irresponsible; some may be dismissed as impractical; some may be condemned as just plain silly. But they are offered with sincerity, after much thought. I hope that the readers of this book will at least examine these ideas with an open mind, and accept that my proposals are put forward in a spirit of constructive goodwill.

Of all the many folk I interviewed, inside and outside the Kirk, the one who most forcefully presented what might be termed the case for the prosecution was Steve Bruce, one of Britain's most eminent sociologists and a leading Scottish academic of impeccable credentials. For the past decade, he has been professor of sociology at Aberdeen University. He has made a specialised study of comparative religion, has written many books including *Religion in the Modern World* (Oxford University Press, 1996), and is currently working on a dictionary of sociology.

He has studied the Church of Scotland with special interest, and he was kind enough to give me an unpublished paper he had prepared on contemporary religious trends in Scotland. His prognostications for the Church of Scotland could hardly be bleaker. But, before we move to the particular, let us place his gloom in a more general but equally dark context – that of our pluralist, secular, postmodern world, which has been much analysed by sociologists such as Steve. Ironically, this world was to a large extent created by the great Protestant Reformation of the sixteenth century, which hastened the rise of individualism and rationality. There was nothing necessarily wrong with that, except that individualism threatened the communal basis of religious belief and behaviour, while rationality removed some of the point and purpose of religion and rendered many of its core beliefs implausible. (To be fair to the great Scottish reformer John Knox, he always wanted to instil what he would have called 'discipline' into the Scottish Reformation. He was concerned to develop social responsibility, and his blueprint for Scotland certainly did not envisage a country of individuals, each out for himself or herself – quite the opposite, in fact.) These powerful trends of individualism and rationality have been in evidence for over 450 years, but they have recently been accelerating at an exponential rate, to the extent that we in the West have now largely lost the reality of community.

We have, of course, gained as well as lost. The intellectual achievements of the Western Christian world over the past 500 years have been staggering. The Reformation helped to end the dark ages of the mind. The forces of intellectual repression and cerebral collectivism have not yet recovered from Martin Luther's incredibly courageous and far-reaching assault on them. But the downside, and it is a terrible downside, remains. Despite the fondness of certain modish politicians, and possibly of more sincere clerics, for invoking communal values, the view of Steve Bruce, a learned and far-sighted sociologist, is that a collection of individuals voluntarily associating is not a community.

His views might be too academically aggressive for some; but, after listening to him, I found it salutary that, every time I was writing the word 'community' in this text, I would stop and realise that I was not really sure what I meant by the word. It is a word that is probably overused – it is certainly overused by people in the Church of Scotland – and often wrongly invoked. Nonetheless, it does crop up occasionally in the chapters that follow.

In a paper delivered to an academic conference in Norway, Steve asserted: 'Even a deliberately formed community is not a community in the sense in which sociologists normally use the term . . . we can always walk away. The sovereign consumer of late capitalism is too self-regarding, too knowing, to step back into a condition of naïve sublimation to an organic whole.' This implies, to quote Steve once more, that we all live with what he calls 'the cancer of choice'. Again: 'Far from creating a world in which religion can thrive, diversity and competition undermine the plausibility of religion'. All this is crucially important. The Church of Scotland is operating in an environment that could hardly be more alien and – worse – more indifferent.

Now, having set the context, let us move to the particular. I went to see Steve in Old Aberdeen on a hot and languid August morning. The cloisters and courts of King's College were mellow in the sunlight, and when I found Steve's office he received me warmly. But what he had to say about the Church of Scotland was chilling. 'The Church of Scotland is not a sect, or a cult. It is a denomination. It has members, but it is on relatively easy terms with the rest of the world – but should it be? It doesn't require its members to be cut off from others around them, to be distinctive, to be different. Denominational religion is doomed: it is withering before our eyes. If you are a liberal Presbyterian, you have absolutely no pressing need to make your children share your beliefs: nothing will happen to them if they reject these beliefs.

'The line of membership will reach the bottom not very far from now. Where's the change, the uplift, to come from? People have been talking about reversing the trend for a long time; but, in trying to recruit new members, you may well be losing your existing ones. The Church of Scotland has become more liberal, more tolerant, more merged with the surrounding secular society. The Church of Scotland is not seen to be set apart, as say the Catholic Church is. The Catholic Church has huge problems, but at least it is seen to be different from the surrounding society. And I'm not sure you are going to get young people to join if you are constantly saying "We are not distinctive – we are building bridges to the secular world all the time".

'And does the Church of Scotland have a clear position? Does it have external or even internal cohesion? What does it believe? Does anybody in it know? I reckon that these days you can get into its ministry believing more or less anything you like. Its ministers believe many different things, and the Church will not tell you exactly what it is that its key people, its ministers and elders, must believe in.'

Steve went on to contrast the Kirk with the Catholic Church. 'The Catholic Church is clearly set apart. Its priests dress differently. They are celibate. They have rituals. And because they have rituals, they can get away with their very real disagreements over belief. You take the Mass – all sorts of different things are going on privately among the celebrants. The Church of Scotland should be a church founded on belief, presenting a religion of belief, not of ritual – yet it appears to lack core belief. Presbyterians do have collective acts of worship and they should have a distinctive lifestyle; but neither of these is central to Presbyterianism. The citizens of our secular society in Scotland may not understand why a Catholic fiddles with rosary beads, or goes into a confessional box, or lights candles, or kneels a lot, or goes to Mass regularly – but they have no trouble seeing these as religious rites. The net result is that when secular people – for example, film-makers – want to portray religion, they find it much easier to do so with the Catholic faith than with Presbyterianism.

'Another point is that most Scots, especially those under 60, have almost no knowledge of the history of their national church and no interest in it. I'm sure that the suspicion – generally ill-founded, it must be said – that Presbyterianism's recent past is nothing to be proud of must be an important factor. I'm very struck by the contrast with Finland. Although, like most Scots, most Finns are not personally religious, they do retain a considerable respect for their Lutheran national church and its heritage.'

I asked Steve if he had any prescriptions. 'More sectarianism', he said quietly. I looked up from my notebook in shock; there was just the flicker of a smile on his face. 'I'm serious', he said. He went on to explain that he was by no means advocating the *excesses* of sectarianism. 'But I am saying to the Church of Scotland: if you want to revive, don't keep trying to merge with surrounding society. Be different and be distinctive. Retrench, and become more conservative.'

I suspect that many people in Scotland, both Kirk members and non-members, will concur reluctantly with much of Steve Bruce's analysis. I also suspect that many others may find his prescription for renewal slightly provocative. Yet it was not too far removed from that of one of the more interesting ministers I encountered in my travels round Scotland, Derek Morrison of Gairloch in Wester Ross.

Derek told me: 'The Church of Scotland has many gifted people, but they are not always delivering what non-church people are looking for, which is authoritative moral and spiritual leadership. There is in our church great latitude given; there is a huge range of theological positions. But we would be helping all those around us if we were much clearer about the central issues in which we believe. More clarity is definitely needed. Doctrinal clarity is most important. What is the source of our authority? Christ came with Grace and Truth, and we don't always emphasise the Truth enough.

'We need courage, the courage not always to go with the flow. We need to be more of a counter-culture. We don't necessarily need to follow the world around us. Sometimes we have to say to the world, with compassion: You are going the wrong way. This approach can be caricatured; but we don't need to, and indeed we must not, use inflammatory language. I do believe that we have gone soft on the central issue of our faith: the uniqueness of Jesus Christ. Belief in Jesus Christ as the Son of God must be central in everything that we do.

'Maybe there has been too much fluidity in the Church of Scotland. We have got overmuch into the secular mindset, and I think this is particularly true when it comes to issues of sexual ethics and family life. The Church of Scotland does an enormous amount of good out there, but the church is not just about social action; it is about the motivation that lies behind that social action. So I say: we do need a consistent system of belief, particularly when the outside world is looking for moral and spiritual leadership. The church is here to deliver a propositional message, a message that must lie at the heart of our faith. We must do more than just peddle our own individual points.'

That is Derek Morrison's credo, and there is certainly no lack of clarity there. One of the themes he touched on was the diversity, the excessive diversity, in the Kirk. I come back to this point of almost self-indulgent democracy. A wide range of positions can be a strength; but it is not a strength if the Kirk is atomised, and it presents a disparate and disjointed face to the world, and there is no centralising, uniting force. A good example of this is the amazing diversity of Sunday services I attended. Derek himself preached for thirty-five minutes; some other ministers saw no need or point in preaching at all. At times, when I looked at the Kirk, I would think: this is the pick-'n'-mix church.

Derek is a relatively young minister, and he has not been in the Church of Scotland for long; until recently, he was a minister in the Associated Presbyterian Church. Ron Ferguson, on the other hand, has been a Church of Scotland minister for very many years, the last eleven of them in Orkney. By the time this book appears, he will have retired; when I spoke to him in Kirkwall, he was on the last furlong of a long and at times arduous journey in the service of the Kirk. He is a former leader of the Iona Community, and he also worked as a minister in Easterhouse, Glasgow. As an experienced and wise insider, his viewpoint could hardly be more different from that of Derek Morrison, the tyro insider, or Steve Bruce, the academic outsider.

'A lot of people would like a church that is clear and certain. But certainty can end up killing people, or anyway excluding them. It is fine to have certainty if you are not a gay, or you are not going through a painful divorce, for example. When I was much younger, when I was in Easterhouse, I used to take a hard line on baptism. A woman came to see me wanting her child baptised, and I said no, I don't think so; and then as I had a further conversation with her I learned that in every part of her life she had been rejected, and here I was rejecting her once again, and the Church was rejecting her through me.

'You need a church, and in terms of providing back-up for an organised church you need a ministry. But the church must not be the be-all and end-all. It is not an end in itself. That is Christianity. I know that what I call the fundamentalist wing is growing in strength, and I know that the fundamentalists like to present people with certainties. But I am uncertain about the answers to many fundamental questions. You are talking here about things that are almost beyond speech.'

In other words, the long and distinguished ministry of this compassionate and thoughtful man has led him to reject the very certainty that Derek Morrison is so eloquently seeking. Ron Ferguson is not exactly advocating diversity as an end in itself; however, he well understands that his views make dogmatic leadership very difficult. And certain and clear leadership might have the effect of driving out some of the Kirk's most caring and committed pastors.

My juxtaposition of these two utterly different viewpoints is artificial, but it is also valid because it has the merit of highlighting the acute dilemma at the very heart of the Kirk: its ministers, who are its local leaders, believe in wholly unrelated and diverse approaches to their calling. Here, in sharp relief, is its core problem. As long as this chronic and ongoing divergence of approach obtains, the Church of Scotland will be a multiform church, devoid of coherence. It will be relaying contradictory messages, not just in words but also in actions, to a complex and pluralistic society that has lost the concept and the reality of community.

At this point, for what I hope will be the one and only time in this book, I am going to cop out. I am not going to offer an opinion or a way forward. I am not going to say that the Kirk has to choose between compassion on the one hand and certainty on the other, or between mystery on the one hand and clarity on the other, although one day such choices may very well have to be made by the Church of Scotland as an entity.

I wish to conclude this Introduction by quoting, as an antidote to the eloquent and scholarly pessimism of Steve Bruce, the words of Marjory MacLean, one of the key people in the Kirk. She is depute clerk at 121 George Street; for six and a half years until November 1998 she was minister of Stromness in Orkney, and she is not unsympathetic to the evangelical position. She said: 'I'd be very, very sad if the Church of Scotland was so worried about arresting its decline that it took Steve Bruce's medicine, and became so distinctive that it could not communicate easily with our society, and instead became a kind of chaplain to those with extreme beliefs. I'd rather carry on doing the friendly and kindly things we are doing. The professor's solution is really for us to become a cult, and I think it's a horrifying one.'

WHERE'S THE CROSS?

❖❖

I want to present a few impressions of the General Assembly 2001. I watched the proceedings from an eyrie at the far end of the dress circle in the Usher Hall. (This vantage point was directly above where the former moderators sat, and observing their body language during the more obscure debates became something of a diversion for me.) This particular Assembly was characterised by Muriel Armstrong of *Life & Work* – it would be ungallant to describe her as a veteran observer, but she has brought her very shrewd eye to quite a few Kirk occasions – as unusually gentle and harmonious. For this, she gave most credit to the firm but patient moderating of John Miller.

Many commissioners told me that they thought the highlight came on the Monday, when the report of the Special Commission anent Review and Reform in the Church – or, as I shall call it, the *Without Walls* report – was debated. (To its shame, *The Scotsman* regarded this debate as the only one worth reporting during the whole week.) But I was grievously disappointed with this session. At first, I sensed that I was about to listen to an intensive, questing debate on a great institution which was desperately ill-at-ease with itself. Yet it soon dawned on me that I was not listening to a debate or even a dialogue of any kind, but just a series of isolated points that were being made from the floor. Furthermore, almost all of these points were made by men; it was as if the women of the Kirk had no say or interest in its future. It took fifty minutes, and ten different speakers, before the first woman was called.

No, the highlight for me came during the education debate. For a start, it was a genuine debate. Also, an intervention from the floor changed the Assembly's mind and saw the wishes of the convener of the Education Committee, Jack Laidlaw, overruled. The dramatic moment came when a young minister from Lanarkshire, Ian Watson, demanded that the Assembly should strengthen its approach to the Scottish Executive on the vexed issue of sex education. He made an impassioned plea on behalf of marriage – 'it works', he stated baldly – and said that sex education was being provided in the context of the one-night stand. He wanted sex education in Scotland's schools to give priority to marriage, to suggest abstinence from sex before marriage as a viable option and to stress the responsibilities of parenthood.

This was greeted with loud applause; but Convener Laidlaw demurred. He asserted that the Assembly (and by implication his committee) had 'to deal with the realities of where young people are'. The matter went to a vote, and Ian Watson's addendum was carried by 330 to 240. This, it seemed to me, went to the very heart of the Kirk's dilemma. Is it to go with the tide, and make its voice heard by accommodating the realities of the way people live now – or is it to make a stand? Meanwhile, here is a sketch of the week's proceedings.

The very first impression was not good. The Lord High Commissioner and his considerable party – the Lord Provost of Edinburgh, the Purse-bearer and many others from the ranks of the great and the good – arrived in the hall amid excessive pomp and circumstance and sheer deference. John Knox, who was nothing if not chippy, would have been displeased. Media representatives attending the Assembly were given two official handouts explaining the role and position of the Lord High Commissioner. The first dealt with protocol and included this paragraph: 'During his or her period of office the Lord High Commissioner is granted the dignity and courtesy of the crown (he or she is addressed as Your Grace, that being the title by which the Scots king was addressed before the Union of the Crowns) and he or she ranks next to the Queen and the Duke of Edinburgh and before the rest of the Royal Family. It is customary for gentlemen to bow and ladies to curtsey on first meeting Their Graces, on parting from Their Graces and when recognising their presence in public places.'

The other handout dealt with the official party of this particular Lord High Commissioner, the Rt Hon. Viscount Younger of Leckie. This group included Viscount Ridley, Lord Steward of the Queen's Household; Lord Luce, Lord Chamberlain to the Queen, and Lady Luce; Vice-Admiral Tom Blackburn, Master of the Queen's Household; Sir Joseph Barnard, chairman of the National Union of Conservative and Unionist Associations, 1990–1, and Lady Barnard; the Earl and Countess of Airlie; Viscountess Runciman; Lord and Lady Lang of Monkton; the Bishop of London and Mrs Chartres; the Earl and Countess of Dalkeith; Sir Jeremy Morse, former chairman of Lloyds Bank, and Lady Morse; the Earl and Countess of Ferrers; Sir David Landale, former director of Jardine Mathieson, Hong Kong, and Lady Landale. And so on. I do not wish to labour the point, but I was beginning to suspect something heavily anachronistic, something inappropriate to the work of a democratic Kirk.

Lord Younger delivered a graceful and concise speech; in replying, Moderator Miller saw fit to pay tribute to the Lord High Commissioner's service as chairman of the Royal Bank of Scotland over ten years, during which he had consolidated Scotland's role in the international world of finance. Everything was getting a little too worldly.

After all this, not a great deal happened in the first morning of the Assembly. The actual handover by the outgoing moderator Andrew McLellan to John Miller had been an effective, simple and dignified ceremony; thereafter, there was a little less dignity in the way the gathered former moderators crowded on to the dais to encircle the new moderator. There were just enough seats, and there was just enough room, for all of them – but the way some of them scrambled up to the raised area indicated that they feared they were going to be left below. I can just about comprehend the concept of 'first among equals', but this looked suspiciously like 'quite a few firsts among equals'.

I don't think the Assembly really took off until the third session, on the Sunday evening. Andrew McLellan's review of his modera-torial year was warm, at times very funny indeed and at times desperately serious. Here was a moving account of a year well spent, delivered without a hint of self-importance; if anything, the outgoing moderator was too self-deprecatory. His peroration, in which he reiterated the credo of his year: 'I have longed for a passionate church in a gentle Scotland. It is the poor and the weak and the despised who will lead us to a passionate church in a gentle Scotland', possessed genuine spiritual power, and for the first time I felt was attending a gathering concerned with the spirit rather than with ceremonial and bureaucracy. Altogether, Sunday evening was convivial and happy. What was bleakly described as the 'presentation of delegates and visitors' was almost jolly, with a palpable sense of fellowship and friendship in the air. And there was a crisp and amusing speech of thanks by Trevor Morrow from Ireland.

The third day started with the celebration of Holy Communion, which was beautifully organised and impressive to watch – yet I could discern absolutely no sense of joy in the proceedings. The sacrament took place in total silence, and I wondered if some appropriately numinous music could not have been played. Then we moved on to what should have been the great debate on the *Without Walls* report. Peter Neilson presented the report with flair; but, as I have already noted, what followed was a series of random and disconnected points from the floor. Two years earlier, the Assembly had appointed a special commission to re-examine the primary purposes of the Church, to re-examine its shape and to formulate proposals for continuing reform. Peter Neilson, convener of the commission, emphasised to the 2001 Assembly that the completed report was the start, not the end, of a journey. But after he had spoken, I waited in vain for a response which evinced any measure of vision or passion or serious spiritual commitment. Instead, there seemed to be confusion, a certain amount of scepticism and a lack of understanding of where the Kirk was to go now.

I'm certain that part of the problem was that many of the most active people in the Kirk do already 'listen to the local voice and serve the local church', to quote the report. *Without Walls* is essentially about empowering local congregations; but, if the report was presented as the beginning of a journey, I reckon that many commissioners thought they had already started the journey and, indeed, were well on the way. Moderator Miller said he felt sure that the report had been a significant step in the life of the Kirk. Norman Shanks, leader of the Iona Community, warned that the Kirk had been here before: other big reports had been debated and discussed but had then fallen aside, largely unimplemented. One commissioner asked simply what his kirk session had to *do* about the report. Another, in contrast, said there were too many instructions in it. There was a general absence of strong feeling, and there was certainly none of the excitement that should attend the start of a great journey. This should have been a major moment for the Kirk; instead, it was flat, anticlimactic, uninspiring and wholly unmemorable.

If there was any passion at all, it came in the response to the report's survey of the Kirk in the Highlands, which was very critical. The most articulate speaker in this context was Andrew McGowan, principal of the Highland Theological College in Dingwall, of whom there is more in Chapter 11. Here, the debate almost flickered into life; but this was, overall, a most dispiriting session. I noted during it that the Lord High Commissioner and his party were not present, although this should have been the key session in the entire week. While Lord Younger could perhaps be commended for his prescience in avoiding the debate, his absence again made me wonder about the relevance of the Lord High Commissioner's role.

If there was an unfortunate absence of passion on the Monday, there was plenty of it on the Tuesday evening. First, the Assembly debated the future of the St Ninian's Training Centre in Crieff, and then it debated whether to readmit an adulterous former minister to the ministry. There was a real forensic edge to both of these sessions, although the St Ninian's one did get bogged down in petty legalism. Time and again, the principal clerk, Finlay Macdonald, performed heroics to prevent the Assembly from rushing up legal cul-de-sacs. Then we had the adulterer petitioning to be readmitted to the ministry. Put like that, this particular session might sound like something straight out of the seventeenth century; but in fact it was an invigorating and eloquent debate in which decency, penance, high seriousness, humility, judgement, earnest enquiry and heartfelt concern were all very much in evidence.

Judgement – that might not sound very Christian, but this was the Assembly sitting as the Kirk's supreme court, and there was a distinct whiff of courtroom drama about the whole affair. Glasgow presbytery had already objected to the applicant's petition; now he was appealing to the Assembly. He stood at the bar with a representative of the Board of Ministry (in effect his adversary) alongside him. They spoke well, and this added to the tension. Eventually a vote was taken, electronically, and the petitioner was back in the fold, by 198 votes to 156.

There were not many commissioners present at these two sessions; but those who were there showed every sign of intense concentration, and many were very eager to speak. For the first time, the atmosphere was highly charged. Two important issues were at stake: the future of a much-loved training centre, and the future of a former minister. But these were hardly as important, in the wider context of the Kirk's entire future, as the *Without Walls* report. It had been received blandly the day before, whereas on Tuesday evening there was an abundance of passion on display. Has the Kirk lost sight of the big picture? Even more pertinently: does it want to grapple with its future? On the evidence of the first few days of the Assembly, it is much better, and much more engaged, when dealing with the particular than when addressing the fundamental.

In the very recent past, the Church and Nation debate tended to be the high point of Assembly week. Not this year. I did not like the tone of the discussion about Trident. I accept that the Church and Nation Committee, and indeed the Assembly itself, regard both the use and the threatened use of nuclear weapons as morally illegitimate. Even those who disagree with that premise must surely accept that the Kirk has taken a high moral position here. But I felt I could sniff not a little self-congratulation and self-delight, and even perhaps the self-righteousness of the Pharisee, when those who had been arrested during their demonstration against Trident at Faslane recounted their experiences.

A former moderator, the Very Rev. John Cairns, sought to puncture this mood: he said he was all in favour of the rule of conscience, but he suggested that it was relatively easy, in just about any historical context you cared to choose, to be arrested by laughing policemen and then to be allowed to sing defiantly in the cells. This point was perhaps made too subtly; a more bludgeoning intervention came from a frequent contributor to the week's deliberations, the Rev. Gordon Kennedy from Stranraer, who demanded to know what was the point of encouraging people to take part in the political process if the Kirk was going to ignore, time and again, the politically expressed will of the people and to encourage unlawful action.

In any case; the mood of the Assembly was clearly very much against Mr Kennedy. It was thus all the more surprising the very next day, during the low-key debate on Kirk chaplains to HM Forces, that the Second Sea Lord, no less, was given a most enthusiastic and warm reception by the Assembly after he had addressed it. I do not believe in discourtesy, and I'm not suggesting that he should have been booed from the hall or anything like that; but, if the Second Sea Lord's finger is not one of those on the proverbial red button, then whose is? The Assembly is clearly not always a model of consistency.

To return for a moment to the Church and Nation debate – I discussed it later with Dan Mulhall, at that time the Irish consul-general in Scotland, who was an interested observer. He told me that he was impressed with the wide-ranging engagement with so many secular issues, but he could not discern any theology behind the discussion. A point he did not make – and this surprised me, for it was a point that was being made by many other observers – is that the Church and Nation Committee may have lost some of its point, and certainly some of its thunder, since the Scottish Parliament came into being.

As the Assembly progressed to its close, I realised that two visual concerns had been gnawing at me without my really confronting them. First, where was the cross? Here was a great Christian gathering – and there was no cross in evidence anywhere, at least not as far as I could see from the gallery. There was a huge screen behind the moderator, on which the proceedings were displayed; there was a huge table immediately in front of the moderator, where the principal clerk and his various assistants and aides sat. But on neither of these two focal points was there any evidence of a cross, the great Christian symbol and, indeed, the greatest symbol of all. I am not sure what this absence says about the Kirk; but, when I gave it some thought, it made me uneasy.

Second, as the week progressed, I noticed that fewer and fewer of the ministers were wearing dog collars. Quite a few did at first; but, by the end of the week, only a small handful were. Indeed, those wearing them looked very much like men and women apart, a small minority of outsiders. This seemed strange, particularly when the moderator, the principal clerk and his deputy, and the convener of the Board of Practice and Procedure, sitting at the head of the Assembly, all sported their appropriate ecclesiastical kit throughout the week. Again, for a self-consciously democratic assembly, there was a sense of the wrong signals being transmitted.

It was as if, without really thinking about it, the Assembly had sorted itself into three distinct groups – the high heid yins running the show, the majority of commissioners in their secular mufti (and some them were very casually dressed indeed), and the small minority of traditionalist ministers still defiantly wearing their dog collars. This might not seem to matter overmuch; but it did look wrong to me, as I gazed down from the gallery, that those ministers signalling that they *were* ministers looked so very much men and women apart.

Ministers, and for that matter elders, *are* different; otherwise, what would be the point of ordaining them? I understand that many folk inside the Kirk dislike the dog collar, and outside it can be regarded as a joke. But I strongly believe that all ministers and elders should wear, at all times, some badge, emblem or symbol to show that they are different; for that is just what they have chosen to be. I shall return to this theme in Chapters 4 and 7.

I hope that these impressions, outlined above, do not appear over-critical. On the whole, I was genuinely impressed. The commissioners who spoke were for the most part articulate, committed and concise. There did not seem to be a bore among them. But that begs the question: did the ever-courteous but brisk chairmanship of Moderator Miller inhibit the Assembly at times? Nobody was allowed to bore it; on the other hand, few spontaneous debates took place.

And the Assembly did seem at its most animated when it was most introverted – when it was discussing what seemed to me fairly arcane matters to do with ministerial support, or the future of one of its training centres, or whether to readmit an errant minister. I wondered, from time to time, what pertinence the Assembly had for the ordinary folk milling around on the sunny Edinburgh streets outside the hall, for instance the drinkers sitting at the outdoor tables of the Shakespeare bar, just across from the hall on the edge of Festival Square. And then I realised, as the week progressed, that some of these drinkers were in fact commissioners, indulging in a little gentle truancy (yes, I truanted on occasion also).

The issue of pertinence is a difficult one in the context of Edinburgh, for I suspect that Edinburgh is pretty apathetic about the Assembly anyway, and hardly notices whether it is there or not. True, the capital's great and good, or a proportion of them, enjoy the garden parties and the receptions and the dinners which the Assembly brings in its wake every spring. But, without being too chippy or puritanical, I reckon that such occasions are pretty irrelevant to the core of the Assembly's work. The point is: Edinburgh takes the Assembly for granted, and no longer connects with it. I mentioned earlier that Edinburgh's morning paper, *The Scotsman*, virtually ignored the 2001 Assembly. I suspect that the great majority of the capital's citizens are unaware of the Assembly's presence amid them.

This would not be the case if the Assembly moved around. In the July 2001 issue of *Life & Work*, the then editor Rosemary Goring wrote a thoughtful editorial in which she suggested that 'a peripatetic Assembly might be in the best interests of the Kirk'. I concur wholeheartedly. For a start, it would give a real fillip to the life of the Kirk in the area it visited. Second, it would – and I write this in no spirit of condescension to the supposed provinces – be seen as a tangible way for the Kirk to be supporting life in Scotland beyond the capital.

Suppose, for example, the Assembly were to go to Dumfries (a town where I have some connections). I know that it would be welcomed with open arms; its very presence would be a boost not just to the local economy, but also to the general morale of the area. Some might say that there are no suitable halls in towns such as

Dumfries or Ayr; but I'm sure that, with a will, any logistical problems could be overcome.

Furthermore, a peripatetic Assembly would help to counter the tendency whereby more and more is being sucked into the capital, a boom city. One of England's problems, for many years, has been its overweening capital; London's prosperity and its cosmopolitanism and its self-delight are resented elsewhere, more so than many Londoners realise. I hope we are not going to make the same mistake in the new Scotland. Some readers might think all this is somewhat fanciful – but just look at a map. Neither London nor Edinburgh is anywhere near the centre of its respective country; instead, both are situated in uncannily similar spots in relation to the overall geography of the respective countries – firmly in the south-east.

Such matters – whether Edinburgh's relationship with the rest of Scotland is becoming problematic – might seem to have little to do with the Kirk. I'm not so sure; it is, after all, a national church. And I referred above to the 'new' Scotland. New, mainly because it has a new Parliament. This will affect the Kirk significantly, and that is yet another matter that will be explored later in the book.

Meanwhile, here are my final two points on this General Assembly. First, I thought the education debate was, for once, a real and a strong debate; and, in a way, it was thrilling to see a young minister, through the sheer force and sincerity of his intervention, overturn the wishes of headquarters at 121 George Street. This was also about an issue, sex education, which had meaning for the wider community. But, in a spirit of humility, I have to report that nobody else I spoke to – and I did speak to quite a lot of people, outside observers as well as commissioners – thought that the education debate was the highlight of the week. So, impressions are subjective and quite possibly erroneous.

Second, I return to the vexed matter of the Lord High Commissioner. It is difficult to write this, for I have no wish to offend Lord Younger, or any member of his party, or indeed any of the various Lord High Commissioners of recent years. One of them, Lord Macfarlane of Bearsden, held this office three times; he is a personal friend, and I know him to be a fine and decent man who does a lot of very good work modestly, behind the scenes. I know also that he took his work as Lord High Commissioner very seriously, and that it gave him and his wife Greta and their family great pleasure. I emphasise that what follows must in no way be construed as an attack on any individual. It is, rather, an attack on the institution, which I regard as outdated, as dangerous insofar as it sends out completely the wrong message about the nature of the Assembly and the Kirk, and as essentially fatuous.

The office of Lord High Commissioner was born more or less at the same time as the Kirk was born; that is, in 1560, when it was agreed that Mary Queen of Scots, a Catholic, could send a commissioner to observe the proceedings of the Church of Scotland in its General Assembly. I, more than most, would not want the Kirk to lose touch with its roots; but it hardly needs to be said that the conditions which obtained in 1560 do not obtain now. The Lord High Commissioner, as I understand it, now has two functions – to represent the sovereign during the Assembly, and to report to the sovereign on the deliberations of the Assembly. How on earth is the latter task to be undertaken when the Lord High Commissioner is absent during the most of the proceedings? Again, it is not an attack on the Lord High Commissioner to say that he is absent most of the time; he (or she) has a lot of ceremonial and other duties to undertake beyond the Assembly.

The Assembly is a formal gathering and, as such, it is quite rightly conscious of its dignity. But, far from enhancing its dignity, I think that to see the Lord High Commissioner turning up at the start of a session, listening to a debate for a few minutes, and then departing, actually diminishes its dignity. The reality is that the Lord High Commissioner is a complete outsider who can address the Assembly only when asked to do so and who has no constitutional right to do anything significant or dramatic, for example to dissolve the Assembly. The Church of Scotland is a Presbyterian church – probably the most famous Presbyterian church in the entire world. I associate Presbyterianism with, among many other things, an absence of show, an absence of unnecessary flummery and a matter-of-fact determination to eschew what is meaningless. The office of Lord High Commissioner should be abolished forthwith.

HIGH AND LOW

❖

This is a second chapter of impressions. I want to describe some very varied experiences of Sunday worship around Scotland. In his book *Our Church* – by far the best basic introduction to the Scots Kirk – R. D. Kernohan writes: 'The pattern of worship in the Church of Scotland varies quite widely. Sometimes this is a reflection of the taste and style of the minister who is responsible for the conduct of worship. Some ministers are sensitive, however, to the needs and wishes of their congregations.' This was written some time ago; it is all true, but significantly understated. I found, in my travels around Scotland, a quite remarkable diversity of Sunday worship. This is an area where power has been devolved to the local minister; and, from what I have seen, the ministers are not slow to make use of their freedom.

A thin drizzle fell on a thin line of worshippers as they walked down the pathway from Lothian Road to St Cuthbert's Kirk in Edinburgh's West End. It was a Sunday in late July – a dreich day, and the weather matched my mood. I was apprehensive as I embarked on what I then regarded as a chore, a dreary round of Sunday service samplings.

I am not quite sure why I chose St Cuthbert's as my starting point; perhaps it was because this was the church of Peter Neilson, whom several people had described to me as the 'coming man' in the Kirk. Or perhaps because it was here that the Kirk's greatest churchman of recent times, George MacLeod, first made his mark in the ministry. From 1922–6 he had been an assistant at the High Kirk in Edinburgh, but it was when he moved to St Cuthbert's, as collegiate minister, that he really began to be noticed. Indeed, some have claimed that his ministry at St Cuthbert's was the high point in his life. The church, and it is a very big one, was filled to capacity every time this charismatic figure preached; as Ron Ferguson notes in his superb biography of MacLeod, 'the crowds attending worship testified to his popularity, and his ability to communicate with all classes was marvelled at'.

I was not expecting any charismatic preaching, and I was not best prepared for worship; but my negative mood was soon dispelled. The welcome at the door could not have been warmer, and the beauty of the church stunned me as I entered it. Even Presbyterian churches can transform by their beauty; and this church, designed by the great Edinburgh architect Hippolyte Blanc, is no ordinary Presbyterian church. There is a fine mosaic floor and a great white marble communion table, and the pulpit is supported by four red marble columns from San Ambrogio in Verona. If you reckon that this suggests a high or even a slightly Romanesque ambience, you would be right; that, I was to learn later, is St Cuthbert's reputation.

As I waited for the service to begin, I studied the order of service and the 'Welcome Card' which was given to visitors. Both reiterated the welcome and extended an invitation for tea or coffee after the service. The card went further: 'It is good to have you with us today. We do hope you enjoy your time here and that you will be refreshed by the Presence of the Lord . . . if you can bide a while, join us for tea or coffee after the service or ask if one of our welcome meals is due.' And there was contact information for any visitor seeking specific assistance. (I understand very well that St Cuthbert's is a relatively wealthy congregation and that other churches could not afford to dispense a similar 'welcome pack'. That does not diminish the fact that, in this particular matter, the congregation of St Cuthbert's have used their money well.)

The actual service was rich, distinctly high in tone, and smoothly orchestrated by no fewer than three ministers: the parish minister Tom Cuthell, the associate minister Peter Neilson, and the probationer assistant minister Ian Andrew. (This did seem a high-powered team, particularly as there were only about ninety people in the church, including quite a few who were obviously visitors.) There were three particular highlights for me. First, a girl sang Schubert's *Ave Maria* with plangent beauty (when I later described this to a distinctly 'low' minister from the West of Scotland, he said: 'But Mr Reid, that was *entertainment!*'). Second, there was a magnificent, if somewhat stagily delivered, sermon by Peter Neilson, based on Luke 11 ('seek, and you shall find') and on the theme of prayer. And third, my favourite hymn, Wesley's *Love divine, all loves excelling*, was sung to what I regard as the correct tune, Hyfrydol.

At the close, the three ministers strategically placed themselves at each of the three exits, so that they could give a smile, a few kind words and a handshake to those who were not staying for tea. I left, not exactly uplifted, but in much better spirit than I had been in seventy-five minutes earlier. The service had without doubt been a bit west-endy, and perhaps too mellow for some Presbyterian tastes; but it had been charged with real warmth and grace, and this excellent start meant that I went to other services all over Scotland in a much less sour frame of mind.

The next service I went to was in Cramond, on the western fringes of Edinburgh. This was notable mainly for the best children's address by far that I was to hear. Delivered by the minister, Russell Barr, with gusto and humour on the theme of 'Where is God?', it had not just the kids but the entire congregation laughing uproariously. The church was well over half-full, and there was a friendly atmosphere; yet there seemed less of a sense of engagement than I had experienced in the emptier, and bigger, St Cuthbert's.

And now I come to what was without doubt the most extraordinary service I attended anywhere in Scotland. This was at Cults, a few miles along Deeside from Aberdeen, and was a joint service held by two congregations, Cults East and Cults West, held in the parish church of Cults West. Perhaps I was paying insufficient attention, but it took me several minutes to realise that the female figure in front of me, clad in trainers, slacks, a bright yellow T-shirt, a fluorescent bib and a yellow hard hat (certainly no sign of a dog collar here), was in fact the minister conducting the service. The penny at last dropped when she introduced a bunch of children, similarly attired, who crowded round her. She was the Rev. Mrs

Flora Munro, minister of Cults East, and she conducted an exceptionally informal service. The theme was 'Breaking new ground for Jesus', and the kids and Mrs Munro were summing up their summer mission week, run for the young people of the two parishes. There was no sermon; there was plenty of happy music, and it was all a bit shambolic. Mrs Munro got the order of service mixed up a couple of times, but she excused herself with the words: 'on a building site, anything can happen!'

Anyone seeking ritual, formality, Biblical exegesis, any kind of sermon, or indeed any sense of a traditional service at all, would have been quite bereft. On the other hand, there was a sensation of palpable joy about the proceedings; the kids were clearly enjoying themselves, and as the service progressed I found myself more and more won over. But had I been, say, a visitor from abroad experiencing my one and only chance to worship in the Church of Scotland, I would have been left with a pretty peculiar notion of the style of service in today's Kirk. This led me to reflect that there must be some better of way of advertising what specifically is on offer at Sunday services throughout the country; indeed, such advertising is more or less non-existent. I shall develop this theme later in this chapter.

Not too far away from Cults as the crow flies, but right in the very heart of Aberdeenshire, is the parish church of Kirkton of Rayne. This lovely building, much larger inside than it appears from outside, is set in a hard-worked but benign landscape of large fields, gentle woodland and distant hills: the much-loved profile of Aberdeenshire's favourite hill, Bennachie, looms a few miles to the south. The places hereabouts have eccentric names such as Baldyquash and Meikle Wartle, and you are always aware that you are in the midst of the biggest single swathe of agricultural country in all Scotland. Here, on a sunny Sunday morning in early September, I experienced a simple and joyful family service, most pleasantly conducted by Mary Cranfield, the minister of Culsalmond, Daviot and Rayne.

Again there was no sermon, but there were two simple talks for the kids. The only problem was that there were very few present – fewer than twenty, of whom ten were youngsters. (There had already been a more traditional service at Daviot earlier that morning, and there was to be a united service, for all three parishes, at Daviot that evening.) In a way I find hard to describe, this was the most pleasing worship I attended. Now, I know that worship is about more than pleasing; it is about challenging, and explaining, and glorifying. All these things were going on, in a very gentle kind of way, in Rayne Kirk that early autumn morning. For some reason, I was put in mind of an elemental service by pioneers in the west of America.

Now we move on the north-west, to Aultbea, in the vast parish of Gairloch and Dundonnell. Before I describe what was by far the most intense and Bible-based worship I experienced, I have to deal with the nonsense that is the division of Presbyterianism in this beautiful part of Highland Scotland. It is an area that is sparsely populated; yet there are no fewer than five Presbyterian denominations active in the vicinity. These are the Church of Scotland, the Free Church of Scotland, the Free Presbyterian Church of Scotland, the Associated Presbyterian Churches (APC) and the Free Church Continuing. Absurdly, there could have been a sixth: the United Free Church is active elsewhere in the Highlands but, for reasons no-one could explain to me, not in this particular parish. (To add to the mix, there is also in the parish of Gairloch a Scottish Episcopal Church, St Maelrubha's at Poolewe; and the local Roman Catholics hold services in Gairloch Community Centre.)

The minister of Gairloch and Dundonnell, Derek Morrison, is an affable, outgoing man in early middle age. He used to be minister of the APC in Poolewe, but he switched to the Church of Scotland and is now based in Gairloch. I attended evening service at Aultbea, a few miles to the north of Gairloch. This was the third service Derek had conducted that Sunday; he had taken morning service in Gairloch itself and had then moved on to take lunchtime worship at Badcaul, quite a distance further north. The Aultbea service took place in the village hall, a fairly grim edifice; it was a converted Nissen hut. It did not take me long to realise that the atmosphere was less cheerful than I had experienced elsewhere. For all that, there was a warm enough welcome. This was delivered by one of two elders who took the early part of the service; it became clear that all Derek had to do was preach. It also became clear that the sermon was very much the centrepiece of the service, so the word 'all' is hardly appropriate. There was robust and hearty singing of traditional Victorian hymns, with the men's voices (in Church of Scotland services, it is usually the women's) to the fore. The congregation was predominantly middle-aged to elderly; the smallish hall was nearly full. There were heaters along the walls, and they were switched on; even so, there was a chill in the air. Then, when the time came for Derek to move forward and preach, the heaters were switched off.

The sermon was the most powerful, the most detailed and the best structured of all the sermons I was to hear. It was based on an intensive reading of the Bible; and, during the long address (thirty-five minutes), most members of the congregation had their Bibles out, following the appropriate texts in the Book of Joshua. It was perfectly paced; as Derek reached his peroration – on the lines of 'Don't tell me you don't know the way to the City of Refuge; the signposts are all around you' – I was at once moved, shaken and, I have to admit, just a little scared. Although his delivery was well-nigh perfect, towards the end he seemed conscious of the time; he kept glancing nervously at his watch, and he later told me that he tried to keep his sermons to thirty minutes. This discipline was self-imposed; he was under no pressure from his parishioners.

What I have written perhaps makes this sermon sound like something dismal yet over-the-top, delivered by an old-style hell-fire preacher. Nothing could be further from the truth. It was out of time, or at least out of tune with our times, and there was undoubtedly a component of grimness in it all, yet there was charisma here too. There was no joy, but there was hope; there was a sense of uplift as well as of warning, and it was definitely a sermon I'd like to hear again. (Later, Derek told me that he had taken eight hours to prepare it.) To listen to Derek Morrison preach was to experience something strong and life-enhancing.

Finally in this section, we move to Inverness, where a short stretch of the River Ness in the centre of town must surely be the holiest neighbourhood in all Scotland. On one side of the river stand a large Episcopal cathedral, a kirk, a Roman Catholic church and a Methodist church; on the other bank there are three Church of Scotland churches and a (very big) Free church. Among the more modest of these buildings is Ness Bank Kirk, although this, too, was to prove bigger inside than it appears from outside.

Two large wooden notices on either side of the church had informed me that, in July and August, Sunday morning worship took place at 10am. But when I turned up shortly before ten on a bright August Sabbath, the church was clearly closed. I did however find the beadle, who apologised profusely and said that because the school holidays had ended, they had reverted to 11am services a week earlier than usual. He helpfully and ecumenically suggested that I could go to the Episcopal service across the river, which was about to start; but he assured me that no Church of Scotland service anywhere in the city would be starting before 11am, although other signs might also suggest differently.

When I returned, and entered the church just before eleven, I had a new experience: it was difficult to see any space among the crowded pews. A lady steward eventually found me a place near the front, and I looked around as the service was about to start. The church was just about full. All age groups seemed well represented. There were to be two baptisms and a series of Sunday School presentations, and these in part explained the fine turnout; but I was to learn later that this is a church which is generally packed. The service itself rattled along in a brisk, accessible kind of way; there was nothing special to note. It was perhaps the most mainstream worship I attended. There was a crisp, shortish sermon from the minister, John Chambers, based on Psalm 84 and on the subject of 'longing'. The two baptisms were conducted beautifully. The feel was of a congregation at ease with itself, and of a minister very much in tune with his congregation.

When I was leaving, I fell into conversation with a gent beside me. We had more than the usual exchange of superficial pleasantries, as the church was so full that it took quite a time to shuffle out. I said to him that it was encouraging to see a church so well attended. He told me that, in his opinion, the congregation had been transformed since the arrival of Mr Chambers three years previously, but that there was now a shadow hanging over them: there was a proposal that they should be linked with another local church, and they might even lose their church building. I was genuinely astonished; why on earth, I asked, should such a vibrant church be asked to link with another? He said he was unable to explain, but added that the uncertainty was creating a lot of un-happiness, just when the congregation was enjoying a strong revival. I later contacted Mr Chambers, who confirmed what I had been told. The proposed linkage was with St Stephen's; to add to my confusion, he told me that, had I attended worship there, I would probably have found it equally well attended. In other words, two strong and good-going congregations could in effect be diluted; it did not make sense.

I sought elucidation from the convener of parish reappraisal for Inverness presbytery, Fergus Robertson, and the presbytery clerk, Alastair Younger. Both these ministers were courteous and tried to be helpful, but having spoken to them I was not much the wiser. Mr Robertson told me that he had just taken over as convener and he had still to have detailed discussions with the clerk. He assured me that nothing would be happening in the near future, and indeed he said there was no specific timetable for action. Mr Younger told me that the Board of National Mission in Edinburgh required that all presbyteries in Scotland should have a 'presbytery plan' and that this would generally include proposals for unions or linkages. Such a plan was being drawn up for Inverness presbytery, and the overall plan did include a proposal for the union of Ness Bank and St Stephen's. But Mr Younger went on to emphasise that these matters had to be negotiated over time, and, even if a decision did eventually go forward, Ness Bank would still retain the right to appeal to the General Assembly.

I made contact again with Mr Chambers, who said he had first heard about the proposal in detail after Ness Bank had put forward plans for major fabric work on the church. These included develop-ment plans for disabled access, for new kitchens and for renovated church halls to deal with the expanding youth work that was under way. Because this was development rather than maintenance work, the presbytery had indicated that major rebuilding work could not go ahead until the long-term future of the church itself had been resolved. But Mr Chambers repeated to me that this proposal meant that two of the strongest parishes in Inverness could be united.

All this came as the first strong intimation to me of one of the problems which is gnawing at, and debilitating and indeed vitiating, the Kirk at local level: unions and linkages. Parish reappraisal sounds a bland bureaucratic term, but in its wake can come much tension and even misery. How the Kirk handles such issues in the next few years may well be the defining measure of its maturity, sensitivity and (centralised) organisational ability. Sadly, this is all about managing decline; but then I must point out that I saw no sign of decline, none whatsoever, at Ness Bank.

One other point occurs: if there were to be fewer presbyteries, would that help or hinder this process? On the one hand, it seems pretty obvious that if there are significantly fewer presbyteries, there will also be significantly less local sensitivity. On the other hand, there might be less chance for local and petty jealousies to fester; and I'm afraid that not even the Kirk is bereft of such unpleasantness.

The other, and very different, conclusion I want to draw here concerns the advertising of services. When such a diversity of worship is on offer, it seems inadequate to rely on word of mouth or localised insider knowledge as being the only means of indicating what is available at particular churches. Obviously, congregations have to look after their own, first and foremost; and presumably congregations have a pretty fair idea of what they are getting, and are likely to get, at their own church. But visitors are important also – and such visitors may be chance passers-by, they may be tourists, or holidaymakers, or business people; they may be incomers, they may be simply the glibly curious or they may be people with specific needs and wants. All of these people are important; the parable of the lost sheep comes to mind.

In just about every service I attended, there was a real and kind welcome offered to visitors and strangers. My point here is that more should be done to attract these visitors and strangers in the first place. There are many methods of doing this, and I shall look at these in greater detail in Chapter 4; but surely presbyteries could think about improving signage outside churches, and improving local information networks, and making more use of local media, information centres, libraries and the like, so that visitors to an area could find out easily just where and when worship takes place and also – though this is more difficult – what type of worship is on offer. At the moment, it can be something of an initiative test to find out simply where the kirk is and when the service takes place. A small example of what can be done is that when I was in the north of Scotland, I came across, not once but several times, a leaflet detailing all the Episcopal churches in that vast area, and when the services took place. Even this elementary service does not seem to be provided by the Kirk.

Now I wish to move on to some other experiences of Sunday worship – first, a pleasant enough service at Dean parish church in Edinburgh. The phrase 'pleasant enough' might suggest a gentle put-down; and I think this would have been a more engaging worship if the congregation had been a bit more responsive. I sensed a certain lethargy, or dourness, in the air. The mood was fairly flat. The big church was only about a third full, and, although there were quite a few (noisy) children present, the worshippers were, for the most part, elderly.

The minister, Mark Foster, was trying hard, but I detected a grimness among the older people in my area of the kirk. Somehow, I felt that the disposition of the congregation was not as positive as it might have been. It was almost as if some of them resented the presence of the children throughout the duration of the service; the youngsters did not leave for Sunday school, because it was harvest thanksgiving. The pupils did various presentations, including an imaginative liturgical dance, interpreting Psalm 100. The highlight was a baptism, movingly conducted as ever. (The simple baptism sacrament represents, I think, the Church of Scotland at its very best. The words and music of the Aaronic Blessing are among the most moving ever used in worship. Ministers can have a difficult time with funerals, and even with weddings; but baptisms surely cannot avoid being joyful and hopeful occasions.)

The next two services might represent some indirect threat to the established ministry. Although I am very pro-minister, it is obvious that there are not enough ministers to go round, and this problem is going to get considerably worse before it gets better. Ministers and, indeed, congregations cannot be complacent; they certainly cannot assume that the traditional model of 'one minister, one congregation' is set in stone. The two services I am now going to describe, briefly, were both conducted, in their entirety, by non-ministers; and both of these non-ministers acquitted themselves well.

The first was at St George's, Dumfries, on a very wet morning in mid-October. The minister, Donald Campbell, was on holiday, and the service was conducted by a Reader, Mrs Jeanette Piggins. It was the first time she had taken a service at St George's, a large square church with a pleasantly intimate feel about it. Despite the appalling weather, there was a good attendance. Mrs Piggins seemed nervous at first, but she soon got into her stride. In her sermon, she talked about the so-called war (my phrase, not hers) – it was just over a month after 11 September, and the bombing of Afghanistan had recently begun. She dealt with this most contentious of subjects in a low-key and almost oblique way; and, although I would have liked something a little more spirited, her address was thoughtful and gentle. And no doubt it would be insensitive for a visiting Reader to be too controversial.

One other point about the St George's service is that the welcome at the start extended well beyond the routine invitation to shake hands with your immediate neighbour. There was a near-riot of handshaking, yelled hellos and other greetings, and even back-slapping; and, although this was among people who already knew each other, there was a palpable sense of good fellowship which was extended to the stranger in the midst of the people around me. I'm sure this way of beginning a service could and should be tried elsewhere.

The other service was at Kirk o' Field on Edinburgh's south side. This, obviously enough, is not the famous Kirk o' Field which was burned to the ground in 1544, nor has it anything to do with the infamous and mysterious murder of Lord Darnley in 1567, which is frequently described as having taken place in Kirk o' Field; the dark deed was done near the site of the old kirk. The current Kirk o' Field is on the fringes of Dumbiedykes, about 300 metres to the south-east; it is a smallish and relatively undistinguished Scots Gothic building, built in 1910. When I attended worship, the minister, Dr Ian Maxwell, was in Portobello, attending to his duties as interim moderator of St James' parish church there. Tasha Blackburn, a young American student from nearby New College, took the service in its entirety. I thought she did exceptionally well; she had prepared a particularly imaginative and clever children's address, which required some participation (and yes, I know it's easier if you don't have to do it week in, week out). Although she had to work hard to get some response from the children, she won through, being helped out by a couple of cheerful older people, while her main sermon was crisp, simple and very effective.

Kirk o' Field is typical of some of our city kirks: it has an active membership of about 150, who are really involved and committed, although the bulk of them are elderly. In the kirk that morning, there were a few young people, including a handful of Taiwanese students who are apparently regular attenders; Dr Maxwell has worked hard to build links with the University of Edinburgh, offering pastoral services and support to the students who live in his parish. As so often, I was warmly greeted when I arrived, but in a more pawky manner than elsewhere; the elder at the door demanded to know if I was a southsider, and threatened to deny me entrance if I wasn't. This was an obvious joke, delivered with cheeky bonhomie; and, inside a kirk which I had expected to be dreary, there was an atmosphere of geniality and good humour.

One of the best-attended kirks in Scotland, and one of the most generous in terms of giving, is New Kilpatrick in Bearsden, just north of Glasgow. Given that there are two other good-going kirks within a quarter of a mile of New Kilpatrick – Bearsden North and Bearsden South – its success is remarkable. 'Leafy' is the hackneyed adjective most often employed by feature-writers when describing the prosperous purlieus of suburbs such as Bearsden, and there were leaves aplenty lying on the pavements as I made my way to New Kilpatrick on a drizzly morning in early November. This contributed to a muffled, dank and almost stagnant atmosphere outside, and Alan Sharp's wonderful phrase, 'a paralysis of insulation is in the air', sprang to my mind. But, as had happened before, any negative thoughts were dispelled by the warmth of the welcome I received inside the church. It was about three-quarters full, with nearly 500 inside, and I noticed that the worshippers – particularly the women – were by far the best-dressed I had encountered. Nothing showy or sleek; just a neat and traditional display of what was presumably the Sunday best.

New Kilpatrick places a strong emphasis on music; the choir made a grand entrance (and later a grand exit), the men in robes, the women in traditional collars and cuffs. There was also a multi-age band, or 'music group' as they were called in the Order of Worship, and in the middle of the service they played Norton's Ragtime, a jaunty and upbeat but totally secular piece. The congregation evidently loved it, and burst into spontaneous and loud applause when it finished; but I did wonder what on earth this had to do with Christian worship. When I later put this point to the minister, David Scott, he said simply: 'Well, all kinds of music can speak to the inner person'. Mr Scott's sermon was excellent: quite long and very well constructed, it started with an elaborate joke; he certainly had me kidded for a couple of minutes. David Scott belongs to the school that takes sermon-writing seriously, and places it at the very core of ministry; he starts his background reading and preparations on a Tuesday, continues them through the week, and devotes much of Saturday to the actual writing of the address.

New Kilpatrick has approaching 2,000 members, and they give to the tune of almost £300,000 a year. Mr Scott emphasised to me that this 'congregational liberality', as he termed it, does not just happen. 'A lot of groundwork has been done by the kirk session, and we work hard at this each year. We have visitations which review giving on an annual basis.' He did not say so, but I was left with the impression that the folk of New Kilpatrick parish, many of whom are obviously well-off by any standards, are striving hard to avoid any smugness; they seem to understand well that prosperity has its responsibilities.

Before I move on to describe a quite superb Remembrance Day service, held in an unprepossessing hall in a working-class area of eastern Edinburgh, I'd like to offer a few reflections on the Kirk's ambiguous relations with the military. I have already noted that during the General Assembly the Second Sea Lord was given a warm and enthusiastic reception, despite the distinctly anti-militaristic tone of the Church and Nation debate the previous day. There is a paradox at the heart of the Church of Scotland's response to the notion of service with HM Forces in defence of our country, which is well exemplified in the turbulent life of the Kirk's greatest figure of the twentieth century, George MacLeod. He became a militant and vociferous pacifist, as various Assemblies were to hear, but not before he had served with conspicuous gallantry in the Great War, receiving both the Military Cross and the Croix de Guerre.

The writer and historian George Rosie discussed with me what he called 'the astonishing number of casualties to the Kirk's clergy families in the trenches'. Describing the Church of Scotland's response to the Great War, George said: 'The minister's son was expected to set an example by volunteering. Being educated, he became a junior officer. The attrition rate among junior officers was appalling. The blood sacrifice was high.' (Incidentally, George traces some of the Kirk's despicable anti-Catholicism of the 1920s and 1930s, one of the few really shameful periods in its entire history, to the earlier war years. He points out that, when the Irish rebelled in 1916 and the Catholic Church fought conscription, the Kirk saw the Irish as stabbing Britain, and its own sons, in the back, despite the fact that many thousands of young Irishmen fought on all fronts.)

The tradition of managing to combine stalwart support for, and engagement in, HM Forces with the accommodation of a powerfully anti-militaristic and even pacifist wing within the Kirk continues to this day. Three relatively recent moderators of the General Assembly, Robin Barbour, George Reid and Fraser McLuskey, were holders of the Military Cross. The Church of Scotland currently provides no fewer than twenty-nine chaplains to HM Forces, plus another seven to the Territorial Army, as well as eleven to the Army Cadet Force.

I mentioned in the Foreword the visiting preachers who came to Beechgrove, Aberdeen, in the 1950s; one of them, the Rev. Prof. Murdo Ewen Macdonald, had seen active service as a chaplain to both the 4th Camerons and the 2nd Paras, and was awarded the US Bronze Star. The minister of Beechgrove in the 1950s, Stuart McWilliam, had also served as a chaplain. Much later, he told me of his near-despair after he landed on a beach in Italy in 1944; he was not in immediate physical danger, but he was lonely and utterly confused. As he searched for his unit, with the mayhem of preparations for battle all around him, he pined for the young wife and the new child he had left at home. His successor at Beechgrove,

Bill Cattanach, had also served in the Second World War, and indeed he resolved to become a minister when his life was saved at a moment of desperate peril.

As an antidote to all this, however, I recall my own father, who served in North Africa and Italy, telling me that, in his experience, Catholic chaplains were rather more assiduous in attending to their duties than Protestant ones. Anyway, the generations for whom two world wars meant such danger, privation and sacrifice are, sadly, dying away. I believe that it is vital that we continue to remember their enormous contribution, which is almost beyond words, and also that we reflect on whether the freedoms they achieved for us are not being rather wasted. At the same time, many in the Kirk are, as I have noted, uneasy with both the military inheritance and the military present, and most in the Kirk are certainly uneasy with anything which might, even indirectly, appear to glorify war. All of this makes the conduct of remembrance services a peculiarly tricky and sensitive matter.

And now, after this extended preamble, I come to the Remembrance Day service on Sunday 11 November, at St Margaret's parish church, Restalrig South, Edinburgh – except that the service was not in the church, which had been subjected to a particularly nasty arson attack. The congregation was now gathering in the slightly poky church halls across the road. The appearance of the minister, Ewan Aitken, that Sunday morning was striking, not to say saturnine, or even a little piratical. Whatever his aspect was, it was clearly not militaristic. Sporting a large earring and a heavy beard, Ewan eschewed a dog collar and instead wore a dark poloneck with a big cross hanging round his neck. He commenced the service by announcing that, at long last, rebuilding work was to start on the church the next day. There was a spontaneous outburst of joy; almost, but not quite, whoops of glee and yells of hallelujah, American gospel-style. The hall was packed; indeed, there was standing room only at the rear. I counted just over 170 souls crammed into the cramped space. (Of course, representatives of the uniformed organisations were there, swelling the numbers somewhat.)

What then took place was a powerful and immensely effective fusion of the traditional with a more modern, even experimental, style of service. The main formal elements were as follows: first, the two-minute silence, impeccably observed despite the presence of quite a few young children. Second, Laurence Binyon's beautiful lines, 'They shall grow not old as we that are left grow old; Age shall not weary them, nor the years condemn. At the going down of the sun, and in the morning, we will remember them', were spoken with simple dignity by an elder standing at the back of the hall, whereupon the entire congregation intoned simply: 'We will remember them'. Third, the names of the fallen from the parish were read out by representatives of the uniformed organisations. And fourth, the National Anthem was sung lustily at the close of the service.

The more modern aspects came during Ewan's address, which he spoke very softly, with a strumming guitar in the background. He bravely pointed out that this Remembrance Day coincided with the start of Ramadan, and he went out of his way to mention Muslims in a most inclusive manner. He returned to this theme in his prayer later. He offered no certainty in his reflections; indeed, at one point he said: 'Salvation – whatever that might mean to you'. (He told me later that, in his view, doubt is part of the nature of faith, and that he was also aware that he was speaking to several people who were not church members and who only attended on Remembrance Day.)

The word that springs to mind when I review my reaction to this intense service, conducted among ordinary folk in a working-class area of eastern Edinburgh with no sense of false ceremony or pomp, is *regeneration*. There was also a sense of solidarity in the face of adversity. Ewan mentioned, to loud applause, how one 80-year-old member of the parish had asked for his birthday gifts to be given in the form of cash. He had then handed the total sum received over to Ewan for the rebuilding fund. Once again, it occurred to me that the Kirk is maybe at its best when it has an obvious fight before it.

On a final, and lighter note, this service was also marked by the most disgusting (in the nicest way) children's address I witnessed, when the student minister Graham Wilson dished out multi-coloured sweeties to the kids, and got them to suck them and then hold them up, to a chorus of groans from the watching adults, as by this time the little globules were all wet and grey. The point was, of course, that we are all different externally but remarkably similar internally. The other point was that this would not have been tolerated in the middle of a more traditional remembrance service.

Next, and by way of contrast, we come to the most formal, most high and most posh service I attended. A couple of miles or so west of St Margaret's, Restalrig South, is the pseudo-cathedral of St Giles. I use the term pseudo-cathedral advisedly; in *The Buildings of Scotland*, vol. 2, *Edinburgh* (Penguin Books, 1984), by John Gifford, Colin McWilliam and David Walker, there is the following long and magisterial sentence: 'St Giles has four personalities: the vast medieval Burgh Kirk, the late Georgian gothic casing of the exterior, the dour Victorian "restoration" of the interior, and finally the character of the reformed worship that was quite at home in the various post-Reformation subdivisions but is still somewhat embarrassed by the complex and sullenly impressive spaces of a pseudo-cathedral' (reproduced by permission of Yale University Press).

Rather than call it a cathedral, or even a pseudo-cathedral, I prefer to think of St Giles by its other designation, that of the High Kirk of Edinburgh. It is a complex, dark building that has been much extended, restored, altered and generally tinkered with over the years, not always for the better. It utterly lacks the simple grandeur of, say, St Magnus Cathedral, or even the smaller St Machar's Cathedral in Aberdeen; inside, it has an atmosphere of brooding muddle. A great deal has happened here over the years; this Kirk is particularly associated with its most famous minister, John Knox, and of course the feisty Presbyterian militant, Jenny Geddes (see Chapter 7, p. 150); and you cannot help wondering what these two worthies would make of what is going on in St Giles these days, particularly as the ubiquitous Bishop Richard Holloway is now there in an associate capacity.

Saint Giles, incidentally, would appear to have had nothing whatsoever to do with Scotland. He was a hermit, and the patron saint of beggars and blacksmiths; he was also a patron of cripples, lepers and nursing mothers, and he became the subject of a huge cult in the early Middle Ages. Although some say he was an Athenian, it is more likely that he was a Frenchman from Provence. It has been suggested that the French link – the Auld Alliance and all that –

explains the Edinburgh connection to Saint Giles; but, considering that this kirk's greatest figure, John Knox, came to it at the very time that the Scots and the English had combined effectively to drive the French out of Scotland once and for all, that notion seems somewhat inappropriate, to put it mildly.

St Giles is where the main General Assembly worship takes place, though personally I don't see why this should not be spread around a bit; Edinburgh has plenty of overlarge churches. I attended one of the regular Sunday morning communion services at St Giles along with Finlay Macdonald, his wife Elma and my wife Julie. I had read the above 'architectural' paragraph the night before, and the phrase 'sullenly impressive' kept echoing in my head as the service progressed. As well as Finlay, the moderator-designate, I spotted three former moderators in the smallish congregation. Also worshipping were a former Lord Provost of Edinburgh and the principal of New College. There was just a whiff of 'the establishment at prayer' abroad, although there was none of the pomposity I had been half-expecting.

The service was very 'high', though perhaps not much more so than the one I had attended at St Cuthbert's, just down the hill. But whereas the service at St Cuthbert's had been cheerful and uplifting, I found this one dreary and dispiriting. It was taken by the Very Rev. Dr Gilleasbuig Macmillan, Commander of the Royal Victorian Order, who is convener of the Kirk's twenty-eight-strong Panel on Worship, which has as its official remit 'to witness to the importance of worship as a primary function of the church'. He is also Dean of the Order of the Thistle and Chaplain to the Queen in Scotland, and of course Minister of the High Kirk. If all this suggests someone very grand, he certainly did his best to disguise it. If anything, I thought his demeanour was excessively modest. He was dressed in a sort of off-white surplice, and his address and his prayers were softly spoken, so that they were hard to follow. The content of the address matched the style of the delivery; it was low-key, thoughtful, and diffident almost to the point of being apologetic. There was absolutely no declamatory certainty here. The burden of it all was something cerebral but not inspirational.

When we came to communion, most but not all of the worshippers gathered in two big circles round the communion table.

The sacrament ended with a shaking of hands, which was undertaken with solemnity. There was a distinct absence of joy in the air. The responses, the spoken confession, the way the choir in their peculiar porridge-coloured cassocks processed round the kirk at the start and end of the service, the way the servitor held a cross as he headed the procession, the great communion silver by the burning candles on the great table – all of this stirred some faint atavistic unease in my Protestant soul. Had the service been more colourful, more joyous, more infused with the life-changing import of the greatest sacrament, I would have been happier. But I was to experience all that the following week, in Glasgow.

When, at the end, the four of us repaired across the High Street for coffee, Finlay sensed my unease and sought to reassure me. I felt a bit churlish at my slightly sullen reaction; but then I thought that, despite the beautiful music, it had been a slightly sullen service. I may well be out of step here. I am aware that Gilleasbuig Macmillan has quite a fan club in the capital and beyond. Several people have told me that they would travel many miles to worship at St Giles (and some do). Throughout this book, I am trying to eschew negativity if at all possible; but the negativity I felt that morning lingers on. It has been honestly described.

Now we move across to Glasgow and the city-centre church of St George's Tron, which is situated on an island site in Nelson Mandela Square, where West George Street intersects Buchanan Street, right at the centre of Scotland's biggest city, just 100 metres or so west of George Square. In the immediate vicinity of this church, there are many hotels of various sizes and standards; there is a main-line railway station, a suburban-line station and an underground station. The Royal Concert Hall is a one-minute walk away, up the gentle slope of Buchanan Street. The vast Buchanan Galleries shopping complex is even nearer. The bus station is only three minutes' walk away, a second main-line station is five minutes' walk away, and two major art galleries are very close by. And the splendid City Chambers are of course situated in the almost-adjacent George Square. Many of Glasgow's busiest restaurants and most celebrated pubs are very proximate. Double-decker buses pass by, literally within feet of the side windows.

St George's Tron is externally very beautiful, with unusual baroque features, including a fanciful tower and obelisk; it was designed in 1807 by William Stark, who was inspired by a visit he had made to St Petersburg. Inside, it is more functional (even stark), but the point I wish to stress is that there can surely be no other kirk in Scotland that gives such a physical sense of being at the very heart of urban life. I wanted to visit St George's Tron for two reasons: I had been aware of the congregation's excellent outreach work when I lived in Ingram Street, on the fringes of the Merchant City; and I had been told, more than once, that its senior minister, the Rev. Sinclair Ferguson, is one of the best preachers around.

When I arrived, slightly late, I enjoyed a pleasant experience I had not been through since my visit to Ness Bank, Inverness: I had to squeeze in at the end of a very crowded pew. St George's Tron is not a big church: it has just 500 members, and the building is pushed to accommodate more than 600 worshippers; but on this sunny December morning it was absolutely packed. Those present were, as ever, predominantly middle-aged to elderly; but there was a healthy leavening of younger folk, and, judging from the way people were dressed, there was a huge mix both of backgrounds and of attitudes to churchgoing. The dress ranged from the smart and formal to the raffish and shabby, not to say downright scruffy. I was aware of the traffic noise outside; but it did not intrude.

I soon realised that this was communion Sunday, for the silver was on display, and early in the service Dr Ferguson conducted what more or less amounted to an informal mini-communion with the kids. Then they departed for Sunday school, and the main service began in earnest. Dr Ferguson preached a very lucid exposition of the significance of communion – 'this little drama', as he described it more than once. He explained with simple and persuasive eloquence how you experienced the presence of Jesus Christ although the bread and wine were symbolic. This might seem fairly elementary to regular Presbyterian churchgoers; but for me, a marginally sceptical outsider, this sermon was, in its clarity and its grace, almost epiphanic.

When the sermon started, I had had no intention whatsoever of partaking of the bread and wine; but such was the understated eloquence and force of Dr Ferguson's moving address, with its parallel exposition of a church of diversity where everyone had different things to offer, that, when the bread and wine were being passed along the pew towards me, I suddenly decided to bite the bullet (perhaps not the appropriate phrase) and take part. I'm not sure if this was technically proper, as I was not a church member; but Dr Ferguson assured me later that he had no problem at all with my participation. Now – whatever this book is and is not, I want to make clear that it is not a description of a personal spiritual journey, with bells and hallelujahs a-ringing out at the end. But I do want to record, simply and quietly, that this was an important moment for me, for at this point I decided that I would join the Church of Scotland.

The sacrament ended with everyone shaking hands with each other. The young woman beside me turned to me, took my hand and said simply: 'Peace'. And what could I say to her in return but: 'Peace'? Then, just before the end of the service, Sinclair Ferguson told us that his son had been very seriously injured in a terrible car accident a few days before. He was making progress, but only after more than fifteen hours of surgery. (I learned later that Dr Ferguson had spent the whole of the previous day in Cambridge at his son's bedside. He was remarkably calm and assured in the aftermath of this personal crisis.) And then he sent us all out into the Buchanan Street sunlight with the exhortation to 'go and serve this broken and dying world'. Here was a man of gifts; a man of charisma, clarity and expressive grace.

Maybe I am slightly ingenuous; maybe I am a sucker, as some will already have suspected, for evangelical certainties. In any event, I have to report that I was deeply impressed. All I am trying to do in this chapter is describe my spontaneous response to very different experiences of Sunday worship in the Church of Scotland; worship that I tried, admittedly not always successfully, to attend with an open mind. Anyway, being Scottish, I did have some cavils. I did not like the way the grimly suited elders, all men, were ranged on the dais at the front of the church, under the dominating pulpit. This looked forbidding and oppressive. And Dr Ferguson himself, while very dapper in a sharply cut suit, wore no dog collar or anything else to signify that he was a minister.

St George's Tron is to some extent a 'gathered' church for those of the conservative evangelical tendency. This of course means that it draws from a much wider area than its own immediate parish. And when I spoke to Sinclair a day or so later, he told me modestly that its good attendances were also a function of its geographical situation: it attracted people who were staying in hotels, or simply passing through the busy city centre (and, even on a Sunday morning, that part of Glasgow gets very busy indeed). He explained that he had inherited an all-male eldership on his arrival three and a half years earlier, and that his main concern since had been to reduce the existing number of elders. 'My conviction is that the eldership is wonderful when it is working well, but that almost every church has too many elders. I believe that we need to develop pastoral care in a different and more dynamic way than visitations by elders. And to have fifty trying to lead a congregation of just 500 is lop-sided. So I have been reducing the number of elders from what I inherited.' He went on to say that not all elders were good at visiting members, which had traditionally been seen as their principal function; and he was now trying to encourage the St George's Tron elders to give more real spiritual leadership.

I asked about the lack of a dog collar. 'There is no doubt that many of the older folks would like to see me in a gown and a dog collar. And where it is seriously expected, for example in the service for the Normandy veterans, then I would wear clerical attire. But you must understand that people come to the church from all backgrounds, and I would say that more than 50 per cent of them are not dyed-in-the-wool Presbyterians. That is our culture. In some ways I personally enjoy a higher liturgy, but the central motif to our worship is that we are members of a family, and nothing should hinder that. And, you know, we can be hindered by so much, even by the building.'

I asked him next about his closing remarks. 'I always try to end with a little exhortation just before the benediction. I can assure you that is unprepared and quite spontaneous.' But his actual sermons weren't spontaneous? 'Oh no. I prepare them thoroughly, but I do not write them out. Writing rather than speaking is my preferred mode, and I have had to work very hard at communicating verbally with people, and trying to communicate well by the spoken word.'

And finally, I said that although I had found the communion service exceptional, I still thought that it would have been more joyous had it been accompanied by music. 'Well, you are right in that communion services can sometimes be exceedingly funereal, given that we are celebrating the fact that Christ is alive, not dead. We have tried singing during communion, and maybe we should try it again.'

I conclude this chapter with brief accounts of sermons by Finlay Macdonald and Andrew McLellan. Finlay, as principal clerk, does not preach very often. In a way, that made me all the more keen to listen to him when I had the chance. So, when I heard that he was to take a service at Newbattle parish church, a couple of miles south-west of Dalkeith (currently a vacant charge), I made my way there, on a bright but bitterly cold winter morning.

The people in the characterful little church (built in 1727 to a classic T-plan design, by Alexander McGill) could not have been friendlier. I had hardly sat down when an elder came up to apologise for the coldness of the kirk. Then another came up to ask if I had managed to park all right. (The church is situated right on the edge of dense woodland and there is no parking on the road outside, so parking can be tricky.) Then Mrs Ann McCarter, the session clerk, stood up to read the intimations. It became apparent that her microphone was not working, so she had to shout, but she carried on with aplomb. When she came to the bit about a *warm* welcome to any visitors, there were sniggers from the back of the kirk. It certainly was very cold, but there was a cheerful atmosphere in anticipation of the visit of the principal clerk and moderator-designate, which, in a low-key kind of way, was obviously regarded as quite an honour. Mrs McCarter explained that tea and coffee would be served at the close of the service in the hospitality suite (in fact the northern wing of the little church) – and then Finlay took over.

He conducted the service with gentle assurance, and he preached with brisk clarity, and he certainly had the merit of brevity; it was just about the shortest sermon I heard. But it had other merits too. Talking in the context of a post-11-September world in which, as he said, more and more people seemed to think that it was difficult or even pointless to believe in God, he neatly asserted the old verities: we should talk less about the church (and that made me feel just a little guilty) and much more about Jesus Christ, and try to live out his teaching – and also study the Bible. It was straight-forward and, in a restrained kind of way, exceedingly effective, and it certainly seemed to go down very well with the friendly rural congregation. Then Mrs McCarter's husband yelled out an apology for the breakdown of the heating system, and we all gathered for our tea. The coldness had become the subject of constant mirth. The moderator-designate and his wife mingled, and everyone was talking easily and happily. There was no stiffness; everything was jolly and just a little haphazard. I thought briefly and mischievously of Steve Bruce, for here there appeared to be the genuine warmth of a community at ease with itself.

And finally, we return to Edinburgh, to the beautiful circular church of St Andrew and St George (the scene of the Disruption in May 1843, when almost 500 ministers walked out of the General Assembly which was being held there). This is the Very Rev. Andrew McLellan's church, and no doubt cynics will reckon that I would find it difficult to write anything critical about the performance of my mentor. Well, I am happy to say in all candour that the sermon he preached on Sunday 16 December 2001 was the best I heard, and the cynics can sneer if they want to. It was a dismal, dreich morning, and Edinburgh's normally costive traffic was rendered even more gridlocked than usual by a major Countryside Alliance demonstration that was taking place elsewhere in the city. Despite the drizzle, Andrew stood in his robes out on the George Street pavement, beyond the portico. He was greeting his parishioners as they arrived for the 11am service (the third he took that morning), and he was also greeting any strangers who might be tempted into the church. It was a simple and effective form of welcome; but I realised that I had seen only one other minister (Mary Cranfield) greeting arriving worshippers in this manner.

The service was straightforward enough and efficiently conducted by the probationer assistant, the Rev. James Aitken. The highlight was Andrew's sermon; I had never before heard a sermon by him, but I had been told by several 'experts' in such matters that he was one of the Kirk's preaching 'stars'. The address started with John the Baptist languishing, pathetic and forlorn, in Herod's dungeon; but it ranged all over the place while managing to hold both its tight structure and its eloquent coherence. I have no hesitation in describing it as a *tour de force*. It was not particularly long; but, among other things, Andrew contrived to get in a plug for Amnesty International, a discussion of two poems by Matthew Arnold, a most thought-provoking and sensitive evocation of the horrors of being imprisoned (Andrew famously had visited every one of Scotland's prisons during his year as moderator) and, what for me was the centrepiece, a helpful and clear exposition of what people should do if they thought their faith was deserting them.

What I particularly liked about this last part was that, at the very heart of this complex sermon, charged as it was with literary allusion and Biblical scholarship and fluent phrases, Andrew had some very simple and pragmatic advice for people needing spiritual assistance – those who, in the words of the hymn, were asking: 'Where is the blessedness I knew when first I saw the Lord?' This advice had five components, which I shall now seek to summarise concisely. (1) Talk to Andrew, or his assistant, the Rev. Tony Bryer, or your district elder. Or, if you don't want to talk, write a letter to them. (2) Go to a different church for a month or two. (3) Do your best to avoid giving up prayer, which is *the* spiritual medicine, even it has become weakened and diluted. (4) Read Mark's gospel, if possible in one sitting, and then get hold of a commentary on it and work your way through that. (5) Don't blame yourself. If your faith is no longer bright and happy, it doesn't make you a bad person – and we all have to face obstacles in our life of a kind that some other people never have to face at all. I thought that this clear advice managed to combine reassurance, understanding, compassion, practical advice and gentle sympathy in equal measure. Some achievement!

There was a reasonable number of worshippers – over 100 – which I did not count as a poor attendance, considering it was the third service of the day (after the earlier communion and then the family service), the streets outside were jammed because of the protest, and the rain was drizzling down. Nonetheless, I thought that this exceptional address did deserve an infinitely larger audience.

That ends my account of my impressions of Church of Scotland Sunday worship. The three core conclusions I reached were that there is enormous diversity on offer, that visitors are offered a genuinely warm welcome and are usually invited to stay for tea or coffee after the service, and that the standards of preaching vary considerably (where there is a sermon, that is – and sermons are not guaranteed these days). When I write that the standards varied, I have to report that I did not hear a bad sermon. The worst one was more than adequate. I shall look at preaching in Chapter 8, but I must note here that at least three of the sermons I heard (by Peter Neilson, Sinclair Ferguson and Andrew McLellan) were of an exceptionally high quality, in both content and delivery. Peter, and to a lesser extent Andrew, were quite stagey in their delivery; but, if the presentation enhances the message, I have no problems with that. I doubt very much if better sermons than these are to be heard with any regularity anywhere in the English-speaking world. Indeed, I would not hesitate to describe these three sermons as 'world-class'.

Derek Morrison in Aultbea preached a sermon that was very long but beautifully paced and splendidly delivered; yet it was probably just too intensively based on Old Testament text exegesis for most modern tastes. The young American student at Kirk o' Field, Tasha Blackburn, gave a crisp and impressive address, and I also heard very good sermons from David Scott in Bearsden, John Chambers in Inverness, Finlay Macdonald in Newbattle, Midlothian, and the Reader, Jeanette Piggins, in Dumfries. Mrs Piggins, incidentally, was the only preacher who began to grapple with the *political* aftermath of 11 September, though she did so in a pretty oblique way. I could probably have done with a lot more overtly political sermonising; but again, I shall discuss this in Chapter 8. I also heard a superb children's address by the Rev. Russell Barr, and another that was almost as good by Tasha Blackburn. Ewan Aitken's reflections on Remembrance Day, spoken softly with a guitar strumming in the background, could not really be called a sermon, but in their way his remarks were both brave and delicately judged.

Funnily enough, the service that I enjoyed most lacked a sermon; and it was also the least well attended. Yet Mary Cranfield's simple family service at Kirkton of Rayne in Aberdeenshire pleased me more than any of the others (even more than the one at St George's Tron in Glasgow, where I enjoyed something close to an epiphany), for reasons that I find hard to describe. Maybe it was just the utter unaffectedness, the winsome plainness, of this most happy service on a late summer's morning in a lovely sun-drenched church deep in the Gordon countryside.

So, that was the service that I *enjoyed* most. But this book is about Presbyterianism, and presumably most Presbyterians would argue that worship is about more than mere enjoyment. For spiritual uplift, challenge and succour, the sermon remains essential. Thus, I would personally prefer it if sermons could continue to be regarded as the pivotal point of Sunday worship, for the spiritual nourishment of the worshippers. And if you are lucky enough to hear a world-class sermon, as I did on the three separate occasions described above, then you, and your soul, are privileged indeed. Meanwhile, it will have been noted that I have written nothing above about the prayers that were offered. The standard here was consistent; the prayers were clear and helpful. But I never heard a prayer that was really arresting or unusual.

I did not set out on my round of Sunday service samplings with a particularly light heart. I thought it was going to be a necessary chore. But, at the end of it, I can fairly report that in this, one of its core functions, the Church of Scotland is doing not badly at all. Indeed, the challenge must be to get more Scottish people to sample Sunday worship. I reckon many of them would be most pleasantly surprised.

As a postscript to this chapter, I should mention that various Kirk people told me in the course of my investigations that far more people attend Church of Scotland worship on a Sunday than pay to watch Scottish professional and semi-professional football matches on a Saturday. This theory, and I suspect it is a theory rather than a fact, seems to be so widespread in its propagation that I thought I would discuss it here. Perhaps the claim would be accurate were attendance at other Christian churches, namely Catholic services and also those of the other Protestant denominations, to be taken into account as well; but, at present, I think there is a bit of delusion around.

I am not happy to draw such a conclusion, for I think that if more people attended worship they might well be both delighted and surprised. As someone who has watched more Scottish football matches than I care to remember (and yes, most of them have featured Aberdeen FC), I think I can now safely say, without being too frivolous, that the entertainment value may quite possibly be better at church, and obviously there is spiritual sustenance on offer which you cannot receive at a football match. But, of course, the problem is that many people attend football out of a tribal allegiance or an atavistic loyalty that seems, for so many Scots, to possess a potency and a pull that the Kirk no longer has. (Indeed, cynics say that more men change their wives or their bank accounts than change their football teams – that applies to the long-suffering supporters, not the mercenary players, I hasten to add.)

It would be an interesting exercise for the Kirk to do an official attendance survey on a few selected Sundays in the coming year. This proposal reflects the truism that the more the Kirk knows about what is, or is not, going on – the more concrete information it has about its current audience – the easier it will be for it to begin to address its many problems. I am not suggesting that worshippers should have to go through turnstiles; but, at present, the football authorities do provide apparently accurate figures regarding attendances. Let us take a typical Saturday: 1 December 2001 (though this might not be all that typical, because the conventional wisdom is that in December football attendances decline, as even macho Scottish men are inveigled or cajoled into Saturday afternoon shopping expeditions). Anyway, the attendances on this Saturday were as follows:

Bank of Scotland Premier League:

Aberdeen vs St Johnstone	17,369
Celtic vs Hibs	59,415
Dundee vs Rangers	11,085
Hearts vs Dunfermline	11,176
Kilmarnock vs Dundee United	6,130
Livingston vs Motherwell	5,426
Total Premier League:	110,601

The Bell's Scottish League aggregated attendances were as follows:

Division One:	11,947
Division Two:	4,087
Division Three:	1,639 (one postponed match).

The total from the Scottish Premier League plus the three divisions of the Scottish League was 128,274.

If we also take in the seven Highland League games played, plus the considerable number of semi-professional 'Junior' games that took place across the country on that Saturday, the aggregate attendance would undoubtedly rise to more than 140,000 – in all likelihood a little over 150,000.

And that of course begs the question: are there 150,000 people, or more, attending Church of Scotland worship on your average Sunday? More's the pity, but I very much doubt it. On the Sunday immediately after the Saturday for which the above statistics were provided, I attended worship at St George's Tron in Glasgow, a good-going 'gathered' congregation. The church was full and the attendance was certainly over 500. But the sad fact is that St George's Tron is not at all typical. Most Kirk services on an average Sunday will be attended, I would guess, by well under 100 people. If we take a (very) generous estimate of 1,250 services on a typical Sunday, that would give an overall attendance of 125,000. I believe that one of the Kirk's most immediate tasks is to get people back to Sunday worship. Some ideas as to how this might be achieved are offered in Chapter 4.

3

ISOLATION AND OVERLOAD

❖

I wrote in the Introduction that the Kirk's ministers were its elite troops. I reached this conclusion quickly in my investigations, and it was a conclusion that seemed to surprise and even irritate certain senior figures in the Kirk, including, funnily enough, some very eminent ministers. I understand very well that ordinary members of the Kirk have a big role to play if there is to be significant renewal, and that the eldership will have an even greater role. But I envisage the leadership at local level coming from the ministers, and I envisage the elders supporting the ministers, rather than vice versa.

Whatever this book is or is not, I want to make clear that it is very pro-minister. (A certain cynic, who must be nameless, told me that if I wanted to make myself popular it should be very pro-elder, and sceptical about the ministry. 'Apart from anything else,' he said, 'there are far more of us elders than there are ministers, and we do have our doubts about the ministry.' I have managed to ignore this worldly advice.) The Kirk asks a great deal of its ministers, particularly those in the parishes. A simple, stark sentence in *Without Walls* says much: 'Ministers speak of isolation and overload'. The Kirk has tried very hard to establish support systems, but these are mainly organised centrally at 121 George Street and through presbyteries. I reckon that elders and other individual members of congregations could often be doing more to support their ministers. For ministers have a very tough time.

What do they do? I have read many accounts of the minister's role, but I would say there are five key tasks: to proclaim God's word, to administer the two sacraments (baptism and communion), to lead worship, to provide pastoral care, and to sustain the life of the congregation, socially as well as spiritually. In addition, there are the two very important sub-tasks of conducting weddings and funerals. The latter can obviously be particularly stressful, and of course you cannot plan for them. Bereavements can occur at any time of the year, and often at the most awkward time for the minister. And like buses, they tend to come along in twos and threes. To write that is not to be frivolous or insensitive; it is simply to point out that the minister has no control over the timing of a major part of his or her workload.

In theory, all Church of Scotland ministers are equal; but this is clearly a nonsense, both symbolically and in practice. I remember watching all the former moderators scrambling on to the dais at the General Assembly, each of them resplendent in his best ecclesiastical kit. More importantly, I have observed the huge differences in style and size of the manses I have been invited into. I have also been made aware of significant differences, not in workloads but in local support systems. It might be a waspish point, but I have also noted that very few ministers seem to move from fat-cat congregations to poor ones, rather than from poor to rich, or from jobs in 121 back to the grass roots.

And, as if all this is not bad enough, *Without Walls*, while being generally sympathetic to the ministry, wants to add to the general burden by getting ministers to take on the additional (big) roles of apostle, prophet and evangelist (on top of those of pastor and teacher). I reckon that the ministers are well placed to help with outreach and with a new emphasis on ecumenism; but, given their current workload, they will need more support than they have received up until now. Finally, there is the bureaucracy. 'Far, far, far too many meetings', the Rev. Shirley Blair said to me, with great feeling.

Some of the ministers I talked to were single; most were married. Obviously, a supportive spouse can be an immense help. But here I come to what was probably the most worrying meeting I had during my researches; it certainly showed the Kirk in a very bad light. The meeting was with a minister's wife. For reasons that will become apparent, she did not want to be named. (Of all my principal inter-viewees, she is the only one who will be anonymous.) She also wanted me to avoid giving any clues or hints as to her identity. Suffice to say, then, that she lives in a manse near but not in one of our great cities. Let us call her Celia. Her problem, in essence, is that she has no faith; she does not believe in God. This might not be a problem for many people in our secular society, but it is certainly a huge problem for a minister's wife. Celia told me: 'When my husband was studying for the ministry, I knew that our lives were going to change. I wanted to support him in his ministry, but it required inner contortions. It was making me ill. In effect, I had to fight for my soul. I didn't want to profess things I couldn't believe. If you are the minister's wife, so many things are expected of you. You must not say certain things. You are not supposed to have your own mind.'

(In an interjection here, I would point to interesting echoes of the Conservative Party, where, notoriously, the male candidate's wife is expected to be wholly and almost mindlessly supportive, and not to stray from the party line in any circumstance. There are other parallels, too: the Kirk and the Tories both reached their apogee in Scotland in the mid-1950s, and have faced accelerating decline ever since. Both organisations have given the impression of having lost their way, of having been unable to connect with the wider Scotland and with a new generation's changed priorities and needs. Mischievously, I could suggest that the Scottish Tories and the Kirk should get together to reflect jointly on their problems and possible solutions. If anything, the Scottish Tories seem to have started their revival before the Kirk has.)

Celia told me: 'I haven't met any minister apart from my husband who begins to understand the problems. If only they could *not* believe, then they might understand better. There is this tremendous judgement against you. I found that the only way other ministers would try to help me was to tell me to pray. They saw the problem as religious. They seemed afraid, and it was as if they always had to stick to the religious line. They kept telling me that God would help me. They didn't or wouldn't understand: I don't believe in God. Now I never go to church at all. I did go when my husband was inducted, but now I feel it's much better to stay away. I don't think the Church of Scotland is aware of how people really are. People kept saying to me: God will help. But you need more than that. I do think that many ministers' wives are completely intimidated. And I know of at least one other minister's wife who is in exactly the same position as myself. My views on the Church of Scotland are coloured by all this experience. I have had a terrible, terrible time. I tried to explain things to an elder's wife, who seemed sympathetic. But I soon realised that she did not understand, *because I was the minister's wife*. Everything was seen through the eyes of the Church.'

Celia is an intelligent and successful woman. She is strong and feisty, yet she is living a disjointed life. And she wants to protect her husband. Her parting words to me were: 'Please don't let me be identified. Don't write anything that will give the game away.' Her account was disturbing. In effect, the dedication of one person to the Kirk has made another person miserable. Obviously, her story does not reflect well on the Church of Scotland; but indirectly it also serves to indicate the pressures all ministers and their families are under. So much is expected of them, often unfairly. This burden of expectation is not shared by others in the Kirk.

I want now to relate the experiences of four very different ministers, two women and two men. Two of them serve in rural parishes, one of which is extremely remote. The other two serve in a small town and in a busy port respectively. Each of them has had to grapple, or is grappling, with problems that may be particular but are by no means unique. Thus their stories and their experiences may serve as useful indicators of the ministerial burden, for these problems are very much additional to those of the normal day-to-day workload. I cannot emphasise strongly enough that, although they confided these difficulties in me, they did not do so in a whingeing manner. Far from it; these are people of spirit and resource, and none of them evinced an iota of self-pity.

Let us begin with Mary Cranfield, minister of Culsalmond and Rayne linked with Daviot in Aberdeenshire. On my way to meet her, I turned off the busy A96; and shortly, as I was heading east on a much quieter road, I passed what looked to be an impressive and handsome church. I was soon to learn that this building, Culsalmond

Kirk, splendid as it appeared, had been the cause of considerable grief and pain. In fact, one of the first things Mary said to me was: 'You don't want to buy it, do you?' (I am not wealthy, and I don't think I look like the kind of person who would go around the country buying redundant churches; but Mary was not the first minister to ask me that question. It is a mark of the Kirk's current plight that getting rid of unwanted church buildings is one of its greatest immediate problems.)

I write there 'unwanted'; but then, of course, a few people do want very strongly to keep these buildings. And that is understandable: if you have worshipped for many years in a lovely church, and tried to maintain its fabric and its substance, then it obviously becomes part of your life, a tangible part of your spiritual life, and you will not want to see it festering, forlorn and unused – or sold and used for blatantly commercial purposes. Mary told me of her 'five-year nightmare', up until September 1998, when Culsalmond finally closed. 'My predecessor had three churches and three congregations. I was presented with two congregations, but three buildings. The Culsalmond church was in a dire state. I was aware of the great affection for it, and it took me two years to decide that we had to have death before resurrection, as it were – in other words, to get rid of it and to form a new life for the united congregation round one building, Rayne. It was very painful. Some members of the united congregation simply could not see beyond their building at Culsalmond. People would be insisting to me that there was nothing wrong with it when cracks half an inch wide were appearing in the structure. I was scared to go into it; bits would regularly fall off inside the church.'

With that problem eventually overcome, Mary was, when I spoke to her in September 2001, wrestling with a very different one. She had been appointed interim moderator to handle the ministerial vacancy at St Andrew's, Inverurie (the nearest town). St Andrew's is a surprisingly big congregation for a rural area: it has 2,000 members, whereas the total membership at Culsalmond and Rayne linked with Daviot is less than 500. During the vacancy, Mary had, crucially, to arrange for someone to take the services at St Andrew's. (On a normal Sunday, she conducts two services, at Rayne and Daviot.) She also had to conduct the St Andrew's kirk session meetings and to provide pastoral care for 2,000 people. 'Bereavements alone are a large burden', she told me. 'I do about fifteen a year for my own two congregations. At St Andrew's, there are obviously far more. And funerals are urgent; you have to abandon everything else to prepare for them.' A retired minister was to be helping out from the end of September; but, as Mary said, all the phone calls came to her, as well as all the matters to be attended to in the day-to-day running of an unusually large congregation, the second-largest of the thirty-two in the presbytery of Gordon. And there was no certainty as to when the vacancy would be filled; it could be in late October – or much later than that.

The subject of funerals also loomed large in my conversation with Shirley Blair, minister of Leith St Thomas's and chaplain to the Port of Leith. She is also chair of the Leith Churches Forum. Because of the nature of the parish, with its large proportion of elderly people and the serious social difficulties attendant on a major port, Shirley has to take a lot of funerals. 'I do like funerals to be life-centred. I need to get a feel for the dead person and to find out about him or her – that takes time. I thought I would have had more drug-related funerals, and more prostitutes' funerals, than I have had; but I have had a few, and they can be very harrowing. You are never sure what you are going to meet at a funeral, or after it. I once had thirteen funerals in one week. My worst time was when a woman drowned in Leith harbour. I simply could not fit that one in. Then the person who was supposed to be covering for me became ill. Another minister actually refused to help me, but eventually I got help from another local woman minister. Weddings and baptisms you can plan, but you obviously cannot plan for funerals. If you have made elaborate plans, they will almost certainly be interrupted.' I asked about elders taking funerals. Shirley thought that the concept was a good one, but the bereaved would have to be assured that they were not attending a second-class funeral. If the practice became commonplace, that would obviously become less of a problem. 'I think it would be excellent to have a few appropriate elders, who had been properly trained, taking funerals regularly', Shirley told me.

Pressures of a different kind – and, you could argue, of a self-inflicted kind – loom in the ministerial life of Derek Morrison at

Gairloch and Dundonnell in the far north-west. For Derek takes preaching very seriously indeed – so seriously that he spends at least eight hours preparing each of his sermons. When you learn that he preaches three different sermons each week, you will understand the amount of time he devotes to this aspect of his ministry. Preaching is not taken lightly in this part of Scotland (Derek was brought up in a tradition of sixty-minute sermons); but, even so, some might regard as excessive a period of over twenty-four hours each week devoted to sermon preparation. I am not so sure, having been privileged to hear him preach for thirty-five minutes at Aultbea one early autumn evening, in his third address of the day. I can testify to the care and craft with which the sermon must have been composed.

Derek has to cover a very large area, from Badcaul on Little Loch Broom in the north down through Aultbea and Poolewe to Gairloch. It is a glorious ragged littoral of peninsulas and sea lochs and islands; there are many scattered communities (Steve Bruce will, I hope, forgive me for using that word in this particular context). Travelling around is time-consuming. In the not-so-distant past, there were four Church of Scotland ministers covering this area. And at Gairloch, the main centre of population, incomers are now moving in and the little town is actually growing, which is unusual in the Western Highlands. Derek has two school chaplaincies, a youth club and two homes for the elderly which he has to keep an eye on. He also does a lot of door-to-door work asking people why they don't go to church (mischievously, I asked him if it was because of protracted sermons). He said that people were clearly looking for spirituality, but not within 'the old institutional authority-structure' as he calls it. The point here is that he has a lot of pastoral work to do, and a lot of ground to cover. On top of this, the intellectual burden of his sermon-preparing must be colossal; not that he was complaining.

Finally in this section, I come to Ian Watson, the minister of Caldercruix in North Lanarkshire, whose dramatic and successful intervention during the General Assembly I described at the beginning of Chapter 1. Like the other three ministers, Ian is working very hard indeed; but, more than this, he is grappling with a serious ongoing problem: he does not like the way his church is going, to the extent that he believes it is not inconceivable that one day he may have to leave it. I am going to recount his views at some length, because if a minister is seriously ill-at-ease with his own church then his burden extends well beyond matters such as the nature and size of his workload. His unease will gnaw at him constantly, to the extent that his church, which should be a prop, a constant source of strength and personal renewal, almost becomes the enemy. These are my words, not Ian's; but I am trying to explain the impression I was left with after an intensive conversation with him in the manse at Caldercruix, high in the bleak post-industrial uplands of North Lanarkshire.

The first questions to be asked are whether Ian is alone, or whether there are other young ministers who feel much as he does. From what he and others have told me, I think he represents a significant minority in the Kirk, and one that it will ignore at its peril. Ian is a son of the manse; he first worked as a solicitor in Fife, and, as he was dealing with divorces and the aftermath of crime, he soon found he was spending a lot of time in effect counselling people. It was not that big a step to decide to join the ministry. 'When I was training for the ministry, I kept my head down, but now I'm going to start raising my head above the parapet. I'm not alone, but I don't know who else is prepared to speak out. I believe that there are like-minded ministers who are busy getting on with their parish work but are not speaking out. Our views are not being taken seriously.'

What are these views? Ian could be described as a conservative, an evangelical or even a fundamentalist, but he didn't seem particularly comfortable with any of those designations, and especially not the last. Without getting into theology, he emphasises two essentials that he thinks the modern Kirk is evading: one, the central place of the Bible in the Kirk's work, and two, the uniqueness of Jesus Christ. 'Everything else flows from these. A lack of grounding in Scripture upsets me – it upsets me very much. You can't pick and mix from the Bible. And the only way of salvation is through Christ. I don't think the Church of Scotland has anything like enough confidence in the gospel. I wish it would act as if it believed in what we say we believe. There is far too much equivocating. It is clear that the views of myself and people like me are not taken seriously. We are educated people, but we are presented as Bible-belt fundamentalists. A broad church is fine in theory. I'll go to seminars and listen to people like Andy McLellan and Ron Ferguson and John Bell, of course I will, and I can respect them, and yes I do respect them. But will people like them listen to us and respect us? We don't have anything like the Iona Community. And some people who think like me are frightened of being seen as a threat to the Church. They don't want anybody to question their loyalty to it. They do their visits, they preach, they go the prisons and the hospitals – but they don't want to get involved in church politics. But I think people like us are going to have to get involved in church politics. I don't want to be a part of or even to head up a disruption or something like that – but the day might come.'

What, I asked, would be the likely breaking point? He thought, and said: 'If I was told, by my presbytery, that I could not refuse to marry a homosexual couple. If that happened, if I was asked to do that, I'd say I'm not doing it. If the presbytery insisted, I'd have to leave – or I might already have gone.' I asked if he could not be considered judgemental. 'I don't think so. A local girl, from a church family, got pregnant. She was 15. She loves the baby. I baptised the baby, and I also gave her support and help. I don't think I'm judgemental. I just believe in the Bible.'

Ian talks of the loneliness of the ministry. 'Of course it is a lonely job. I don't think the support systems are working. The presbyteries and 121 should be supporting the ministers more than they do. I've got good friends – they are my support group. The ministers who have burnt out – they are the real loners, the guys with nobody to help them. It is easy for ministers to create work for themselves and to lose confidence in themselves. I'm not sure that I was trained properly. I was certainly never taught how to grow a church. These days, when you should be training, you are in essence doing a secular university course and doing what your lecturers happen to be interested in. So many of the students in the divinity faculties are not going to be ministers anyway.'

Ian did not say so, but the essentially lonely nature of the job is presumably exacerbated if the minister feels that the church is not supporting him or her. Furthermore, if the minister is making mental preparations, however tentatively, for the possibility of having to quit the church one day, that obviously represents a most onerous additional burden. Equally, if he or she is having to gird up for a major fight within the church to try to prevent that day coming, then that also will create an enormous extra strain.

Wherever the minister stands in the church, whether he or she belongs to the conservative or the liberal wing, whether he or she is old or middle-aged or young, whether married or single, whether he or she has a big congregation or a small one, whether he or she is serving in the city or the town or the country – it makes no difference to the fact that serving as a Kirk minister in today's Scotland must be a much harder job than it has been for at least fifty years. There are still jokes about ministers having a one-day working week. There is still a feeling in some quarters that if the minister plays his cards right, he can spend far more time on the golf course than most professional people. One of the greatest figures in Kirk history, Thomas Chalmers, helped to perpetuate the myth of the minister with ample time on his hands when he declared: 'After the satisfactory discharge of his parish duties, the minister may enjoy five days in the week of uninterrupted leisure for the prosecution of any science in which his taste may dispose him to engage'. (These were words which he later regretted uttering.)

The Church of Scotland must understand, even if the wider world doesn't, that the modern minister has a complex and very taxing job. And the few who are coming forward for the ministry will have to be sustained as never before. The four case histories above illustrate some of the variegated pressures on the ministry in the field; but they only scratch the surface. There is not yet a serious general crisis affecting the 1,000-plus ministers who are out there, but there could be before too long; the danger signals are there. Ministers have to deploy a lot of very different skills, in often stressful situations, in a context that is not always sympathetic and is sometimes downright hostile. Like schoolteachers, ministers aren't granted the respect that was almost automatically granted even a generation ago. Unlike schoolteachers, they are for the most part operating in isolation. If the Church of Scotland is to go though a great period of renewal, ministers will be the key personnel; but their burden will be increased, not diminished. They need more support now, and they will certainly require much more support in the future. In the short term, things are likely to get worse as the crisis of supply deepens.

Most of the above refers to Scotland at large, and within Scotland the Kirk at large; but at the more micro level there are often acute problems within congregations. In Chapter 2, I mentioned how surprised I was at just how much is devolved to the minister when it comes to the conduct of worship. In effect, the ministers can do more or less what they want, provided of course that they take with them the kirk session and most of the congregation. But such freedom is often attended by more stress and strain. In many ways, it is to the Kirk's enormous credit that the responsibility for the conduct of worship is a wholly devolved function; but, if ministers had to operate within strict guidelines, their lives would be easier, if more constricted.

If the minister is keen on experiment and innovation, it is all the more crucial to take his or her people with him. Many congregations are dominated by older people who tend, naturally enough, to prefer the safety of well-kent ritual and tradition. Jack Holt, the minister of Birse and Feughside, told me that he liked to surprise his congregation every Sunday. He was an electrical engineer before he became a minister, and his previous life had clearly influenced his approach to worship. When I chatted with him in his manse, which has a particularly lovely situation, looking south across the strath of the Feugh to that most kenspeckle of local landmarks, the hill of Clachnaben, he insisted: 'You need much more than words. Lighting and sound systems are very important. I like to surprise the congregation. I like movement within the church, and I like to have people participating from all parts of it. I aim to have something different each Sunday, and I've never had a problem with a kirk session or anyone else.' Jack is a very upbeat individual, one of the more sanguine and optimistic of the ministers I met; but I should imagine that his determination to keep ahead of his congregation, as it were, must impose its own stresses.

Then there is the question of who exactly the minister is serving. The congregation that has called the minister, obviously; but who, if anyone, else? 'Some members want you to serve the whole community, but others want you to serve the members only', Shirley Blair told me. Many people expect ministers to conduct sensitive, well-informed and dignified funeral services, even if the deceased and the bereaved haven't been near a church for years. Then there is the question of outreach, raised eloquently in *Without Walls*. I didn't mention anything about outreach in what I identified as the five key tasks. But if you read the marvellous parables in Luke 15 carefully, you may well come to the conclusion that a minister should, as the first priority, be serving just about anybody except those who are actually in the congregation. As I say, it ain't easy.

I think the first thing the Kirk has to do for the existing ministry is to encourage more support from church members, and particularly the elders. Marjory MacLean, who as depute clerk is now at the epicentre of the Kirk's administration, but who until the end of 1998 was a parish minister in Orkney, has an interesting perspective on this. 'There was a time when the Church allowed its professional ministers to do everything, and it was not at all inclined to let the laity do the things it could do, and do well. Any congregation, however small, has people with a multiplicity of skills. And ministers are not good at everything. Almost anyone in the universe could do a better children's address than I can, for example. There is then an ongoing process whereby the professional ministry is trying to devolve what it has been unnecessarily doing. Another example: why should the minister be editor of the parish newsletter? But it would be a very big mistake to undervalue the professional ministry; in other words, to devolve too much away from it. Yet another example: amateur preaching is usually excruciatingly bad. You need a well-trained elite to do that.'

The Rev. Gordon Kennedy, of Stranraer St Ninian's and Port-patrick, who was a member of the *Without Walls* commission, told me that most congregations contained a number of tremendously gifted people who could be serving the church much more effec-tively. 'You don't need to send people off to conferences or college or anything like that. There are a lot of people who could be trained locally by the minister, trained to lead worship and so on. The minister would become more of a team leader. We are going to have to rethink the whole relationship between the minister and the congregation. That is going to have to happen, unless we suddenly find more than 200 brand-new ministers.' Greater support for the existing ministry is crucial; yet even more important is the recruitment of new ministers. Even if ideas about greater involvement of the appropriate laity are implemented with remarkable speed (by Kirk standards), I reckon that minister supply, or rather the lack of it, remains the Kirk's most immediate and pressing specific problem.

The potential pool of recruits was, in effect, doubled in the late 1960s, when the Church of Scotland started ordaining female clergy. The Kirk deserves credit for this move, but no doubt some of those who overcame their hostility to the change were prompted by pragmatic expectations that it would enhance ministerial recruitment. And of course it did, for a time; yet now, over thirty years on, the crisis is worse than ever. And, as Steve Bruce has noted, had the Kirk been as powerful or the clergy as prestigious as they had been a century earlier, then the change would probably have been more aggressively resisted.

If we move forward twenty years from the admission of women to the ministry, to the summer of 1988, we can refer to an eloquent article in the *Glasgow Herald*, by the Rev. Norman Bowman, on the bleak future of a church 'starved of ministers'. The logical end of the recruitment deficit which then obtained, Mr Bowman wrote, was 'a Church disappearing into a Black Hole'. This most prescient of articles pointed to exactly the crisis which the Kirk is now facing – or not facing, as the case may be. Mr Bowman's conclusion was lucid and straightforward: 'New ministers emerge from the existing membership, out of existing congregations . . . When the demand is really there, it will attract the supply.' Well, if that is true, the demand is not there yet. Maybe congregations are too complacent. Maybe their minds are only concentrated when they have to deal with a vacancy.

I have dealt with some of the most pressing problems facing the modern minister; but there are many others. Time management is a skill they soon have to learn. Much of their work, for one reason or another, takes place in the evenings and sometimes well into the night; yet, if they take compensating time off during the day, that might well be misconstrued. Not all members, and certainly not all elders, are always sympathetic to problems of ministerial workload. They can be difficult and even truculent in other ways, too. Principal David Lyall of New College recalled that, when he was a parish minister in Ayrshire, one particular member of the 'awkward squad' used to attend kirk session meetings carrying his copy of Cox's *Practice and Procedure in the Church of Scotland*. As David put it: 'He sat there waiting to pounce'. From what I have heard, the crabbit or carnaptious elder is still a fixture in many kirk sessions. Indeed, ministerial candidates seem to be warned in advance about a number of congregations where kirk session 'mafias' operate.

Another related point is that ministers are not afforded much time to be truly private. Almost everything that they do is carefully observed and picked over, occasionally malevolently, often critically. Ministers must be discussed more behind their backs than even, say, lawyers. As Ann Allen, one of the Kirk's leading figures in recent times, and herself the wife of the minister of Chryston, put it to me: 'The minister's words, deeds and actions are constantly scrutinised and discussed by a large number of people'.

Again, the manse is not the minister's property, and I have heard depressing tales of ministers having a hard time before they can get even elementary repairs and maintenance attended to. The peculiar nature of the manse, which is often as much an office and a meeting place as a home, makes it less of a retreat than the family home is for most professional people. It is difficult, if not impossible, for most ministers to ring-fence their domestic life.

I do not want to present the ministry as a bunch of belly-aching bleaters and moaning minnies, given to excessive repining; but I do want to convey fairly their grievances, which seem to me to be, for the most part, perfectly legitimate. Indeed, this is one of the most difficult tasks I have – to communicate sympathetically the discontents of the ministry in the field without suggesting that I have become used as the ingenuous and manipulated mouthpiece of a peevish rabble of malcontents. I am sure the morale of the ministry in the field is not helped by the fact that many people in senior positions in the Kirk talk (generally off the record) of a decline in standards; whispers are bound to reach the parish ministers, who are, not unnaturally, going to be displeased if they are aware that, behind closed doors, they are being unfavourably compared to their predecessors.

And it has to be asked if their predecessors did such a grand job anyway; the 1950s in particular were a fat and good period for the Kirk, but the alarming decline that has set in since then may well be rooted in a lack of far-sightedness at that time and in a failure to respond adequately and imaginatively to the fresh challenges that were beginning to emerge. The Kirk had shown energy and courage in sorting itself out, after its dark and bitter years during the 1920s and 1930s; but, having achieved that internal renewal, should it not have looked ahead with more vision? There is much to be said for the old military adage: always reinforce success. If there was indeed a failure to build on a position of new strength, then some of the great figures of the 1950s and the 1960s might be seen, in retrospect, to have been less impressive than they seemed at the time.

I suggested above that being a minister now is much more difficult than it was, say, fifty years ago. Maybe that is, at least in part, because the ministers of fifty years ago did not do a sufficiently rigorous and forward-looking job at a time when the current was, for the most part, with them. Anyway, there can be no doubt whatsoever that, as fewer new ministers arrive on the scene and more of the older ones depart, the burden on the newcomers will be even greater because of the lack of experienced, mature figures to guide them. Of course, tyro ministers do not want to be patronised or subject to officious interference; but I should imagine that they will be looking for an empathetic and wise helping hand from time to time, and there will be fewer and fewer such hands around.

Now, I am well aware that – even with all their pressures and problems – contemporary ministers have it easy compared to some others in our society and to many others elsewhere. And they must always be aware of the struggles of those who built the Kirk, here and elsewhere. To expand on this point, I would like to quote at length from an editorial by the Rev. David Scarle in the *Rutherford Journal* (vol. 8, no. 1), a magazine 'for ministers, church leaders and elders' published by Rutherford House in Leith.

I recently met two different clergymen, both recently inducted into their first ministries. They are both mature men with some experience of life and work prior to their ordination. Both are married and with children. However, both were full of the miseries of life and despairing of doing anything worthwhile in their respective congregations.

What are their problems? By a surprising coincidence, both have very difficult people to minister to. Both have extremely awkward elders. Both have unreasonable demands made on their time. Both are expected to do far too much visiting. Both have complaints about the quality of their preaching. Both find the administrative burden of running a congregation far too heavy. Both are sure ministers in other parishes have a much easier furrow to plough. Both are convinced they have landed in the most difficult community possible where sin abounds, stubbornness is endemic and resistance to the word of God is second to none in the whole land.

Speaking to such beleaguered chaps who are battling against seemingly impossible odds, beset by insurmountable problems, suffering from deep depression on account of the hardness of heart of those to whom they seek to declare the Good News of the grace of Jesus Christ, I felt my heart go out to them in deepest sympathy. What a scandal, I felt, that their people do not appreciate them, support them, and love them and respond gladly to their preaching!

Indignant and vexed, I wondered how it was that God does not judge such unworthy congregations. Don't they realise how fortunate they are to have their own minister in this day of such shortage of candidates for holy orders? Let any one of them try and tackle the work they are heaping on to the bowed shoulders of these newly ordained fellows. Don't they realise how appallingly they are treating them? Once these two were bright-eyed and enthusiastic. Now they are crushed with care, disappointment and disillusionment.

Well, probably by now you have a fair idea of what may be coming next. Mr Searle continues:

Then I recalled a book I read recently about a young couple, Mr and Mrs Stuart Watt, who were the very first missionaries to Kenya in the last two decades of the nineteenth century. Their story, told by Mrs Stuart Watt, with immense restraint and modesty, was one of almost indescribable suffering and privation. It took them five months to trek from Mombasa to Nairobi where they believed God would have them pioneer a work of the Gospel. Their journey took them though many killing fields where they walked among the skulls and bones of unburied victims of savage intertribal warfare. Their first-born son died on the way and was buried in an unmarked grave deep in the bush. Porters carrying their possessions absconded with as much as they could carry. Malaria struck them down and raging fever hindered their onward march to the parish of God's choice.

At last they reached the area where they were sure they should live and work. Unfortunately, no 'fabric convenor' had been appointed and there was no manse. Stuart Watt set to and with his own hands built a house in the African style while he and his wife lived in a fragile tent, cooking on an open fire as they had done during their harrowing safari through trackless forests under a blazing tropical sun.

The local tribes were certainly not friendly . . . That is an under-statement if ever there was one. Repeatedly they attempted to kill the Watts. They poisoned their water supply and even attacked them with spears and arrows. Miraculously God preserved them.

And so it goes on; you will have got the drift. Mr Searle concludes with 'five words' to the whingers. A soldier must be prepared to endure the most harsh and demanding conditions. No effective ministry is possible without plain human courage; in other words, ministers need guts. An understanding is needed of the ways in which God works. Every minister has to grasp that Jesus came not to be served but to serve. And, finally, unless ministers are con-strained by and controlled by the love of God, they will be no more than sounding gongs and clanging cymbals. And Mr Searle adds a postscript: 'Where a minister is living a defeated and despairing life, it only needs a few prayer warriors, either within the congre-gation or from elsewhere, to mount a rescue operation'.

This is an eloquent and persuasive leading article, worthy no doubt of a wider audience than the subscription list of the *Rutherford Journal*. It does verge at times on sarcasm; and the contrast between the putative modern whingers on the one hand and the valiant Watts on the other is crude. But what Mr Searle writes could be construed as an effective wake-up call to the carping tendency. And we do live in soft and ample times; any contemporary who complains about his or her burdens should, if possible, try to recall the struggles and privations of his or her counterparts in other, harder times.

I must also point out that Mr Searle plays a pragmatic part in helping modern ministers. He runs short, sharp, practical courses at Rutherford House which help serving ministers deal with such apparently mundane yet crucial matters as time management, sermon preparation and delivery, and handling cantankerous elders and kirk sessions. At least two ministers told me that they had found these courses more useful than anything they had learned at university. All that said, I have to report that the complaints of the ministers I have spoken with do not accord with the grumping of the two imaginary contemporary ministers in Mr Searle's leader, apart from generalised complaints about excessive admin and too many demands on their time. I certainly did not hear, for example, complaints about the need to visit parishioners, or the expression of any envy of other ministers. No; the most prevalent gripe, by far, centred on isolation.

Let us take Jane Barron, minister of Stobswell in Dundee. She would appear to have absolutely everything going for her. She is still relatively young. She has a sunny disposition. She has experience of the world, having enjoyed previous careers as a teacher and then as a journalist. She is happily married with a supportive husband who is an elder in the Kirk. She has excellent relations with her kirk session and finds it easy to work with her congregation. She has recently become a member of the Church and Nation Committee. As far as I could detect, she is popular and hard-working. She is certainly personable and enthusiastic. So what is the problem? Why on earth should she complain, as she does, of isolation? She explained her concerns to me as we chatted over lunch at Dundee's waterfront on a bright and beguiling day when you could almost have mistaken the city for Naples. (And a journalist did once describe Dundee as the Naples of the North.)

Jane said: 'I think it is when I look back to my previous careers that I can best analyse the loneliness, the isolation. Then, I would be together with colleagues through the day. You would help colleagues, they would help you. You would be dividing and sharing skills and speaking to your peers throughout the working week. Or

I look at my husband. He is an educational psychologist, and he works in a team. They are constantly supporting and, indeed, supervising one another. And they have ongoing training and career development. That seems to be happening all the time. I do feel that this kind of professional development is not provided at all for the ministry. We need pastoral development as well as theological development, and I do think that headquarters, wherever that is – I suppose I mean 121 – should think about laying on much more support. And I would like to have a team around me, and associates I could talk to about our professional problems.'

In fact, Jane does have a very strong friendship with Mrs Lezley Kennedy, the minister of nearby Downfield South. 'We meet twice a week and we go to yoga together. I must admit that we do moan a lot. I sometimes wonder how I would continue if I did not have these sessions.' I said that I could understand how ministers in rural areas felt isolated; but, perhaps ingenuously, I wondered how she could feel this debilitating isolation in the midst of a vibrant city, especially when she had, by her own admission, a 'marvellous' kirk session. 'Well, in a way you are right. I do find a team building around me, and I'm not just talking about my own elders and members . . . I have built relations with neighbourhood development workers, we have good contacts on the council, and local ecumenical relations are very good. But it remains: I do still have this feeling of isolation.'

Jane went on to warn me that minister retention could well become as big a problem as minister recruitment, or an even greater one. She believed that many ministers, less than five years into their ministry, considered giving up. When I probed further, it seemed that at the heart of the problem was a lack of proper communication and structure within the Kirk. Jane (and she is a relatively new minister, recently trained) confessed to a 'massive ignorance' about the Church of Scotland as a whole. 'I want to drip-feed into the congregation lots of information about the Church and what it is doing, but then I get frustrated because there is so much about the Church that I don't know myself.' Jane says, for example, that only about a third of her congregation receive the magazine *Life & Work*. 'It is a hugely territorial church and there is sheer, massive ignorance. You can get really intelligent and well-educated people in your congregation, doctors and lawyers and so on, yet because of the way congregations have been treated they are unaware of so much of what the Church is doing. For example, there is ignorance about how the Assembly works and what it is for, and some members have not even heard of the Church and Nation Committee.' I asked Jane if some of those matters could not be addressed through presbytery, but I got the impression that she did not think that presbyteries, as presently constituted, were of much use. She was looking for really radical change, change that involved risk.

When I talked to Rosemary Goring, the perceptive and sympathetic editor of *Life & Work*, I asked her what, after about eighteen months in the job, had been her most positive surprise as she had learned in detail about the Kirk and all its workings. She replied: 'I have been most surprised by how much is going on in the parishes and how much work ordinary ministers are doing and the huge commitment they offer'. Rosemary comes from a Kirk background and was to some extent steeped in the Church of Scotland even before she took on her editorship, but she said that she was now much more aware of the essential isolation of the minister's job. That was the underside of all the work they were doing; being very busy does not necessarily prevent loneliness or even disillusion.

When I spoke to three ministerial candidates, in their final year at New College, Edinburgh, worries about stress and isolation were never far away as we ranged over various issues. I tried to keep our conversation as open-ended as possible, and certainly did not try to steer them towards the themes outlined above. Yet the theme of isolation kept cropping up with inexorable persistence. The candidates seemed particularly worried about isolation, partly because of what they had heard, and partly because they were aware that in New College they had been studying in a context where mutual support was taken for granted. They were determined that they would keep in touch with each other during their ministerial careers.

The trio were all mature students, family folk with children, still young by Church of Scotland standards but all on that difficult cusp between youth and early middle age. They were Joanne Evans-Bointen, Robin Hill and Fiona Hutchison. All three were happy with their education at New College, run in conjunction with residential conferences organised by the Board of Ministry. They were soon, after graduating, to go out and 'shadow' existing ministers for fifteen months or so. There would be more – intensive – training conferences, and then would come the first call, and ordination. They knew that they were a small band in a buyers' market, but this awareness did not make them in any way cocky or arrogant. Fiona said: 'I think we still have quite an idealised view of it all. I know that there is the business side of things, all the committee work and so on, and this appals me, but I understand that it has to be done.' Robin said that he, too, was worried about admin and committee work, though he realised that this was inevitable in a Presbyterian structure.

Each of them was very concerned about outreach. Fiona said: 'I am aware that members of a congregation don't always like it if their minister goes out and ministers to the wider parish, but I do believe that you are there to minister to all the parish. I think this is important if the Church of Scotland is to grow.' Robin agreed: 'We must serve the whole parish if we are to have any claim to be a national church'. Joanne told me that her two main concerns were working with her congregation, and ecumenism. She said: 'The church cannot survive simply by ministers trying to lead. The minister and the congregation must work together in all aspects of the ministry. I see that as crucial, though it is maybe at times not at all easy. Also, I think that we must try to be outward-looking, and positively ecumenical. We must seek every opportunity for co-operation with other churches.'

Robin said he endorsed Joanne's point about being outward-looking. 'We must get out, and stay out. It is not so much about trying to bring people into the church, it is about loosening our ties on property and institution and getting to situations of pastoral need. This attracts me to chaplaincy, particularly in hospitals and prisons where people are looking for real help.' Robin added that he was concerned about encountering cynicism. 'Ministers go out with high hopes – but then somewhere their dreams are dashed.'

Finally, a brief postscript to this section: Robin told me that he had not attended a single lecture in which John Knox had been mentioned. Fiona said that she had studied early church history, but they had 'stopped before the Reformation'. I found this astounding. Admittedly, knowing a lot about Knox and Wishart and Melville will not necessarily make you a better minister, and it certainly will not help you with practical operational skills; but, once again, I found myself asking – has the Church of Scotland so lost confidence that it no longer cares about the best and proudest times in its history? Later, I raised this concern with Prof. Stewart J. Brown, dean of the Faculty of Divinity at the University of Edinburgh. He conceded that there had been a temporary problem, because of academic staff deployments, but he assured me that this was being put right.

There is one individual in the Church of Scotland who, more than any other, has to sort out all the problems discussed above. Not only that; he also has to sharpen the Kirk's cerebral edge at the same time, given that he has recently been appointed to the key post of professor of Christian ethics and practical theology at New College, University of Edinburgh, where he is expected to be a major internationally published scholar. He is Will Storrar, convener of the Board of Ministry.

If I stress Will's personal responsibility for dealing with the difficulties which beset the ministry, and indeed for addressing the colossal crisis in ministry recruitment and retention, it is not because of any crusading bravado or excessive ego on his part. Not a bit of it. He realises that he has to work with his board as well as lead it, and that he has to persuade the courts of the democratic Kirk. He is more aware of, and sensitive to, the Kirk's traditions than most. He understands that he has to work with rather than against the current ministry.

At the same time, he is a man of great drive who keenly wants the Kirk to be seriously engaged in the wider Scotland's political, cultural, social and intellectual life, as well as its spiritual life. He is a committed Scottish patriot in the best sense of the term. I wonder whether there are all that many such individuals in the Church of Scotland. In any case, few of them are placed, as he is, to start making a significant difference. Thus, if I had to identify not so much the 'coming man' in the Kirk but, rather, an individual who is utterly convinced of the need for really deep and, if necessary, disruptive change – and then, more importantly, has the will and the energy to succeed in delivering such change – that individual would be Prof. Storrar. He is purposive and pragmatic, an enemy of inertia and a friend of vigour.

After this build-up, we come to what used to be called the nitty-gritty. What follows is an outline, in his own words, of the strategy that Will and his board are developing to revive the ministry, no less. 'First, we are looking at the auxiliary, that is, the unpaid, non-stipendiary ministry. There are only just over thirty of them in the whole of the Church of Scotland, although they were suggested by the Committee of Forty as far back as the 1970s. We have about 1,350 full-time ministers, so the auxiliaries are a tiny proportion. The Church of England has about 10,000 priests, and one in ten of them is non-stipendiary. That is the sort of proportion we should be aiming for. The auxiliaries cannot at present work independently; they have to be directed by a full-time minister. But could we not have non-stipendiaries in charge of a parish or a congregation? Our sister churches show us that we could have a far larger number of people working on a part-time basis. Auxiliaries could be given much more freedom and responsibility. Then we are working with the Board of Parish Education and the Board of National Mission to look at team ministries which would cover a larger grouping of congregations, not just those in one parish. We must push this forward.

'There is also the debate about the Readership. At present, a Reader cannot take the sacraments. But Readers are paid at present for conducting a service, whereas auxiliaries aren't. This is an anomaly. A radical option would be to have a non-stipendiary ministry of word *and* sacrament instead of Readers and auxiliaries. We are working with the appropriate boards and the Panel on Doctrine to review all this. Next, we have a new recruitment and assessment project currently being introduced. It allows a local enquiry, which gives potential candidates experience outside their own congregation but still locally. And there are the enquiry conferences being run by the Boards of Ministry, Social

Responsibility, World Mission and National Mission, and Parish Education. These conferences have been a great success in gaining interest and attendance. They are residential and last for forty-eight hours. People can ask questions and decide whether they want to sign up for the local enquiry process. The approach is gentle; it eases people in without commitment so that they can find out about going overseas, or the parish ministry, or whatever. There is good news coming out of the local enquiry process, and we are definitely encouraged.'

Will told me that it would be a year or so before all this bore fruit. He was not talking about wonder solutions; but these cross-board initiatives would help greatly. And what, I asked, about minister retention? 'Well, I agree that this is an issue that the Board of Ministry must address more and more. We have held conferences on clergy stress, and there is now manse support and a counselling service. But much more is needed. We consulted the Alban Institute in Washington to find out when in a ministerial career key stress points were most likely to emerge. These would be after five, eight and fifteen years. I am particularly concerned about the last of these, about supporting ministers in mid-life, those who have done say fifteen or twenty years. They are asking themselves if they want to keep doing this, if they can keep going for another fifteen or twenty years. Believe me, I can identify with this. Ministers are for the most part able and gifted people, but we have to give them more support, and we need to give them more mental refreshment.

'It is important that we are now aiming to recruit collaborative ministers, rather than the solo operators of the past. We are moving towards local teams, as I mentioned. Increasingly, I want to see able ministers in mid-career taking on responsibility for teams; we have not been offering such ministers enough new opportunity and fulfilment.' Like the promotion and career structures other jobs provide? 'Yes.' And would this involve an enhanced stipend? 'The answer is yes, but at this stage I'd prefer to talk in terms of increased fulfilment.'

Will summed up his approach to retention thus: 'We must give good ministers more local responsibility and challenge that is beyond the parish but not linked to 121. I'm sure this would help the problem of isolation. We are also working on a pilot project whereby ministers review their work with their peers. About forty ministers are taking part in this throughout Scotland. This again emphasises the collaborative, team approach.'

I asked if all this implied the end of the parish. 'In urban and town areas, many, including myself, would query the traditional parish model. The key challenge is to retain the vision of being a national church and for there to be worship and witness in every community' (that word again); 'but we must be far more flexible in providing this.' I commented that, in his remarks, he had not reflected much on stress. 'I am well aware of the problem of stress. Paradoxically, as the Church declines, the workload for ministers increases. Three or four ministers used to work in an area where only one is working now. I know that, where the people are older, there is a large number of funerals; and that is a draining, a most draining, personal commitment. And in rural areas, some ministers have three kirk sessions to run. I do understand that there is more administration; I accept that there are more and more meetings.'

Will reflected on his own ministry in Lanarkshire when he had a very active congregation of 1,200 and was chaplain to a primary school, a hospital and a residential home, as well as sharing a secondary-school chaplaincy. In addition, he was convener of a presbytery committee and he was the presbytery representative on the Board of Social Responsibility, for which he convened a special working party. 'That's not excessive, but it was very hard work – about seventy or eighty hours a week. We must find ways of sharing the load more, and that is why I stress the collaborative approach. I am aware that team ministries can produce their own conflicts, like personality clashes, status problems and so on. But the teams would mean that the burdens were shared and the sense of isolation was reduced.'

Many other specific ways of at once easing the ministerial work-load and dealing with shortage of personnel are being looked at, for instance the possibility of appointing lay interim moderators (a sensible innovation, which I would have thought was long overdue). But I do not wish to rehearse all the ongoing work of the Board of Ministry. What I would rather do is draw attention to two aspects of Will Storrar's remarks which strike me as especially significant.

First, if I had to identify just one key word in all that he said to me, it would be *collaborative*. Clearly, his vision is predicated on the loosening, or even the ending, of the old idea of the minister operating in isolation – or solo, to use Will's preferred term. I am sure that collaborative ministry is the right way forward; but the implications are enormous, and the skills which ministers have to offer will perhaps have to become increasingly social as opposed to cerebral. The minister-scholar working long, lonely hours on his or her sermon may well become a thing of the past. In some ways I regret this, but that is by the way; the essential point is that a completely new kind of minister is in time going to be recruited. (This, incidentally, implies a growing dislocation between the academic work being done at places like New College and the practical work being done by ministers in the field, although I reckon Will would dispute this, as he is passionate about all ministers developing their intellectual muscle.)

The other point is that Will was clearly going out of his way to emphasise the interboard and interdepartmental nature of many of the initiatives. This is in the best sense collaborative, so that is consistent; but it is also to me, an outsider, immensely frustrating. Why should a man of obvious drive and zeal be so cabined and confined by the Kirk's Byzantine and increasingly ridiculous multiplicity of boards, departments, subcommittees, panels and working parties?

If meaningful change is to be driven through, the Kirk is going to have to learn to place more emphasis on reform and less on bureaucracy. Change is the most difficult thing to push through in any organisation; it frightens people. But then the Church of Scotland is a reformed church, born in times of mind-bending and cataclysmic change. The Disruption of 1843, however unfortunate some of its consequences, was about dramatic change. And the Church of Scotland is a lean church, and it is getting leaner by the hour. The ability to embrace change should be growing. But is it?

These, I am well aware, are dangerous words, for Will has already been at the centre of a stushie over what, to my eyes, seems a relatively minor change in his board's executive set-up. The Board of Ministry hired outside consultants to look at its structures – and, although having had intense personal experience of different groups of management consultants I am somewhat sceptical about them,

I'd have thought that if there is one place in Scotland that is crying out for the scrutiny of consultants, it is 121 George Street, Edinburgh. The consultants' proposals were duly approved, without dissent.

One of the specific proposals was that the role of general secretary to the board should be split, with the general secretary's role becoming more that of leadership, along the lines of a chief executive. Responsibility for pastoral matters would be allocated to a new post, that of senior adviser (pastoral care and minister support). Early in 2001, the general secretary, Dr Sandy McDonald, a man of outstanding personal popularity within the Kirk, voluntarily and graciously offered to step down and take on the new role of senior adviser. Among other things, he thought that this would make the appointment of the new general secretary an easier process. The job of general secretary with its new remit was thus vacant; it was advertised, interviews were held, two short lists (first ten candidates and then five) were drawn up and interviewed, and eventually an outsider, Mrs Ruth Moir from Heriot-Watt University, was appointed. (She is the first of the board's general secretaries who is not a minister and not a man.) This process was conducted constitutionally and correctly throughout.

However, in the middle of it, the General Assembly was held. At this stage, Mrs Moir had not yet been appointed, but the second short list had been drawn up. There was much disquiet at the Assembly – a lot of gnashing of teeth and outpouring of angst, a little of it personally directed against Will Storrar. Some of this, I suspected, was because the deputy to Sandy McDonald, the Rev. John Chalmers, had not made the second short list. (Mr Chalmers, like Dr McDonald, is a widely liked and admired figure.) But most of the unease, and it was strongly expressed, was about the nature of the new role for the general secretary. There seemed to be a groundswell of feeling that somehow the remit was too managerial, too modern and too secular for the Kirk to stomach.

I reckon that this episode did not show the Church of Scotland at its best. Had anything been done improperly or unconstitutionally, there would have been cause for concern. But, as I say, my understanding is that everything was done by the book. The Assembly is, of course, the Kirk's supreme and sovereign court, and it could, if it wished, have thrown the entire process out. Will

Storrar acknowledged this, and made it clear to the Assembly that it had a choice. He won the day.

When I asked Will to reflect on this stushie, on the record, he demurred – for the best reasons, no doubt, of sensitivity and kindness. But he was prepared to talk to me in general terms, and I think what he said is crucially important: 'We simply must have a more effective organisation of the Church's resources at the centre to secure, among other things, its local mission. The kind of review process we engaged in was trying to address this in terms of providing more effective delivery. The problem cannot be characterised as a purely managerial one, but I would say that for over 200 years we have had a central organisation. The most gifted and able people should be serving the wider Church from this centre. Where appropriate, these people can be ministers; but we should be much more open to people with other backgrounds who can offer their considerable gifts to the Church. I would make the distinction that this is about leadership and organisation, not about management.' I am not sure that I quite understand this demarcation: leadership and organisation seem to me to be very much management matters; but then maybe Will, like so many others, is browbeaten by this peculiar notion that a church, as a spiritual organisation, cannot really be managed.

I knew as I investigated these matters that I was dealing with a great unease. I sensed this from the virulence of the debate at the Assembly and from the remarks I often heard to the effect that things were not well within the Board of Ministry. I reiterate my view that Will Storrar is a visionary, the rare kind of individual that the Kirk so badly needs if it is to renew before the current crisis becomes a terminal catastrophe. I formed this view not just as a result of my long discussion with Will, but also as a result of what other people who know him well had told me.

At the same time, I was becoming all too aware that the tensions in the board were deepening, not easing. I also understand that there are two sides to every story; so, I spoke with John Chalmers a few weeks after I had chatted with Will. John said to me: 'I think that Will has tremendous ideas about where the Church of Scotland should be going. He *is* a visionary, and he can read the times. I want to emphasise to you that the Board of Ministry is not in meltdown, whatever any people may have told you. We are getting on with our work. There are a lot of good ideas around, but we need to implement them correctly. You need to move through the steps of change in the correct way.'

Maybe I was both wrong and ingenuous when I wrote above about 'a relatively minor change in the board's executive set-up'. Maybe the changes that are under way are very major indeed, and maybe they need more time to be implemented properly. But I also believe that, in just about any private-sector organisation, change of this kind would be implemented with speed, resolution and rigour. And maybe – this is the rub – that is indeed not appropriate for a church. Maybe what I call the 'peculiar' notion that spiritual organisation cannot really be managed is not so peculiar after all. This is where I am desperately conscious that I am looking at the Kirk as an outsider; a sympathetic outsider, but an outsider nonetheless.

On one final issue, Jane Barron's point about the ignorance of congregations and even of ministers about the structure of the Church of Scotland, Will said: 'When I was a parish minister, I knew about those bits of the greater Church that I was involved in, but I never had the opportunity to find out much about what is a very complex organisation. So, yes, I do think there is widespread ignorance. Even today, after the years of decline, it is still a very large organisation. It is difficult, if not impossible, to get a handle on it all, even if you are right at the centre – so, if you are a parish minister, it is well-nigh impossible. We do have to make much greater efforts to help congregations understand what is going on. And, of course, while the ministry will become more collaborative, congregations – particularly older ones – may well still want to retain a more traditional approach.'

I had earlier discussed some of these issues concerning the future of the ministry with one of my most thoughtful interviewees, Helen McLeod – and Helen should be thoughtful, for she is convener of the Assembly Council, the Kirk's nearest animal to an internal think-tank, though I am not yet sure if it is quite thinking the unthinkable. She made a simple but immensely effective point when she said: 'Never forget that the congregations have the right to call a minister. As the ministry shortage becomes acute, we are going to have more and more vacant charges which will be very lucky indeed to find a minister. Even a prestigious congregation might now get only one or two applicants when, in the relatively recent past, they might have had twenty or more.'

Helen was suggesting that the impetus for reform of the ministry might eventually be driven up, from the congregations, as well as down, from the board. Not that she is an unfailing admirer of congregations – she was the first person whom I heard use the term 'congregationalism'; and, like the similar word 'parochialism', I guessed that it is pejorative. What Helen McLeod said was: 'We are having to fight congregationalism all the time. If you are only concerned with what happens in your own congregation, it is obvious that you will not see the wider picture. But we'll soon have to answer some major questions. What are we going to do with more and more congregations as we find we cannot get ministers for them? Do we need to develop a territorial rather than a congregational ministry? Will congregations have to learn to exist without a minister?' Although her perspective is different, you can see ideas there that are not far from Will Storrar's.

And these questions lead me towards the conclusion of this long chapter. Pro-minister as I am, I want to draw attention to the little congregation of Tenandry, in deepest Perthshire, right at the heart of Scotland. The story of Tenandry is a salutary one for all ministers. Essentially, Tenandry has survived, and indeed flourished, for many years without a minister. Now, nobody could claim that this exceptionally beautiful rural parish (the church itself is situated in lovely woodland high above the River Garry, a few hundred yards north of Garry Bridge) is in any way like most parishes in Scotland. But it is remarkable not so much for its physical beauty as for the fact that, against all the rules, it has carried on its life and work strongly and happily without an official minister for more than twenty years. It has managed to do so partly because of the efforts of an exceptional individual, Robin Barbour.

I discussed the Tenandry saga with the presbytery clerk of Dunkeld and Meigle, a veteran minister called John Russell, who was particularly helpful, candid and genial. The first thing he told me was that at times, over the years, the presbytery had simply not known what to do about Tenandry. 'I suppose it was really a continued vacancy. Robin Barbour acted as *de facto* minister without

a stipend for about twenty years. His services were much appreciated. So, technically you are right: there was no minister as such.
Instead, a small congregation had a most gifted man looking after
it over a long period. Robin is now over 80, and he has decided that
this cannot go on. When a vacancy at Blair Atholl and Struan
occurred, we decided to have linkage, and the new minister has
now been called for the linked charge. But I cannot deny it: there
was a vacancy for twenty years.'

It has to be explained here that the Very Rev. Robin Barbour is
one of the outstanding figures in modern Kirk history: war hero,
eminent theologian and academic, former moderator. As Mr
Russell put it, 'Not every rural parish has such an active and distinguished churchman willing to help out just through the goodness
of his heart'. He continued: 'Some ex-moderators can have their
heads in the clouds, but Robin Barbour, with his family's farming
background, is very much rooted in this part of Perthshire. And
I have to say that he has brought the very best out of this little
congregation.' A heart-warming story, but one that has within it a
warning for the ministry.

To end this discussion of the ministry, where it is and where it is
going, I wish to recount some of the thoughts of one of the most
sensible and sanguine ministers I met – the Rev. Iain Cunningham.
Iain, who was both vice-convener of the *Without Walls* commission and its representative on the Assembly Council, has what is in
many ways a typical parish, if such a thing can be found in Scotland.
He has been minister of Kirkton Church (850 members) in the
Lanarkshire town of Carluke for the past five years. In the course
of a long conversation, I found him somehow to be realistic, weary
and hopeful, all at the same time.

He told me: 'There was a time when the Church was really
respected, and its ministers were considered as authorities. Now
we are much more marginalised. Yet, I'm not complaining about
that. In a way, I believe that it is healthier. We must always seek to
speak with an authentic compassion for other people and not with
the authority of some abstract laws or regulations. The Church has
lost its status; and, if a minister gains respect nowadays, then it is
for the person, not the office. What I have to do as a minister is to

make the Word relevant to ordinary people, so I'm not so much a chaplain to my congregation as someone who is there to help to equip them to be Christians in the wider world, in the workplace, in their home life, in their leisure life.

'But, at the same time, we have to keep the Church running as an institution, and that is what absorbs so much energy. There is the constant, growing list of things *not* done, and that is a real source of stress. There are fewer and fewer of us, and we simply cannot expect people to work ninety-hour weeks. I do wonder if we should still be looking for omnicompetent folk who can do everything, rather than people who can be part of a team. Until the teams become a reality, you are going to get more and more ministers suffering from burnout.

'And yes, I am optimistic. We are very much in a process of transition. The old picture is breaking down, but the new picture has not yet emerged. There are signs of new life in the old Kirk. Other parts will just die. I agree with you when you say that we are not at the moment a coherent church; but that is coming again, I really believe it is.

'Meanwhile, I must say that the strain of preaching does not get any easier, though I started twenty years ago. I don't find it difficult in the pulpit; what is difficult is gathering the material and getting it into the sermon. If it doesn't excite me, I don't think it is worth communicating. It is a very real strain, and people are constantly comparing you with people on television, or even in films. And we have very little help in building our own spiritual life. Most of us ministers are pretty pathetic at that. You are left to your own devices, for example when you are praying. We are supposed to be spiritual leaders – but are we?'

4

THE SHADOW
OF THE CARDINAL

❖

This chapter deals with the vexed issue of communication. As someone who laboured in the vineyard, if that is the appropriate phrase, of Scottish journalism for thirty-two years, I must guard against a tendency to exaggerate the significance of this issue. Many journalists, friends and former colleagues, on hearing that I was writing this book, immediately told me that communication, or the lack of it, was the Kirk's biggest problem. But then they would, wouldn't they?

What worried me more was the number of others I spoke to – ordinary church members for the most part – who were concerned that the Church of Scotland was not making its voice heard in the wider community. And I soon learned that there was something of an obsession with two prominent Scottish clerics outside the Kirk – Bishop Richard Holloway (who now appears to be half in the Kirk, incidentally) and, in particular, the late Cardinal Winning. Why, I would be asked, were these two gentlemen constantly in the news in recent years? Why was there no comparable figure in the Kirk, speaking out for the Church of Scotland? Why wasn't more media attention paid to the moderator? Why were so many people left with the impression that the cardinal was the leading churchman in Scotland, the church leader who was prepared to speak out?

These often-voiced concerns led me to believe that there is a genuine issue here; it is more than a matter of mere journalistic preoccupation. Here are two quotes I was given by two prominent figures that neatly sum up the problem. Douglas Mill, secretary of the Law Society of Scotland, said: 'The Church of Scotland has not been punching anything like its true weight for many years'. John McGurk, editorial director of *The Scotsman*, the Edinburgh *Evening News* and *Scotland on Sunday*, said: 'If you were to go round the principal news editors in the Scottish media, broadcasting as well as press, I doubt if any of them could name you six current Church of Scotland ministers'. For whatever reason, the Kirk is not making its mark in the Scottish media.

If we take a historical perspective, there has without doubt been a dramatic decline in the attention paid by the Scottish press, and to a lesser extent by Scottish broadcasters, to the Kirk. In his most popular book, *The Thirty-nine Steps* (Thomas Nelson, 1922, p. 115), John Buchan at one point has his hero, Richard Hannay, holed up with malaria in a roadman's cottage near Tweedsmuir. The novel was set in the period immediately before the Great War. Hannay writes: 'Not a soul came near the place. When I was getting better, he [the roadman] never bothered me with a question. Several times he fetched me a two days' old *Scotsman* and I noticed that the interest in the Portland Place murder seemed to have died down. There was no mention of it, and I could find very little about anything except a thing called the General Assembly – some ecclesiastical spree, I gathered.' Fast forward ninety years, and *The Scotsman* virtually ignores the 'ecclesiastical spree'.

Ron Ferguson has noted, in his biography of George MacLeod, that in the 1920s the sayings and doings of prominent Scottish churchmen took up many column inches in the Scottish press. When MacLeod was called to St Cuthbert's in Edinburgh in 1926, the *Glasgow Herald* took care to record the significance of the appointment of such a young man to 'one of the great congregations in the Church of Scotland'. Even thirty years ago, when I was a young reporter on *The Scotsman*, the paper assigned a team of senior reporters to cover the Assembly (and also the Guild). I was sent up the Royal Mile to cover some of the late afternoon and evening sessions, as a sort of back-up. I was made well aware that the Assembly was to be taken very seriously indeed; and indeed it was treated with consistent respect by the paper's news desk, by its sub-editors and by its editor. Meanwhile, people like Bob Kernohan and Vernon Sproxton would be giving erudite commentaries on the radio, and these commentaries implied that the deliberations of the Assembly were of serious national import. The Kirk was still the focus of much media attention, and the Assembly was regarded as a major and protracted news event, worthy of extended reporting and much analysis.

Again, when Hugh Anderson's 'shock report' on the state of the Kirk was completed in 1971, *The Scotsman* obtained an advance copy. A senior reporter on the paper, George Barton, had worked hard to get his 'leak', and he was rewarded with not just the lead story; the whole front page was cleared, so important did the paper regard the future prospects of the Church of Scotland. It is interesting to contrast this with how the *Sunday Herald* handled a similar exclusive thirty years later. The paper got hold of an advance copy of the *Without Walls* report. The story was regarded as being of front-page significance and was given a reasonably prominent show; but it was not the lead, and the bulk of the story was consigned to inside.

When I moved into various more senior positions in the Scottish press – features editor of *The Scotsman*, deputy editor and then editor of *The Herald* – I always took the Kirk seriously and did my best to cover its affairs responsibly and thoroughly. I also worked with my old friend Stewart Lamont on both papers. Stewart is an ordained Church of Scotland minister, and he has served two very different Scottish parishes well in that capacity; but I always think of him as first and foremost a journalist. I supported him as he developed his iconoclastic and at times irreverent commentating on religious affairs. Stewart's commentaries often irritated and sometimes offended people within the Kirk, but he always knew what he was writing about, and he had the happy knack of making internal Kirk matters available and relevant to a wide audience. While this was going on, I had intermittent contact with the Kirk's communications staff. It was obvious to me that the Kirk's approach to media relations was very reactive, and to some extent hands-off.

This could not have contrasted more strongly with the approach of the Catholic hierarchy in Scotland. Archbishop Winning and his then press adviser, the indefatigable Father Tom Connolly, made it their business to get to know my then editor, Arnold Kemp, and me – and the four of us were soon enjoying occasional lunches. I was then invited down to a retreat near Girvan to address the Scottish bishops' conference. (It soon became clear that, although they wanted to hear what I had to say, I also had to listen to what they wanted to say. Fair enough. And the next day, a leading television executive was coming down to go through the same process.) The various contacts I had with the two Toms were conducted in a relaxed manner (communication became a little less regular and perhaps a little more formal when Tom Winning was elevated from archbishop to cardinal), but there was a serious point to them. Tom Winning was not slow to make it clear if something in *The Herald* had upset him; we certainly had our ups and downs, and our sessions could be quite disputatious, but they never became fractious. Indeed, Tom Winning became someone I regarded as a friend, and I was happy to attest to my respect for him, a few months before he died, in an interview for Radio Scotland with Johnston McKay.

The last time I saw the cardinal, paradoxically enough, was at a great Kirk social occasion: the final supper party Andrew McLellan held at the official moderatorial residence before he stood down as moderator. I told the cardinal then that I was shortly to embark on the writing of this book, and he said he hoped I would include him among my interviewees. He was an effective and a hard-working communicator, but he was by no means a natural one. I remember watching him deal with questions from a packed audience after he had delivered a 'Town and Gown' lecture at Strathclyde University. He was superb when dealing with an awkward question about denominational schools; he was far less impressive and assured in dealing with an equally difficult but surely equally predictable question about why there were no female priests. In other words, his high media profile did not come without sustained effort.

The late Tom Connolly was a more emollient character, but he too kept in regular touch, and at times he would let me know, in his charming way, that he felt *The Herald* was not being fair to his church. At one stage, he started mentioning that *The Herald* did not have an overtly Catholic commentator, although it had at least two who were writing from a clearly Protestant perspective. I said that was a fair point, and we would discuss it further. 'Let's have lunch,' Father Tom said; 'I'll introduce you to the very man who could do a great job for you.' When I recently recounted all this to a very senior Kirk figure, a former moderator, he seemed thunderstruck. When he recovered his composure, he told me he was amazed that the Catholic hierarchy had been so assiduous in their wooing of the media; he was also seriously concerned that the Kirk clearly did not regard this as any kind of a priority.

Now, it is obvious enough that the Church of Scotland is not a hierarchy. It is a Presbyterian church, and it lacks cardinals and archbishops and the like. But it presumably has something to say, and the big question is: who is to speak for it? Many would say the moderator; but I am not sure that the moderator has the authority to speak for all the Kirk's multifarious committees and boards (when I have raised this point, I have been given different answers by different people). Again, the convention has grown that the moderator only serves for one year, although there is nothing to stop him (or her) being renominated and re-elected. So, just when the nation might be getting familiar with him (or her), he (or she) disappears.

In a sense, the Kirk is hoist with its own democratic petard; it has no clear leader as such, and it has many voices. Yet the wider world is looking for one strong and easily identifiable voice. Winston Churchill famously said, when being congratulated on being the lion who had led Britain to victory in the Second World War, that it was the British people who had been the lion; he had had the privilege of giving the roar. Who is to roar for the Kirk? This might seem to be getting somewhat fanciful, but the point remains: the media, and I suspect much of the wider Scottish community, still seek a Kirk with a loud and strong voice.

Let me now quote, at some length, the views of someone who speaks on these matters with magisterial clarity. Ramsay Smith has worked for *The Scotsman*, the *Daily Mail* and various other papers, in Scotland and beyond. He edited the *Scottish Daily Mail* between 1997 and 2000. He now works as executive director of the big Glasgow public-relations outfit Media House. He was brought up in the Kirk, and attended Sunday school; his father is still an elder in Aberdeen. He told me: 'The Church of Scotland has to learn, and learn soon, before it is too late. It's about markets and about audiences. These are maybe not words that it likes, but they are words that the Kirk must learn to think about. You must tell the people of Scotland what you are about, and you must tell them what you are doing. When I was editing the *Scottish Daily Mail*, I was always aware that even when someone in the Kirk did speak out, his was clearly not the voice of authority. Other dissenting views were always there to be found by the media. I'm not against debate or dissent; of course I'm not. But the media do like clarity, and they do like to have clearly defined conduits. It always seemed to me that there was a really hard edge to the Catholic publicity effort, whereas the Church of Scotland often seemed muddled and soft by comparison. Ann Allen, at the Board of Social Responsibility, was maybe an exception. There were far too many committees and boards, and, if you bothered to find out what they were saying, they were often saying different things. And few Scottish journalists had any kind of working relationship with the conveners or chairs of the various boards. Even fewer understood the different responsibilities and the demarcations between them.'

Ramsay continued: 'If you look at the Special Commission for Review and Reform [*Without Walls*], this could have been sold to a wider audience, beyond the Church, in terms of positive and solid publicity. But nobody seemed to have the energy or the desire or the commitment to do that. The approach to the media seemed half-hearted. Here, as so often, outsiders were not sure what the Church of Scotland wanted. I'm not sure if the Church itself knew what it wanted. In my view, many organisations, and not just the Kirk, do not give communication anything like the appropriate status within their structure. Communication should not be regarded as an add-on, something that has to be done but is merely tolerated. Instead, it should be an integral, absolutely key part of the operation. Look at our government: see how important communication has been to the success of the New Labour government since 1997. The Kirk may be Scotland's national church, but I have to say that in this area it undoubtedly lags behind the Catholic Church, which I reckon is much more aggressively professional and much more pro-active in its attitude to the media. The Church of Scotland has great concerns, of course it has; but too many of them are never aired on television or radio or in the press.'

I mentioned to Ramsay the fact that *The Scotsman* only reported the General Assembly on one day of the 2001 gathering, and ignored it for the rest of the week. 'Well, if *The Scotsman* ignores the General Assembly, they might say that that is *The Scotsman*'s problem. Personally, I do think that *The Scotsman* should have reported the Assembly every day, but that it is not the paper's problem. The problem is the fact that *The Scotsman* did not deem the Assembly to be an essential, newsworthy event. But the Kirk is losing it at the local level too, and that could be even more worrying. Local papers don't bother to cover presbytery meetings any more.'

Ramsay summed up his views thus: 'You cannot even begin to deal with the Church's membership problem unless you are telling people out there why the Church is relevant to them. You must be in the frame all the time; you must be in the mind's eye all the time. If you don't tell the people what you are doing, the drift away will continue.' That is the verdict of an experienced, sympathetic and respected Scottish media figure. I'm sure that many, probably most, senior journalists in Scotland would concur with Ramsay's views. But I am not sure that these will resonate much within the Kirk.

The other point of view, from the very heart of the Kirk, was put with care and lucidity by Finlay Macdonald in the October 2001 issue of *Life & Work*. As previously mentioned, Finlay is principal clerk to the General Assembly, secretary to the moderator, secretary to the powerful Board of Practice and Procedure, and now, as I write this, moderator-designate. He knows more about what is going on in the Kirk than any other individual (every report from every committee crosses his large desk), and he is the nearest the Kirk has to a chief executive. Some people think that, in addition, he should be the Kirk's chief communicator; but he does not share that view. In his *Life & Work* article, Finlay explored the connected issues of communication and leadership. He pointed out that the moderator's role is largely ambassadorial and representative – the holder has no real authority within the church's decision-making structures – whereas, it seemed to him, what made certain church leaders interesting to the media was the fact that they did have real power within their churches.

Finlay was sceptical about any notion that a leader should be artificially created so that he or she would get headlines and the Kirk would be noticed. He went on to say that it seemed a matter of strength to him that on contentious issues the Kirk had room for differing views, rather than being bound by the enunciation from on high of a party line 'from which we dare not dissent'. This most interesting article clearly expressed the communication difficulties of a church that is at once conservative and democratic, at once cautious and diverse. I'm sure it is an excellent exposition of the position from within the Kirk; but then there is the question of what people outside the Kirk (all the lost sheep, as it were – all the potential members) are looking for, and the lesser question of what practitioners in the media are looking for. There is also the fact, mentioned at the beginning of this chapter, that many ordinary lay members of the Kirk are worried and confused because their church does not seem to have sufficient presence in the media. Not all, but many of them – particularly younger members – want their church to have a higher and a better-defined profile in the wider world.

Ironically, shortly before this article by Finlay appeared, a former moderator, the Very Rev. John Cairns, had been telling me that the Kirk desperately needed a chief spokesperson, but in his view it could not be the moderator because the moderator had to represent everyone within the Kirk. (This returns to the key point that the moderator's role is essentially ambassadorial.) He told me: 'I don't want a professional moderator, but I want a professional principal clerk'. He was at pains to emphasise that he implied no criticism of principal clerks, past or present. 'They try not to overstep the mark and overreach, though they do have power. Finlay is scrupulous in this respect. Indeed, he will fight tooth and nail not to say a word publicly more than he has to!' The view of John Cairns, however, is that the principal clerk must become, in effect, both chief spokes-person and chief executive. 'I'd want him to articulate what all the boards and committees are thinking, irrespective of what their particular conveners wanted. This would soon become the most important part of the job.'

I am not sure about this. Apart from the fact that the current principal clerk clearly does not think it appropriate to expand his already onerous role in this manner, I think it might vitiate his ability to be the Kirk's sensitive and all-seeing chief administrator. The media can be voracious, and I reckon that external relations would soon be taking up most of his time. I think that, instead, the Kirk should appoint a principal spokesperson. This would be a key role, one of the two or three pivotal roles in the Kirk; the incumbent would work alongside the principal clerk and report directly to him or her. If such a post were to be created, the media at large would no doubt expect it to be filled by a high-powered journalist rather than a cleric. But I am convinced that it should be a cleric. Dare I say it, there are many excellent and reasonably worldly communicators among the ranks of the ministry. Indeed, privately I have two or three ministers in mind for this putative post. To bring in an outsider would create additional tensions when the job would already be difficult enough.

The Kirk strikes me as being somewhat ambiguous about communication. It wills the end, but is wary of the means. It already has a Board of Communication. The convener and vice-convener are both ministers, and they are responsible for a large professional staff at 121 George Street, including a director of communication and a head of media relations. It is clear that neither the board's convener nor these two members of staff have been given the remit to be high-profile spokespersons for the entire Kirk. Indeed, their role is not intended to be pro-active in this respect, although, when I put that point to the head of media relations, Pat Holdgate, she said that she did try to be more pro-active but that her work tended to be reactive because so many people contacted her looking for reaction and guidance on a whole range of issues.

I watched Pat in action during the General Assembly, and she was tireless in the support and guidance she gave to the various media representatives who attended, and to some who did not attend but still wanted information. As is the way with the media, some of them were well informed; others wanted elucidation in a manner that could only be described as crass or ingenuous or downright ignorant. Pat dealt with them all with equanimity, patience and professionalism.

The Kirk must decide two things, and soon. Does it want to speak with one clear voice? And if it does, who is to articulate that voice? If the answer to the first question is no, then it will continue to suffer in the media stakes, and that means that many people who long for it to have a greater public presence in Scotland will continue to be disappointed. And I am not convinced by any arguments about democratic or Presbyterian purity. It might be a glib point, but I don't think that such considerations in any way diminished the power and efficacy of John Calvin and John Knox as communicators.

I have made it as clear as I can that I think the Kirk should speak with one voice and have one generally recognised spokesperson (not the moderator and not the principal clerk). But this is not to say that everyone else should shut up. On the contrary – I envisage a twin-track strategy, and I believe that the appointment of a principal spokesperson would actually liberate many articulate people within the Kirk to speak out much more easily and readily than they do now. They could do so untrammelled by any fear that they were usurping the role of the Kirk's specifically designated official voice. The media would soon come to recognise the principal spokesperson as being just that; the media would also learn to differentiate between the principal spokesperson, as the official voice of the Kirk, and other prominent voices from within the Kirk, such as that of the moderator.

Finally, here are two small postscripts to this section, both reflecting on the media legacy of the late cardinal. Pat Holdgate told me that, following his death, there had been something of a vacuum in media terms, though 'I think we are beginning to fill that vacuum, slowly but surely'. Professor Duncan Forrester of New College counselled me not to become too obsessed with the cardinal's potency as a communicator. His view was that Tom Winning had been very much a one-off as a communicator; and he asked if I could remember Tom's predecessor as Archbishop of Glasgow, and what kind of media impact he had made. The answers were: I could, and just about zero.

Most of the above has been mediacentric, to use an ugly word. But communication is about more than the media. I am concerned that the Kirk, at local level, is not communicating effectively even through such basic tools as exterior church noticeboards. These boards could be used far more effectively; but, even if we ignore that relatively uncontroversial statement, it is unfortunate if these public boards are conveying information that is just plain wrong. Yet, without trying at all, I found a blatant example in Inverness of a noticeboard giving erroneous information. Sometimes it seems that, at local level (the very level that *Without Walls* is so eloquently concerned about), the Kirk exists for the members and nobody else. It is difficult to determine how much of the Kirk's time should be devoted to outreach; but surely everybody in the Kirk must keep bearing in mind the lost sheep and the prodigal son. Surely the job of communication at local level is to get through to a few lost sheep and a few prodigal sons?

It is no good saying that every regular member knows when the next service is and that the information was in last week's intimations, read sonorously from the pulpit. The Kirk should be actively and aggressively encouraging visitors to attend worship; other things will lead on from that. And to get visitors to attend worship, you have to use all the tools at your disposal; not just noticeboards, though they are more important than some might think, but also community newsletters, local papers, local radio stations and so on. I mentioned in Chapter 2 the excellent leaflet I came across giving simple information about the times of services at all the Episcopal churches in the north of Scotland. The Kirk should be producing leaflets such as this, with more detailed information if possible, and flooding them into every likely or unlikely locus: hotels, visitor centres, community centres, cafes, pubs, newsagents, banks, building societies – anywhere that will take them.

In an aside here, I was interested to read Ronald Blakey's editorial comment, in the official Kirk *Year Book 2001/2002*, anent (to use an annoying Kirk word) a plea for some details of Sunday services. I quote him in full (p. xix):

> There was an interesting suggestion that Sunday service times should be shown for each congregation. Apart altogether from the lynch mob of Presbytery Clerks who would want a quiet word up a dark alley if such information were requested, the thought of incorporating accurately the variations that come with communion, summer and various seasons of the Christian Year was not one which the Editor could face unemotionally. When the complexities of occasional evening services and the particular arrangements

in multiple rural linkings, often with fifth Sunday of the month complications, are added in, it became clear that the labour involved would be out of proportion to any benefit that would be gained.

Well, the *Year Book* may not be the appropriate place for such information; but I think Mr Blakey protests too much. We are, after all, talking about public, not private, services; this is not secret or esoteric information, to be hidden away from the general public, as if it were none of its business. And, if the collating of such information is too much work for presbytery clerks, then, to paraphrase Mr Blakey, perhaps these clerks should indeed be led up a dark alley – that's where they belong.

In short, the Kirk must begin to take much more seriously the whole business of telling people what it is offering – which starts with the providing of basic local information. I'm sure the Kirk's own professional communications staff at 121 George Street would be more than willing to help in this effort. And, if we are to move eventually towards a structure of bigger and better presbyteries, then grass-roots communication should be one of their key functions. Outside aid can be sought from the Department of Communication if it is appropriately funded and resourced to provide this service. Public-relations and advertising agencies also have their uses. Here, it is important to explain what I mean by PR. Ron Ferguson told me, in no uncertain terms: 'I'm not against PR as such, but I'm very against glitzy presentation that is about selling myths. PR can never be a solution to any of our real problems. Should the Church rebrand itself? Never! Would people be flooding into the pews if we had better PR? Never!' I agree, up to a point, Lord Copper. PR or even advertising agencies must never be unleashed by the Kirk to do a hard sell as if Presbyterianism were the next commodity to be punted to a gullible consumerist public. On the other hand, they could help, particularly at local level, with specific marketing tasks.

In my career as a journalist, I got to know many people in PR and advertising in Scotland, and I have spoken to quite a few of them about the Kirk. I do not wish to present their views here in case any of them appear to be pitching for the last great account – that of 121 – but I do want to make one exception and quote the constructive and helpful views of one man, Alasdair Gibbons, who is client services director of the small but highly effective Glasgow agency Clayton Graham (and, incidentally, a member of New Kilpatrick, Bearsden). Alasdair believes there is no reason what-soever why the Kirk should not approach advertising agencies. 'After all, it is promoting a product which has an audience, or a potential audience.' But he thinks that an advertising campaign would be unlikely to work at a national level, through television stations or newspapers such as the *Daily Record*, *The Herald* or *The Scotsman*.

Rather, he thinks that agencies could be invited to pitch to develop a marketing strategy that would already have been proposed by the Kirk. It would work from the bottom up, through parishes to presbyteries. This strategy would be to back up a campaign that had already been worked out at local level. 'It could be something very straightforward. Why not get everyone at every church in the presbytery on a particular Sunday to be asked to try hard to bring along a friend, a colleague, a relative or a lapsed member the following Sunday? These folk would be invited along to see what was on offer at local level, because I believe the Church works at its best at parish level, and I personally don't have any wider idea of the Church existing as a great corporate body. All that really matters to me is how the Church manages locally.' (Apart from anything else, this clearly fits in well with the thrust of *Without Walls*.) Alasdair's idea of a 'Super Sunday' is simple but potentially very effective. The key point is that the initiative would be developed locally and announced from the pulpits; the agency would provide back-up and assistance but would not instigate the campaign. And, although he uses terms like market and audience and product, he is sensitive to the Kirk's status, to the fact that it is, after all, a church and not a corporation.

I believe, however, that such sensitivity can be overdone. Let us turn to another Kirk member in the West of Scotland, who is a leading businessman and who works in the media. He is Colin McClatchie, general manager for News International in Scotland. That means he is responsible for *The Times*, *The Sunday Times*, the *Sun* and the *News of the World* north of the border. He is a member of Kilmacolm Old, where his wife Claire is an elder. Colin is very direct on the theme of communication, which he regards as a crucial management function. He insisted to me that the Kirk cannot communicate effectively with its existing members, let alone potential ones, until it knows more about them and about itself.

'I don't believe it understands its members. You cannot communicate with people if you don't understand them. Let's not call them members; let's call them customers. How can the Kirk satisfy their needs if it doesn't know who they are and what they want? We need information, and we need to use that information dynamically and constructively. Why are some congregations rising? Which ones are they? Why are other congregations losing far more? Which ones are they? Let's find out exactly and specifically what the differences are between those two groups. Let's have an intensive survey of the entire membership. And after that, you can get hold of recently lapsed members and find out exactly why they are no longer customers.

'You must understand the market you are in. Market research is your key tool. You must get the data, and then analyse it from all angles to understand what is going on. Otherwise, you will never recruit new customers. Otherwise, you will never be able to communicate properly. At present, the Church is all over the place in terms of its management and communications structures. No businessman of any standing would take on the Church of Scotland as it is presently structured. And there is no point in being the moral or spiritual guardians of the people if you are eventually going to have no church left. Who is going to run the business? Forget the moral and spiritual arguments for the time being. You must look at the executive structures. You must find out about your customers and your potential customers. There is no point in talking about anything else until you have got that sorted out.'

Many people in the Kirk, and possibly some outside, will find that disturbing; the tone comes over as brash and aggressive. But, as I listened to Colin saying these words, I was aware of his passion; he is sincerely concerned about the future of the Church of Scotland, and as a leading businessman he is worried and in a way hurt that it is ignoring what he would regard as elementary professional imperatives. Once again, some will find unfortunate, or even offensive, the use of words such as product, market, customers, business and management in the context of a church. But the Kirk cannot kid itself. For example, if it wants a chief executive – and *Without Walls* thinks it should have one – then this is the kind of language it is going to have to learn to live with.

Put it another way: why should those Christians, who are operating daily as senior executives in the business world, be told that their practice and their language must be cast aside every Sunday? Why must they be told that they have in effect to operate in two different worlds? The Kirk takes their money and it seeks their service; I don't believe it should be too fastidious, or it might become hypocritical.

I personally have never been a businessman, but I have worked for some pretty hard and commercially aggressive employers and some pretty tough executives, and I have operated at the hard end in what is often cited as the most competitive newspaper market in Europe. I have been involved for more than half my life in creating and bringing out a totally new product six days a week – week in, week out. My livelihood has been wholly dependent on the ability of the team around me to sell a sufficient number of products every day in a desperately competitive market place. In doing this, I have come to respect – not despise – people who operate at the cutting edge in the private sector. That is not a political statement; it is an ethical one. Such people have many skills and many ideas to offer, and I don't see why a church should eschew them just because it is a church.

Thus, I do not believe that introducing some good modern management and communication practice is any kind of spiritual affront. Almost certainly, the day will come when the Kirk is going to have to embrace modern business practice. Indeed, I may not be radical enough in this chapter. For example, I have said that my proposed principal spokesperson should be a minister. I know that many business and media people would be aghast at the thought; they would want a proven secular communicator brought in from outside the Kirk. Again, we must remember that the Christian church in the past has used radical and controversial communication techniques.

Paul of Tarsus and Martin Luther were maybe the most effective communicators of all time, after Christ Himself. Who is to say what methods Paul and Martin would or would not be using, were they alive today? The giants of the Reformation period were not slow to avail themselves of the possibilities presented by the new printing press. If we try to get into the general European mindset at the beginning of the sixteenth century, I'm sure that many, probably most, senior people in the Church (unreformed as it then was) would have been appalled at the notion that the Bible could be printed as a mass, popular publication and circulated to ordinary people and – horror of horrors – translated into robust contemporary language in all the vulgarity and accessibility that robust contemporary language always possesses. (The language of the sixteenth century might seem beautiful but a bit archaic to us now; but it certainly did not then – an obvious point, but a most important one.) So, when it comes to communication, I don't think we should be too precious or over-sensitive. We certainly should not cocoon the Kirk in the protective wrapping of the recent past. And, as I say, I'm not being too radical or abrasive here. I'd just like the Kirk to be less cautious. As one minister told me, 'At the heart of the gospel is risk'. I'd like the Kirk to be far more pro-active and more enthusiastic about pro-claiming good news – not just the essential good news of the gospel, but also its own specific good news when that arises, as it often does.

One of my ideas is that all ordained people in the Kirk, all ministers and elders, should wear at all times in public some badge or emblem or symbol to indicate that they are special people with an explicit calling. The design of this badge could be the subject of a great national competition, presided over perhaps by the Committee on Artistic Matters. If such a competition were to be launched, it would, without doubt, create enormous media interest – *provided that an effective communication strategy had been thought through and put in place*. Another of my ideas is that the Church of Scotland should promote a great national revival of Easter as *the* Christian festival. Here again, an effective, pro-active, coherent and imaginative communications effort would be required.

The Kirk has already, in at least one respect, made a bold com-munications decision. The appointment, relatively recently, of Rosemary Goring as editor of *Life & Work* was an enlightened and, in my opinion, very positive decision. *Life & Work* is now being talked about as it has not been since Bob Kernohan's time, several editors back. It has been challenging the Kirk from within, which is all to the good. To allow Rosemary to edit in the spirited and at times controversial manner which is her style indicates to me a maturity and self-confidence that the Kirk has not always shown when it comes to communication in other areas. Sadly for the Kirk, Rosemary's journalistic excellence has not gone unnoticed, and she has now been spirited off to my former paper, *The Herald.*

Such maturity and self-confidence could be deployed, needless to say, elsewhere. I've made it clear that I think a principal spokesperson should be appointed. But – and this is crucial – this could only work if it was part of a twin-track approach. Ministers, conveners, secretaries, clerks, elders, deacons, chaplains, youth workers, development workers, ordinary members, whoever – if they have something pertinent to say, they should be encouraged to say it. They should be given professional support in saying it. The Kirk should not be scared or wary of having many articulate voices, so long as it also has one universally recognised voice speaking for the entire Church of Scotland.

I think it would be necessary for the principal spokesperson to convene a weekly media conference. At first, there might well be a certain amount of indifference; but, if the spokesperson had something useful to say, and if questions on anything and everything were answered fairly and lucidly, then news editors, and indeed the Press Association and other agencies, would soon regard this as a 'diary' fixture – in other words, one of these indispensable regulars on which the weekly news agenda is built.

To explain further: the result of this twin-track approach would result in anarchy only if mischief-makers could present the views of ministers or conveners or others who were speaking out as the views of the Kirk *as a whole.* If you had a high-profile principal spokesperson, clearly articulating the agreed line of the Kirk as a body, then such confusion or anarchy would not arise. (I am, by the way, getting fed up writing about this putative 'principal spokesperson' – such a clumsy phrase. The Kirk would no doubt be able to come up with a suitable and Scottish title for him or her.)

One thing that the Kirk must never do is gag its more creative and articulate members. They are, or should be, among its leaders – and, as Lord Sutherland of Houndwood, principal of the University

Edinburgh (and professor of the philosophy of religion), told me, the Kirk needs to pay more serious attention to encouraging and nurturing and training its leaders, present and future. 'Leadership is essential if the Church of Scotland is to arrest its decline,' he said. 'It must find ways of encouraging its key and creative people to act *more like leaders*. They must learn to interact with the media, and the Church must learn to help them do this. This is where training and back-up are so important. You need intelligent and able people who are pro-active and have a lot to say. I'm sure there are people like this in the Kirk, but we are not hearing from them. We should be hearing a great deal from them.'

Of course, some will argue wearily that there is too much babble out there anyway. And much communication can no doubt be condemned as being ultimately irrelevant or even meaningless. To quote, from 'Vastness' by Alfred Lord Tennyson, the greatest of the Victorian poets: 'What is it all but a murmuring of gnats in the gloom?' But this is hardly a time for good people to be silent. It is a time for the Kirk to be heard, and heard well.

5

THE HOT KIRK
(IT AIN'T COOL)

—————————— ❖ ——————————

GRIM IMAGES OF PRESBYTERIANISM — THE NEED TO
EMBRACE ARTISTS — CORE CREATIVE CENTRES IN
SHOWCASE CHURCHES — THE TEENS ARE MISSING —
THE NEED FOR YOUTH WORKERS

In this chapter, I wish to examine some issues that probably do not each require a whole chapter of discussion. The first is the question of perception – or its corollary, image, to use an overworked word. There is glibness in the way the Church of Scotland is lazily understood to be grim or dreary or repressive by those who don't bother to find out anything about it.

Prof. Duncan Forrester told me: 'A massive cultural change of seismic proportions has led in one generation to the legacy of Calvin and Knox, that was for centuries a matter of national pride, becoming a major embarrassment to many. In the Church, and in theology, there appears to be a crisis of confidence.' Maybe the Kirk should be more active in presenting its joyous face; it certainly has one, but it is admittedly not always the one that is promoted to the world. I agree with Duncan Forrester that there has been a colossal cultural change in the past twenty-five years or so, but I think that the idea of Presbyterianism being in essence miserable and gloomy goes back, in Scotland and beyond, a lot further. The problem is, I reckon, deep-rooted. John Knox has, for a very long time, been traduced as a killjoy; this is the man who in actuality, in the week he was dying, ordered a new hogshead of wine to be opened, and urged his guests to drink freely since he knew he would not live long enough to finish it himself.

The great Frenchman Voltaire, one of the most powerful and celebrated writers of the eighteenth century, mocked Presbyterians, and particularly Presbyterian ministers, in one of his famous *Letters*

Concerning the English Nation (published in Britain in 1722, in France in 1723). I'd like to quote a passage from this particular – and very mischievous – letter, as I reckon it has been extremely influential through the years.

> The Church of England is confined almost to the kingdom whence it received its name, and to Ireland, for Presbyterianism is the established religion in Scotland. This Presbyterianism is directly the same with Calvinism, as it was established in France, and is now professed at Geneva. As the priests of this sect receive but very inconsiderable stipends from their churches, and consequently cannot emulate the splendid luxury of bishops, they exclaim very naturally against honours which they can never attain to . . . The Scotch Presbyterian affects a serious gait, puts on a sour look, wears a vastly broadbrimmed hat, and a long cloak over a very short coat; preaches through the nose, and gives the name of the whore of Babylon to all churches where the ministers are so fortunate as to enjoy an annual revenue of five or six thousand pounds; and where the people are weak enough to suffer this, and to give them the titles of my lord, your lordship or your eminence.
>
> These gentlemen, who also have some churches in England, introduced there the mode of grave and severe exhortations. To them is owing the sanctification of Sunday in the three kingdoms . . . Though the Episcopal and Presbyterian sects are the two prevailing ones in Great Britain, yet all others are very welcome to come and settle in it and live very sociably together though most of their preachers hate one another almost as cordially as a Jansenist damns a Jesuit . . .

In fairness, to balance this, I should perhaps quote from that greatest of Fifers, the philosopher and economic theorist, Prof. Adam Smith, who, writing about fifty years later in his masterwork, *The Wealth of Nations*, asserted that: 'There is scarce perhaps to be found anywhere in Europe a more learned, decent, independent and respectable set of men than the greater part of the Presbyterian clergy of Holland, Geneva, Switzerland and Scotland'.

There was more to the Kirk, however, than its clergy; and, for much of the 130 years after the Scottish Reformation, it was engaged in a struggle for its very survival. At the period when the First English Civil War was breaking out, both the Catholic king of

England, Charles I, and the English Protestant Parliament, asked the Scots to come south and help them. The Scots intervened (quite correctly, in my opinion) on the side of the Parliament, but the consequences of this intervention were to be both protracted and problematic. For one reason or another, not least the Scots' constant involvement in the affairs of England, it was not until 1690 that the Kirk's future was safely secured and that Presbyterianism had finally triumphed.

In a single eloquent sentence, the historian John Prebble summed up the long struggle thus: 'After 130 years the Kirk was finally victorious, but preoccupation with the long struggle had stunted the artistic and intellectual growth of the country south of the Highland line, hampered its industry and economy, and given it a tradition of hard, self-sacrificial intolerance that would dominate its spirit for another century, and more' (from *The Lion in the North*, Secker & Warburg, 1971). I think the last part of the sentence is a bit unfair to what was to become the Scotland of the Enlightenment; but overall Prebble was undoubtedly right, and in this particular context his suggestion of a long legacy of hardness, intolerance and artistic poverty is depressingly valid.

Scotland's pre-eminent literary agent, Giles Gordon, told me: 'My understanding is that for many years the Church of Scotland did suffer from a lack of aesthetic input; as far as the arts were concerned, it just did not want to know. Unfortunately, that is still the case, insofar as it does seem extraordinarily reluctant to embrace Scotland's flourishing artistic community. We have so many excellent young artists, painters, poets, writers, composers ... why is the Church not more of a patron? Why is it not commissioning more new works? Why is this? Does it not have the money? Or does is it somehow think that artists are vulgar and non-Christian?'

Voltaire in the eighteenth century; Rikki Fulton in the twentieth. Dr Graham Walker told me that 'the dominant impression of Presbyterianism in contemporary Scotland is derived from Rikki Fulton's skit on the stereotypical Kirk minister, the Reverend I. M. Jolly'. Dr Walker is an academic, deeply sympathetic to the Church of Scotland, although much irritated by its failures, who tilts eloquently against the facile use of the 'dour' and 'joyless' Calvinist stereotype in Scottish culture; but the stereotype is there, and it is strongly rooted. So, what can be done?

I reckon, first, that although in general I would agree with Giles Gordon, the Kirk *has* made a considerable musical contribution to the greater Scotland. And I think it should now make more of an effort to parade its joyful side through music. I discussed both the Kirk's musical past and its musical potential with Conrad Wilson, doyen of Scottish music critics. (Conrad has had a distinguished journalistic career with both *The Scotsman* and, latterly, *The Herald*; and, if you have ever read one of the excellent Edinburgh Festival concert programme notes, the chances are that you will have been reading Conrad's words. He is also an eminent musical biographer, having written the authorised biography of Sir Alexander Gibson and books on, among others, Giacomo Puccini and Kiri te Kanawa.)

Here are his comments: 'The Church of Scotland has had a most beneficial, if indirect, influence on the musical life of Scotland; for example, its great psalms have influenced some of our finest composers. And there has been a most practical influence too, through the building up of choirs and choruses, and the playing of organ music. The influence of Johann Sebastian Bach on Protestant Scotland was particularly strong, and many Church of Scotland choirs have been quite exceptional in their singing of Bach cantatas. In the bigger churches, the presence of a good choirmaster and/or organist is vitally important. These people can have enormous influence for the good. But I must say that many of the current ones are lousy; too many of them are backward-looking, and no good at all.

'I would say to the Church of Scotland that it must pay much more attention to hiring really good musicians to recruit, train and build up its principal choirs. It will have to learn to pay a lot more, though; most of its organists and choirmasters are not paid anything like enough. And again, with a few honourable exceptions, nothing like enough has been done to upgrade its church organs. But of course this also costs money, serious money. I know that building up a good choir can help to get younger people involved, and I understand that an absence of young people is a problem for the Church of Scotland and other churches. Most excellent choirs have a really good generational spread. A fine church choir is a superb training ground for a young person learning how to sing; you get to sing in parts, for example. I also think the Church could pay more attention to commissioning and nurturing composers. The two most prominent religious composers in Scotland in recent times have both been Catholics: Thomas Wilson (no relation) and James MacMillan. And finally, I would say that, although the determination of some of its churches to encourage silly and trendy music has not helped at all, the record of some of its bigger churches in encouraging good music has been outstanding.'

I asked Conrad to identify such churches, and off the top of his head he listed: St Giles Cathedral, and Greyfriars, Edinburgh; St Mary's, Haddington; Glasgow Cathedral; Paisley Abbey; St Magnus Cathedral, Kirkwall; and Dornoch Cathedral. There is much food for thought there; and I was especially interested in his remarks that choirs could be useful conduits for getting young people on board. This is one of the Kirk's chronic problems, and here at least is one avenue that could be explored more energetically.

When I discussed artistic matters with Sir Timothy Clifford, the effervescent director-general of Scotland's National Galleries, he was fizzing with ideas for the Kirk but much less sanguine about its past contribution to the visual arts. 'The Church of Scotland has historically done very little to patronise the visual arts. Nothing like enough. The opportunities to beautify and enrich its great churches have been there and are still there, but it is not doing enough to seek out benefactors. There are so many good young artists around in Scotland, but the Church seems to be ignoring them. Why doesn't it give them some commissions? Indeed, what exactly *is* the Church doing? Yes, I know it is going out to help, and dealing with social problems and so on, which is so important – but if it really wants to reach out, particularly to younger people, it should start thinking more about smells and bells and, in particular, about visual excitement. This is not papish; it's just about excitement and fun, and that should be part of religion. No wonder if it can't get young people to come along. And the individual churches themselves should be commissioning more; but it must be done in the right way. Look at the choristers at St Giles; they look as if they are permanently habited in sackcloth and ashes. As I say, the Church needs more brightness and more fun.'

What I draw more than anything from these two conversations – admittedly with people not themselves in the first flush of youth – is that the Kirk could engage more imaginatively with the younger artistic community and with more aspiring artists, amateur or professional, as a means of building bridges with the wider constituency of young people. To return to where this chapter started, such artistic engagement would help to dispel the prevalent perception of the Kirk as being dowdy and dismal.

As I reflected on what these two most eminent artistic pundits had told me, I concluded that the Kirk's record in musical achievement has been, and is, superior to its record in visual art. And, in music, exciting things are continuing to happen. The Kirk does take music seriously at all levels; when I attended a meeting of St Andrews presbytery, there was an intensive if not overlong debate about the Worship and Doctrine Committee's revision of the hymnary. Such (to me) recondite matters as the maintenance of the pitch of hymn tunes so that they would lend themselves to four-part singing led to very animated discussion.

Andrew McLellan had told me that by far the best-known current Kirk minister outside Scotland was the Rev. John L. Bell of the Iona Community. Himself a supremely talented musician, John is currently engaged, among many other projects, in revising the hymnary; he is the convener of the committee charged with that task. He is also the man behind *Common Ground*, the ecumenical and worldwide collection of contemporary songs and hymns published by Saint Andrew Press, the Kirk's publishing house, and now found in so many kirks. He has had no fewer than fourteen collections of songs and anthems published all over the world. His material has been translated into ten different languages. When I eventually tracked him down, he had just returned from Indianapolis in the USA, where he had been working with literally thousands of young Catholics, teaching them songs from all over the world.

John has done as much as anyone to cheer up the Kirk in recent years, and in particular to brighten up worship, yet he was remarkably realistic and even in some ways downbeat when I spoke to him. I asked him if the notion of Calvinistic dourness affected the popular idea of the Kirk here and abroad. 'Yes, it does, but I think that to some extent the Church itself plays up to that idea. Inevitably, when I'm working with people in the Kirk, some of them will say: Oh, that is too emotional, or Oh, that is far too outlandish. We did have a severe and censorious past a long time ago, but even now it is difficult to escape from it.'

I asked about music and young people, and to my surprise John said: 'No, I don't believe that music itself will get young people back into church. That's naïve. We don't have a culture where young people would normally sing, as they would have done thirty or forty years ago. This is because the number of youth choirs and the teaching of singing in schools have gone into reverse. The nature of contemporary popular music has changed, too. And I don't need to tell you that the last thing any young person wants is a 35-year-old with a guitar round his neck trying to convince him or her that Cliff Richard is attractive. No, what young people want is *to belong*. They want to be part of a vibrant and transforming church. If the church is stagnant, they have no reason to come along, let alone stay in it. You have to make young people involved, feel that they belong. The Catholic Church is very good at this in various parts of the world; it is good at making young people feel they are part of it, that they belong to it.'

Someone very different from John Bell but also very much an artistic force for good in the church is Donald Smith, director of the Netherbow Centre in Edinburgh, which provides ideas, advice and assistance on artistic matters for any congregation, group or individual within the Kirk. Donald also runs the Scottish Story-telling Centre and the Netherbow Theatre from the same base, next to the John Knox House in the Royal Mile, and he told me that he probably has more artistic freedom than any other arts director in Scotland, which redounds enormously to the Kirk's credit. The Netherbow Centre is to be redeveloped at a cost of over £3 million; and, although the funding for this project has not yet been finalised, at least half of it will come from the Kirk; the other half will come from grants and private contributions. (Sadly, when the plans for the new-look Netherbow were unveiled in December 2001, the editor of the Edinburgh *Evening News*, John McLellan, regarded the story as being of sufficient importance to make it a page lead, with a big illustration; but the Kirk was not mentioned in the story once.)

As so often in the Kirk, this excellent activity and enterprise by people like John Bell and Donald Smith does not always appear to be harnessed for the greater good of the Kirk or brought very strongly to the attention of the wider Scottish public. There needs to be more effort to develop the artistic work that is already under way, and a completely new effort to use artistic talent – and particularly young artistic talent – to assist the Kirk in its outreach activities. In other words, the Kirk has comprehensively undersold itself as a patron of the arts.

One way of encouraging a greater focus on creativity, particularly by and for the young, would be to develop a series of core artistic centres round some of the Kirk's greatest churches, such as its ancient cathedrals. This idea was first put to me by Ron Ferguson, admittedly not in the specific context of artistic endeavour; and I thought initially that it was a bit elitist and contrary both to Ron's personal left-wing credentials and to the Kirk's wider democratic traditions. But the more I thought about this idea, the better it got. After all, the reality within the Kirk, whether it is commonly admitted or not, is that some of its great churches have much higher status and cachet than other lesser churches; and ordinary people, not necessarily connected with the Kirk in any way at all, often take great pleasure in visiting such magnificent buildings.

Essentially, Ron's notion was that 'fantastic' buildings, such as the Kirk's cathedrals, can often in themselves give a kick-start to activities of all sorts, simply because they are deemed by so many people beyond the Kirk to be engaging and exciting places (and, therefore, places that are not generally thought to be dourly Calvinist or Presbyterian). Building on these positive outside perceptions, the Kirk could identify teams of key people who would be at the forefront of various innovative projects, based around the showcase churches. 'These buildings are often subsidised publicly, by the council or by the state, and we should pay back by selecting and encouraging people with particular creative gifts, basing them in or around the buildings and then getting them to develop their gifts in an ecumenical and team environment', Ron told me.

He was, needless to say, at pains to stress that such identifying of a series of key centres for spiritual and pastoral (and, I would add, artistic) creativity would not be at the expense of the Kirk's outreach in less fashionable purlieus. 'The Church in places like, for example, Castlemilk and Easterhouse requires special talents, and we should be doing more to identify the talents that are required to *make it happen* in these places', he said (having already spoken very warmly of the exceptional work that Moderator John Miller has been doing during his long ministry in Castlemilk).

I suppose part of this idea is predicated on the ending of the traditional lottery of the 'call' by a particular congregation, and on getting the Kirk to direct its available talent in more of an organised and planned manner. Put like that, the idea might seem very centralising and non-democratic indeed; it certainly implies that people at the centre, in the Board of Ministry or wherever, should be able to deploy the Kirk's personnel in a way that might potentially antagonise, and remove power from, local congregations. But then, as the team rather than the solo approach to ministry develops, such ideas are going to develop inexorably; so, the Kirk might as well start discussing them now rather than later.

When I was talking to the Rev. John Munro in Kinross, he told me, quite independently, without knowing anything at all of Ron's idea, that one possible future pattern of Kirk worship would be to have small groups of people meeting to worship regularly in houses, and then every so often gathering in big churches and great cathedrals, where you would have exciting, innovative and creative services – and the big buildings would be absolutely packed.

I have touched above on the problem of the Kirk's inability to attract young people. This is an area where I encountered something close to despair. For example, when I was chatting with Principal David Lyall of New College, a man who is a world authority on pastoral counselling, an experienced minister, a distinguished theologian and altogether a wise and compassionate servant of the Church of Scotland, he looked at me long and hard when I asked how we could get teenagers back into the Kirk. Then, after this protracted pause, he said, with quiet, plain honesty: 'I simply don't have any answers'.

The problem is compounded by the Kirk's contrasting, and very real, success with young children. Time and time again, I was told of congregations with good-going Sunday schools, hugely successful annual picnics and nativity plays and the like. John Munro in Kinross told me with great enthusiasm about the writing groups who were now planning and developing their own syllabus for the parish's very successful Sunday school. 'It means we can have a family service, with the Sunday school coming into the church in effect to teach the adults. We are now into the third year of writing our own material, and at least one neighbouring church wants us to help them revive their ailing Sunday school in this way. We have more than eighty in our Sunday school [this in a congregation of just under 750 members], and the regular Sunday-school teachers are not burdened every week because the writing group, having written the new material, can come and present it. The idea came from a Sunday-school elder who was not trained in this work; in fact she is a dental hygienist.' Once again, here was an idea that had taken off at the micro, local level.

The trouble is that the youngsters who are being enthused and engaged by schemes such as these seem to vanish like the proverbial snow off a dyke when they are about 11 or 12 years old. There are various reasons for this; one is that the transition from primary to secondary school coincides with the arrival of adolescence and all its attendant changes. Suddenly, parents become people to be defied; suddenly, image is all-important; suddenly, the concern to be *cool* overrides previous certainties. The Kirk is associated with the previous, primary, life, and with parental values; whatever else it is perceived to be, it certainly ain't cool.

When I was in Orkney, I discussed these and related issues with two very articulate 18-year-olds, both of them committed to the Kirk – Lucy Holt and Katharine Beaven. Lucy told me: 'Your parents undoubtedly have a huge say in your life up to the end of primary school. But thereafter it's not the done thing to go to church, especially if your parents go. And at the age of 12 or 13, sitting and behaving well for an hour or so suddenly becomes quite a big deal. Religion has been around for so long – young teenagers want to be different, although in actual fact the most different thing they could do would be to go to church.'

Lucy had, at one stage, been involved in the planning of a series of early-morning services at St Magnus Cathedral. 'We would take the whole service for the younger kids. It was really good, and we felt really involved. Eventually, the early service stopped because the kids didn't like having to get up early, and also because some of the parents had to take them home before coming back for the main service. But I think we could experiment more. Surely part of the main Sunday morning service could be aimed directly at young teenagers?' (I had certainly witnessed a service just like that in Cults, near Aberdeen; the trouble is, that kind of worship might end up alienating everybody else.) But Lucy's main proposal for getting young teenagers to stay in the Kirk was the appointment of youth leaders. 'We had one who was only here for three days, but he was full of ideas and he made a big impact. The youth leader we have now is quite old!'

Katharine told me that 'the time to hit them is between primary and secondary school. Then you should give them something to look forward to, and emphasise that they are needed and that they have something to contribute. This is the time when they are suddenly trying to look cool in front of their peers. It is a difficult time, but I think you could develop a range of participatory services for the 12–16s. You have to remember that when they start at secondary school they tend also to start a whole range of extra-curricular activity, and it is also the time when they start going out to dances and so on. They do not like Sunday mornings! As for the message of religion, I think it has been lost. Religious education at school is a joke, and the image of the church itself is of a big stuffy building with a lot of white-haired people in it. Young people do not want to have to listen to old folk whom they don't rate. But then they change after about 16; older teenagers want to discuss all sorts of things more seriously. I agree with Lucy: this is where a good youth leader, attached to the church, could help.'

Lucy then added: 'You can't make them go, or do anything they don't want to do. And it's the ones who won't do anything at all who complain most about having nothing to do. If somehow you could get them involved in church activities when they are a little older, without telling them they *had* to do anything, that might get them interested.' I heard a similar story elsewhere: you can more or less write off the 12–15-year-olds, but in the mid-teens a vague interest in spiritual matters seems to develop. How does the Kirk win them back? I wish I knew.

The Kirk has nothing like enough trained and enthusiastic youth workers; possibly this is almost as big a problem as the lack of ministers. I'd like to propose that crash courses for youth workers be developed as a matter of urgency, and that all middle-sized to large congregations be urged to consider appointing youth leaders as a pastoral priority. Meanwhile, the Kirk is certainly uneasy with its young people; I have the feeling that it tends to patronise those young activists it does have, members of the Youth Assembly and so on. And there are plenty of those in the Kirk who believe that the extreme angst about the missing young is overdone. 'Get other things right and they will drift back in their 20s' is a view I heard expressed more than once.

Without doubt, an overconcentration on young people could divert the Kirk from sustaining the elderly, of whom there are going to be proportionately more and more. I understand very well that young people are needed to liven the Kirk up and to give it its strength and hope for tomorrow; but meanwhile there is a huge, and less-discussed, problem with the elderly. Andrew McLellan told me that the Church of Scotland had 'more or less invented' care of the elderly in Scotland; and its Board of Social Responsibility continues to oversee a quite magnificent range of services for older people. But I am more concerned with the pews of old people in the kirk every Sunday morning; some of them look grim, others look beleaguered, as if they vaguely suspect that, despite their past service and their rigorously regular attendance, they are not the people that the Kirk really wants to welcome. Here we are, once again, confronted by the perennial problem of the lost sheep, who is presumably to be welcomed more than these regulars; or, to put it another way, the older worshippers have rather more in common with the elder as opposed to the prodigal son.

In this context, I was fascinated, when I was in Dumfries, to learn that the congregation of St George's Church, having commendably managed to raise the money to employ a full-time development worker, had thought long and hard about appointing a dedicated youth worker before deciding that it was better to have the new member of the team looking after *all* ages. The minister, the Rev. Donald Campbell, told me that there were plenty of old people in the congregation who needed to be looked after, but in addition there was an important job of outreach to be done among the other *older* people in the parish as well. He told me of a survey that had indicated that only 30 per cent, fewer than one in three, of able-bodied over-65s actually attended worship.

There is also the problem that most regular older churchgoers want safety, ritual and tradition; the last thing they go to church for is innovation and experiment. Maybe, as team ministries develop and the old 'one minister, one parish' model willy-nilly breaks down, the Kirk will learn to develop more and more services for specific age groups and indeed for specific interests. This would break down congregational unity, but it might assist the Kirk in outreach.

6

THE KIRK'S BAD MAN

❖

This chapter is the biggest and it is also, by far, the most difficult to write. It is about ecumenism; but I want to start with an extended look at a shabby and atypical episode in the Kirk's recent history when it was aggressively and despicably anti-ecumenical. This dark period is desperately sad, because the Church of Scotland's overall record has been, overwhelmingly, one to be proud of. I am not equipped to comment on whether it has served God well; but, without doubt, it has served Scotland well. It was born in the Scottish Reformation, which was less bloody and more far-sighted than most of the reformations that had preceded it in sixteenth-century Europe. This was a time of radical popular agitation in Scotland, and our Reformation was a genuine national movement, although it somewhat bypassed the Gaelic-speaking Highlands and islands.

In 1560, the young and tyro Queen Elizabeth of England, bravely and after much heart-searching, sent both her army and her navy north to help the Scots drive out the occupying French. This was the time when our Scottish Reformation was secured. The writer and historian George Rosie (who describes himself, incidentally, as an unabashed atheist) told me: 'I believe the Reformation was probably the most important event in Scottish history, the one which shaped our society more than any other. I agree with Thomas Carlyle that it set in motion a process which produced an educated democracy and the sceptical, challenging mindset that created the Enlightenment. It was also astonishingly benign and peaceable compared to the bloodletting that was going on elsewhere in Europe and even in England.'

It has to be admitted that, through the centuries since then, the Kirk has had its occasional grisly episodes and an unfortunate propensity for splits and schisms. (Often the breakaway groups would split again, leading to a ludicrous pattern of tiny churches operating side by side, especially in the Highlands.) It is ironic that the man who helped to split the Kirk down the middle in the Disruption of 1843, Thomas Chalmers, was its greatest Victorian figure, while the man who more than any other helped to reunite it in 1929 was its most seriously bad figure of the twentieth century. I say seriously bad; that phrase takes into account his enormous gifts, which he misused. Had he been a lesser man, his malignant leadership would have been less serious. This man was John White.

White had worked tirelessly for more than twenty years to unite the Church of Scotland and the United Free Church. He was moderator of the first General Assembly of the newly united Kirk in 1929. Union was his great glory – it delivered a national church with more than 2,000 ministers, more than 2,000 congregations and *more than half the population of Scotland* – but there were many other achievements. He was a complex and brilliant man, and he could have served Scotland superbly – as well as any of her great religious leaders. Instead, he divided Scotland, at a time when it was spent and wounded after the Great War. Indeed, he nearly tore it apart.

White was born in 1867, the son of a Kilwinning miller. After studying philosophy and theology at Glasgow University, he served as a minister in Shettleston, Glasgow, and then Leith before returning to Glasgow, where he was minister of the Barony from 1911 until he retired in 1934. There was a gap when he served with distinction, when he was almost 50, as a chaplain to the Cameronians on the Western Front. He inaugurated a vigorous church extension campaign to build churches and halls in the new housing schemes that were being created on the margins of the great Scottish cities. He was the first convener of the Church and Nation Committee, which he helped to found.

So far, so good; but the dark side of White is to be seen in his visceral racist campaigns against Irish immigration to Scotland. To quote George Rosie again: 'I know that White has been compared to Chalmers, but it is a comparison I find odious. Chalmers was a great man with genuine vision, one who argued for Catholic emancipation. One way or another, John White's Kirk gave its blessing to the Protestant mob that stoned and bottled the buses carrying Catholic women and kids to the Eucharistic Congress in Canaan Lane in Morningside, Edinburgh. This was a time when Catholics in Edinburgh stood watch on their chapels and chapel houses to prevent them being burned down or trashed.' Prof. Stewart J. Brown, a distinguished ecclesiastical historian and the Dean of the Faculty of Divinity at the University of Edinburgh, has told me that 'while no Presbyterian clergymen were directly involved in the anti-Catholic rioting in Edinburgh, it was clear that the Presbyterian campaign since 1922 had contributed to the feeling among many Protestants that racist and sectarian violence was acceptable Christian behaviour'.

The way that White led an assault on the Catholic-Irish population of Scotland almost defies belief, from the more enlightened perspective of four generations on. White asserted that in Scotland a 'superior race' was being supplanted by an 'inferior race'. He said the issue was being pursued 'entirely as a racial and not as a religious question', as if racial prejudice were somehow valid. White's campaign was largely fought through the new Church and Nation Committee, which in 1923 was instructed to campaign for the restriction of Irish immigration into Scotland and the deportation of all Scottish-Irish Catholics deemed as 'undesirable'. Mass public meetings were held, and White organised various petitions and deputations to the government, demanding firm state action against the Catholic 'menace'. (Needless to say, such action was not forthcoming. White may have been a formidable ecclesiastical politician, but he was a poor political politician.)

But, despite the lack of political progress, White was unabashed. At a meeting in 1928, he claimed that his campaign was being conducted on the high moral ground of protecting Scots from being 'corrupted by the introduction of a horde of Irish immigrants'. During his moderatorial year, in February 1930, White was still at it, asserting that combating what he continued to describe as the menace of Irish immigration and Catholicism would remain a priority for the national Church of Scotland. 'Rome [not Dublin, note, but Rome] now menaces Scotland as at no time since the Reformation', he announced.

A new Kirk committee was created to lead the campaign against Scottish-Irish Catholics in 1931. It instructed all Church of Scotland ministers to report on both the numbers and the 'race' of Catholics living in their parishes. Yet, despite this new *ad hoc* committee, much of White's anti-Irish propaganda continued to be disseminated through the vehicle of the Church and Nation Committee (how different, and much better, that body has become), which constantly objected to Irish immigration and demanded that the government take draconian action. All this was bad enough, but the most damning factor is that throughout the 1920s and 1930s John White was the Kirk's 'father figure', to use Ron Ferguson's phrase. He was not some peripheral demagogue, whipping up racial tension and hatred on the margins, but the most central figure in the national church. And he was a highly intelligent and sophisticated man. He could have been an outstanding churchman; and many in the Kirk regarded him as such.

Even so, am I exaggerating his significance? Prof. Michael Lynch, in his *Scotland: A New History* (Century, 1991), does not mention White at all, and the Historiographer Royal, T. C. Smout, mentions him just once in his *A Century of the Scottish People* (Collins, 1986) – and that in connection with the union of 1929, not his campaign of bigotry and sectarianism. But both of these books were published more than a decade ago. Since then, Prof. Brown has trawled through the White papers, which are archived at New College. In two key essays, one in the Catholic historical journal the *Innes Review*, and the other in a book called *Scottish Christianity in the Modern World* (T&T Clark), Prof. Brown has brought to the attention not just of historians, but also of a wider public, the full scale of White's repellent campaign.

The best-selling (and best) general Scottish history of recent times is Prof. Tom Devine's *The Scottish Nation 1700–2000* (Allen Lane: The Penguin Press), which amazingly had sold more than 70,000 copies within two years of publication. Tom Devine deals with White's campaign, but his treatment is somewhat restrained. When I asked him why, he told me that he was conscious of his own background (Tom is probably Scotland's pre-eminent lay Catholic), and he did not want to be anything other than 'as fair to the Church of Scotland as I could possibly be'.

Tom Devine (who is a former vice-principal of Strathclyde University, and now director of the Research Institute for Irish and Scottish Studies at Aberdeen University) went on to tell me that he was convinced that White's campaign was born out of fear – fear of the potentially rapid assimilation of the Catholic Irish immigrants into wider Scottish society. He identified for me three key reasons for White's escalating panic as the Catholic Scottish-Irish population grew: the ending of the Irish Question in 1922 by the creation of the Irish Free State, the growing 'demographic dynamic' of immigration, and the growing strength of the Labour Party. This last is perhaps the most important; the 1920s and 1930s were a time of bitter labour agitation, particularly on Clydeside and in the coalfields of Ayrshire, Lanarkshire and Fife, and the Catholic Scottish-Irish had moved almost *en masse* into the Labour Party. As Prof. Devine says, 'The implications of all this, after several generations of sustained immigration, were enormous, not just for the Church of Scotland but for Scotland as a whole'.

John White was a man of such formidable gifts that it is impossible to avoid speculating on the great good he might have done for ecumenical relations had he reacted to this ongoing 'demographic dynamic' more far-sightedly and deployed his talents in a more positive and, dare I say it, a more Christian manner. Indeed, I find it hard to understand why such an otherwise distinguished and courageous individual, with undoubted greatness in him, should have become so mired in a cowardly campaign that was hateful in conception, maladroit in execution and infamous in its consequences, and politically ingenuous to boot. I wondered if it might have been something to do with his great desire to achieve union; in other words, was his campaign in part designed to appease anti-Irish zealots within the United Free Church? Prof. Brown thinks emphatically not; he pointed out to me that the moves towards union were under way, and going well, before White's anti-Irish campaign really started. Anyway, for whatever reasons, rational or not, White, potentially the Kirk's greatest figure since Chalmers, cast a long shadow over the Church of Scotland which was still there as late as

1952, when his creation, the Church and Nation Committee, expressed alarm and dismay over the growth of Catholicism in Scotland and attempted once again to portray Catholics as an alien presence.

It might be as well to remind the reader at this point that this chapter is not so much about the Kirk's shabby past as about ecumenism in the present and future. The point of this extended preamble is to set the context in which any discussion of relations with the Roman Catholic Church must take place. It would probably be necessary to remind people of these shameful years anyway, but to do so has become imperative after the Catholic composer James MacMillan raised the whole question of sectarianism in modern Scotland during a lecture he gave at the start of the Edinburgh International Festival in 1999.

MacMillan's lecture was ill-thought-out and in parts downright silly. To quote George Rosie once again, 'I refuse to take even remotely seriously anyone who can equate John Knox with Pol Pot and Hitler'. I personally was annoyed by MacMillan's lecture, for he attacked the newspaper I was then editing, *The Herald*, on the grounds that it had called for the ending of denominational schools. This was simply untrue, and I would like to reiterate here that *The Herald* did not at any time, when I was deputy editor or editor, argue for the ending of denominational schools. The paper rather stated consistently that if Scottish Catholics wanted to retain these schools, fair enough.

MacMillan had every right to complain about the way his Catholic parents had suffered in Ayrshire in the 1930s. He had far less right to imply that things had not got much better. (Tom Devine agrees with me on this point. He told me: 'My gripe with MacMillan is that so much anti-Catholic discrimination, for example in the labour market, has now gone. He seemed to take no account of this.') Indeed, the assimilation of the Irish-Catholic immigrants into the very heart of Scottish life, public as well as private, has been one of Scotland's few civic triumphs over the past fifty years or so. Of course, there are still far too many mani-festations of sectarianism and religious prejudice; but surely nobody with eyes to see and ears to hear can deny that things have improved enormously. I would have thought that most enlightened Presbyterian Scots would now be far more concerned about the weakness of their own church from within than worried about any extraneous pressures, real or imagined. This is certainly the context in which I think ecumenism has to be examined.

A secondary point is that, as MacMillan so clearly showed, the badness of the 1920s and 1930s has left behind a bitter legacy. The wounds have not all healed. I reckon, perhaps controversially, that the Catholic Church is less likely now to respond to bold ecumenical initiatives (were the Kirk prepared to make them – and there is no immediate sign that it is) than it might have been eighty years ago, when it was in a less strong position in Scotland and indeed in the world. For, since the 1960s, the Catholic Church has gone from strength to strength in global terms. Christianity is by far the world's biggest religion and its fastest-growing religion. Indeed, never before has Christianity spread as rapidly as it has in the last few decades, particularly in South America, some parts of Africa, South-east Asia and even China. This phenomenal growth is due, not entirely but mainly, to the efforts of the Catholic Church, which is big enough to accommodate a huge range of theologies and practices.

Diversity is, for the Catholic Church, a great asset; for the so much smaller Church of Scotland, diversity is more problematic. The Catholic Church refreshed itself, to enormous and benign effect, during the Second Vatican Council of 1962–5. Apart from anything else, the council helped to unleash the prophetic and transforming work of such great South American clerics as Archbishop Helder Camara of Recife. One very eminent figure in the Kirk told me that as he travelled the world he realised that the Church of Scotland was something of a 'tuppence ha'penny' church compared to the global behemoth of Roman Catholicism. His point was that you can look at the statistics as much as you want, but you really need to experience what is going on in different continents before you can understand the colossal sweep and influence of the Catholic Church. (I hasten to point out here that the various Catholics I interviewed evinced no sense of triumphalism whatsoever. They were well aware of their church's strength globally, but equally aware of its comparative weakness here in Scotland. But then, alas, the Kirk, which should at least be strong in Scotland, is weak here also. And, in a historical context, the Catholic Church is a little stronger in Scotland than it was in the 1920s, while the Church of Scotland is much weaker.)

When Pope John Paul II visited Scotland in 1982, he made an impact which was far beyond anything the Church of Scotland as a whole, or any one individual within it, could have achieved in the space of a mere forty hours. One simple example of this is that I cannot believe that the Kirk could in the 1980s or 1990s, let alone the twenty-first century, organise any event which would get literally hundreds of thousands of people gathered together for Christian celebration. (That might be a challenge for it!) But John White could possibly have done that, had he wanted to.

I accept that there has been no great lasting residue from that heady visit in the early summer of 1982, and the huge rallies at Bellahouston and Murrayfield; as a Catholic observer told me, it was great at the time, but it didn't really change anything. (In that respect, it was maybe similar to the whistlestop visits of the North Carolina evangelist Dr Billy Graham.) The Pope asked Scottish Catholics to 'walk hand in hand' with other Christians – and, while they may well have spent some time walking together since, the sad fact is that they have been walking to nowhere in particular.

The burden of these reflections is this: were today's Kirk to offer any considered and serious ecumenical initiative to the Catholic Church, it would be doing so from a position of weakness. The time for such an initiative was surely in the 1920s; instead, what we got then was the exact opposite.

Before I finally move on from the sadness of White's warped legacy, it must be recounted that the Church of Scotland very slowly but surely eased itself away from its position of extreme anti-Irish and anti-Catholic militancy. Prof. Duncan Forrester reckons that the major turning point came with the Oxford Conference on Church, Community and State in 1937. 'For some significant Scottish church leaders, this was their first real exposure to ecumenism, and it gave them an opportunity to hear at first hand what anti-Semitism and racism were doing in Germany. Some who had colluded with the anti-Irish and anti-Roman Catholic policies came to their senses. Most from this time came to see Scottish church life and Scottish theology in a broader global frame.'

The leading player in this belated but beneficent progress was Prof. John Baillie of New College. Here was an intellectual giant, a man who could and did converse on equal terms with titans such as the greatest poet of the twentieth century, T. S. Eliot, and the outstanding existentialist theologian Paul Tillich. Baillie spent sixteen of his best years in the USA, returning to Scotland in 1934 to take up the chair of Divinity at the University of Edinburgh. As Prof. Brown has noted sharply, 'he soon discovered that his American experiences had made him an outsider in White's godly commonwealth'. Painstakingly, Baillie educated the Kirk; his message was one of pluralism and equality. There was personal animus between Baillie and White; but the former won the day, and he helped to shape the more open and inclusive Kirk that developed in the later 1950s. These were good years for the Church of Scotland in terms of membership; but then complacency developed, and a great opportunity for enlightened mission was lost. Baillie himself died in 1960.

The catastrophic decline in Kirk membership set in during the 1960s; but Kirk–Catholic relations continued to improve, and, in 1975, the young Archbishop of Glasgow, one Tom Winning, was graciously received as he addressed a packed General Assembly. The moderator, James Matheson, told him: 'You have won our hearts'. And seven years later, the then moderator, Prof. John McIntyre of New College, greeted Pope John Paul II under the magnificent statue of John Knox in the quadrangle of the college. What, one wonders, would John White have made of that? Indeed, by this time, some commentators were suggesting that the Catholic Church was in the ascendancy in Scotland, though when this notion was put to Cardinal Gordon Gray, he wisely and modestly said: 'I sincerely hope not'.

And so we come to the present, a present in which Kirk–Catholic relations are, at the higher levels, cordial and positive; yet I sense that there is no great desire for any dramatic ecumenical movement. Good and interesting things are happening occasionally at the local micro level; but, at an all-Scotland level, I reckon the position of the Catholic Church could be summed up thus: 'We are friends with the Church of Scotland, and we can work together in many ways. But when it comes to what we would regard as fundamental – our sacraments, for example – we see no need to move towards the Kirk. Why should we bother too much with it?'

Let me quote the views of Stuart Trotter, a leading lay Catholic. Stuart, a former editor and parliamentary correspondent, has now returned to Scotland after a long stint in London. He was brought up in the Church of Scotland but converted when he was still a relatively young man. A shrewd and urbane observer of politicians and priests, of journalists and civil servants, Stuart worked in the Palace of Westminster for many years and at one time served as chairman of the Press Gallery. He is in no sense an official spokesman for the Catholic Church, but in my opinion his observations are exceptionally well informed and carry considerable weight. Here is what he has to say: 'Scottish Catholics generally respect the Church of Scotland for having been our national church for over 400 years and, in particular, for the high standards of personal morality it has taught and often achieved in its adherents. We also respect the high place it has given to Bible-reading and study, and that is something that other churches have come to copy.'

So far, so good – but what about ecumenism? 'All Christians should welcome the fact that different churches treat each other better and work together *when that is possible*. But as far as church unity is concerned, that is as far off as ever. It puzzles me that the Protestant churches have not made more progress towards forming a single main reformed church – and that would surely be a prerequisite before there were even the beginnings of any serious move towards potential unity.' (It is interesting to note in an aside here the paradox that John White, the man who did more than anyone else in the twentieth century to promote and achieve an ecumenical movement within Presbyterianism, was at the same time a vehement foe of Catholicism. White was in one sense a great ecumenicist; he also wanted the Kirk to start negotiations with the Church of England. But, in the context of the overall Christian family, he was an ecumenical disaster.)

Stuart Trotter continued: 'And I see a particular weakness inherent in Presbyterianism, which is after all essentially a protest against a hierarchical system of church government, a system which we hold dear. I'm afraid I would have to sum up by saying that while general relations between the Catholic Church and the Church of Scotland are much better than they were fifty or sixty or seventy years ago, our doctrinal differences are as strong as ever, and I cannot see this changing.' I asked for a hard instance of this, and Stuart said simply: 'The position of the Pope'.

Next, I went to Motherwell and met Joe Devine, Bishop of Motherwell, in his large, modern office (the diocese was created as recently as 1947, by Pope Pius XII) just across the road from Peter Paul Pugin's Cathedral Church of Our Lady of Good Aid, described by the ecclesiastical historian Peter Galloway, in a felicitous phrase, as 'the delightful epitome of a parish church cathedral'.

Joe Devine told me that the Catholic hierarchy's relations with the Church of Scotland had never been warmer. But that was at a general level; when it came to more detailed relationships, these were more problematic simply because the Kirk lacked what Joe called 'leadership stability'. He said: 'I'll give you a specific example. I couldn't tell you who the moderator of the Presbytery of Hamilton is.' (There are two points here: moderators of presbyteries, like moderators of the General Assembly, change each year; and the Presbytery of Hamilton includes Motherwell within its bounds.) 'No doubt I should know, but I don't. In that sense, there is no stability in relations between the diocese and the presbytery. That doesn't help us at all. I understand that the Church of Scotland doesn't want figureheads, that it wants people to manage things for just one year and then move on. This is very democratic, but it makes leadership difficult if you are constantly dealing with different people. In fact, you have to ask: who are the leaders?' That said, he had been particularly impressed by recent moderators of the General Assembly, and he and his fellow bishops had enjoyed excellent relations with them.

As for ecumenism, he said that occasionally there were significant developments at local level. 'About fifteen years ago, two parishes here, one Catholic, one Church of Scotland, decided to do their silver jubilee celebrations jointly. They selected forty folk from each church and sent them out in pairs, and they visited all the homes. They were invited into 96 per cent of them. That was a good result, and since then they have walked hand in hand, with joint services and dinners and other events. But no other parishes have followed this up.' I asked if more could not be done to encourage such initiatives. Bishop Devine said that you needed the will at local level. He had suggested that this good practice be replicated elsewhere, but it had not happened. 'I accept that local priests don't always take ecumenism as seriously as they should. I think this applies to some ministers too.'

I asked if there was anything about the current Church of Scotland that disappointed him; and he was candid: 'At one time away back, the Catholic community here did feel threatened; but I have not detected any serious anti-Catholicism. If there is any, I think it would be out in the backwoods. I do think there is a poor sense of liturgy in the Church of Scotland, and it is getting worse. Liturgy to us is the very summit of the church's work; but that is not the case in the Church of Scotland, and that strikes me as a problem. Also, I think the Church of Scotland marriage service is remarkably dull. I've been to three or four, and these services lack the warmth and the hope which I think we have.'

Joe concluded: 'Let me say: we do take the Church of Scotland seriously, and I admire much of its work. I'd like, for example, to commend the way it handled parish reappraisal – honestly and bravely. We have the same problems in Scotland, but they have bitten the bullet here in a way that we have not begun to. But I do think that the Church of Scotland is not as strong as it should be, and that it is beginning to lose confidence and self-belief. One of the problems it has is a big gap in lay spirituality. It has no significant lay spiritual movements.' No doubt a small number of people in the Kirk will object to a Catholic bishop opining frankly in this manner; but his comments were solicited, and I was grateful for them. Joe Devine is a convivial and open-minded man; he speaks from a position of genuine respect and fondness for the Kirk.

It is a long way, physically if not spiritually, from Lanarkshire to Orkney. When I was staying with Ron and Cristine Ferguson at St Magnus Cathedral manse, they suggested that I should meet the local Catholic priest, Father Ken Nugent. Ron had worked closely with Father Ken; they had got on very well at the personal level, and this had helped them to improvise various local ecumenical experiments. I was delighted to talk to Ken, and indeed I was sorry that our conversation, which was quite protracted, did not last even longer. He was obviously fond of Ron, and proud of the work they had done together; I sensed that he was a little apprehensive about who Ron's successor might be, and whether he would get on with him or her as well.

I started by telling Ken that he was the first Jesuit I had ever interviewed. He found this amusing; but, as our conversation progressed, I understood that I had to keep my wits about me. Ken was very friendly, but I realised that the famous Jesuitical cerebral sharpness was never far away. I told him that he was the first cleric I had interviewed who was actually wearing a dog collar. 'Well, I think there is value in the uniform, as it were; it is a reminder to oneself, and an identity for other people. I don't think that the ministry in any church should become too chummy. You want a warm relationship with your flock, but you should not get too close. I believe it is absolutely necessary to maintain some degree of formality. In the Catholic Church, ritual and formality are still very important. It is all very well popping into McDonald's for a quick burger; but there are other times, many times, when you would like, when you would need, to see the table set.'

Ken Nugent is 71; he came into the priesthood relatively late in life, having been an architect and a distinguished scholar of the Baroque. He first served in Farm Street, Mayfair, the celebrated (and very posh) Jesuit church where Evelyn Waugh famously received instruction from Father Martin D'Arcy, he of the 'fine, slippery mind' who was later to be immortalised by Muriel Spark. From Mayfair, Ken moved on to Bristol and then north to Glasgow, where he was Catholic chaplain to Glasgow University, and then much further north to Orkney, where he is the sole Catholic priest, serving not just the 'mainland' but all the outlying islands as well. This broad experience renders him well placed to comment on the prospects, or lack of them, for ecumenism in the wider Scotland.

'I think personal holiness is what so many people are looking for, in their different ways, but they are wary of piety. In general terms, I would say that Scotland is considerably more religious than England. I have been very impressed by the courtesy of individual Church of Scotland ministers. Sometimes there is clearly unease between our churches, but courtesy can help you across that. But when you get to specific matters, it is much, much more difficult. Moral theology is still important in the training of Catholic priests. This includes the study of the nature of sin, so that you can guide people. I do wonder if the Church of Scotland is losing that sense, that understanding of the nature of sin?'

He went on to say that in that context, he did find it difficult to offer any specific proposals for ecumenical thrust on a pan-Scotland basis. But I pressed him; and, having thought about it, he did come up with one very interesting proposal. 'A practical step to ecumenism could be for all the churches in Scotland – certainly the Church of Scotland, the Catholic Church and the Episcopalians – to find a common voice for communication purposes. In other words, you could create a Scottish Joint Churches Media Office, if the churches were prepared to pay for it. This would allow us to speak out on important contemporary matters where we do have one voice – and I'm sure that we do have one voice on many issues. We also have serious differences on all sorts of things; but, apart from anything else, this media office would create the discipline to help us find out exactly what we could agree on, and to find out relatively quickly.'

As Father Nugent developed his own idea, in extempore manner, he stressed that the existing media offices would remain, to serve their own churches. The new media office would be an add-on, to speak with authority to the Scottish media on certain matters only, and to help to publicise unity and common response and common purpose where it genuinely existed. Since that conversation in Orkney, I have mentioned Ken Nugent's idea to various people, within the Kirk and without, and it has been well received. It would not be a huge step forward in terms of practical ecumenism, but it would be a significant step nonetheless and, for obvious reasons, a very high-profile one. I was particularly pleased that, when I canvassed the idea with some of Scotland's more thoughtful media people, they were very positive.

I am aware that work goes on – sometimes it is almost dormant, sometimes it sparks into life – on areas of co-operation between the two great churches in Scotland. Work has been done in the areas of mixed marriages and of baptisms, to cite just two examples. But such work is slow and unsteady. There is still suspicion around. The Church of Scotland has not been conspicuously supportive of denominational schools. Also, I'm not sure that the organised experiment of an ecumenical parish in Livingston has been a resounding success; perhaps that is unfair, but there has certainly been no apparent rush to pursue similar experiments elsewhere in Scotland.

The Catholic Church, while comparatively weak in Scotland, is tremendously strong globally; it has other priorities. Indeed, you begin to wonder if there is something desperately wrong in our part of Western Europe: Christianity is reviving and flourishing in so many parts of the globe, but here it is in sad decline, and both the Catholic and Protestant churches are having to face up to the debilitating problems of failure. As Prof. Tom Devine said to me, 'One of the saddest things I know is going to a priest's funeral in the west of Scotland. You'll see a scattering of folk with white hair, that's all. I'd say we could be facing a potential catastrophe in Scotland. We are probably losing young people even faster than the Church of Scotland. And yet churches are so successful, are doing so well, in so many other countries. You have to ask: why is religion declining so rapidly in our particular part of the world?' (Andrew McLellan offers views on this, which appear in Chapter 12.)

Meanwhile, if the Church of Scotland is serious about building links with the most powerful and most historic Christian church (and I write this as someone who believes that the Reformation was profoundly necessary, and who reveres its inheritance), then it is first going to have to do some very hard thinking about some imaginative initiatives and, even having done so, it is going to have to be prepared for rebuff. I reiterate; for all sorts of reasons, social and political as well as spiritual, the urgent time for ecumenical vision on the part of the Kirk was in the 1920s and the 1930s. This was when Scotland was torn and broken after the immense sacrifices of the Great War. When the peace came, it came accompanied by a spirit not of renewal but of strife – strife in the coalfields and in the shipyards and in the streets. At the same time, a colossal demographic dynamic, as Tom Devine terms it, was under way.

That placed more strain on an already volatile mix. And that, surely, was when the national church should have reached out to heal, to seek common ground, to be inclusive and far-sighted and compassionate. Instead, its dominant figure spectacularly failed the test, and the Church of Scotland became mired in rejection, narrowness and racism. That was when the Kirk manifestly failed to show any ecumenical nobility – and it is still paying the price.

We are talking about a long time ago: eighty, seventy, sixty years ago. But the more I found out about the White years, the more I was appalled. Maybe the bitter residue of these years has not yet been expunged. Interestingly, two of the more enlightened members of today's Kirk have suggested to me, separately, that something along the lines of a post-apartheid South African-style 'Truth and Reconciliation' exercise might be needed to erase and exorcise the shame, finally and for all time. Meanwhile, most of today's Catholics in Scotland are friendly, and they respect the national church; but they see no reason even to think about moving on their most cherished principles, and I have to ask: why should they? So, rather bleakly, I think we are all maybe going to have to live with what amounts to an ecumenical impasse for some time to come.

Fiona Hutchison, a ministerial candidate in her final year at New College, told me of her enthusiasm when she attended the first Scottish Ecumenical Assembly in September 2001. But then she became very depressed, because the reformed church participants went one way for communion, and the Catholics went elsewhere. 'Up till then, it had been an exciting weekend and we had all worshipped together. Why could we not celebrate communion together?' It will happen one day, but that day is not near.

I cannot leave this discussion of Kirk–Catholic relations without reflecting a little more on the vexed subject of sectarianism. On the other hand, I don't want to say overmuch about this as, following an intervention from the floor of the 2001 General Assembly, the Church and Nation Committee set up a subcommittee to examine sectarianism in Scotland; and its report may well be published before this book is. It could be that yet another unfortunate legacy of the White years (they might be better termed the black years) is that many modern Kirk figures have lost all confidence when it comes to putting what might be called the public Presbyterian position. It is as if they have been somehow so subconsciously blighted by the malign inheritance of those bad times that they are ashamed to speak up for Protestantism in any context.

It is certainly the view of the Scottish academic Dr Graham Walker that the Church of Scotland has lost many adherents among the country's working classes because it is 'running scared', as he puts it. He says that, for whatever reason, the Kirk has completely lost touch with the bulk of the people in many working-class areas of Scotland where some sectarian feeling does survive. 'Where there is Protestant sectarianism in Scotland, it is to a large degree there because working-class folk feel that they have been rubbished by their own middle-class people. They feel that their own church is not speaking for them, certainly not in the way that the Catholic Church constantly and loudly speaks out for its people, for example on the issue of denominational schools.'

Graham, who himself grew up in a working-class part of southern Glasgow, insists that what he calls the 'Protestant identity' is fading fast, and that the Kirk is instinctively blamed for this. 'The Church of Scotland has undoubtedly lost touch with many, many thousands of working-class Scots who now feel alienated by their own Kirk. They have become unchurched. And they resent the loss, they really do. I'd say this process has happened over the past thirty years or so. When I grew up, there was a strong sense of identity with the Church, partly through the Boys' Brigade; but the main point is that we understood that this was *our* church. And while I would not argue that I want to see the present-day Church fighting aggressively for Protestantism, it has to be said that it does give the impression of wanting to avoid any scrap, on any subject, with the Catholics at all costs.'

I asked Graham to outline his prescription to revive the Church. 'Well, I have to say that it should build on the positives which are still there. It has shaped our nation over several hundred years. It is lamentable that so many in the Church of Scotland seem unaware of, or uninterested in, its huge contribution to the making of Scotland. It must not be allowed to squander its greatest resource, and that is its remaining place in our national life. It is still a venerable organisation, and there is still great potential respect for it. It can undoubtedly recover its role as the conscience of the nation.'

But how, I asked, was this to be achieved? 'As an academic, I'm afraid I think in terms of conferences. But the Church needs to improve its communication, it needs to take more initiatives and it needs to be more pro-active. It should be expressing itself more strongly in all sorts of forums it is not even thinking about, let alone using.' Such as? 'Look at the British–Irish Council. It is open to creative input. I am sure that the Church of Scotland could take a meaningful initiative here. It could ask the council to widen its remit and instigate a good, hard look at relations between Protestants and Catholics on both sides of the water. From what I know of the council, such a move would be well received. The Kirk could lead the way on this. It could make the running, setting the agenda. That would attract a lot of interest and publicity, and it would let people know that the Church of Scotland was doing something for its people in a potentially very important civic and political forum.'

I should explain here that, after working at various universities in Scotland and England, Graham is currently in Belfast, where he is Reader in Politics at Queen's University. He told me: 'Here in Northern Ireland, churchmen on all sides are obviously far more active in the political culture; and, while I would not necessarily want the Kirk to go too far down that road, it does seem to me that, in Scotland these days, churchmen are leaving the politics to the politicians – and that is a big mistake. I would strongly urge the Church of Scotland to use the avenue of political engagement, to get back into the mainstream of public debate, and to connect much more regularly with the wider Scottish public. And this, I am sure, would help it to deal with the big problem I mentioned earlier – that so many ordinary working-class Scots feel that what *should* be their church is *never* speaking for them.'

Given that Graham mentioned overtly political engagement, it has to be noted that there was a definite political undercurrent to the Church of Scotland's anti-Irish and anti-Catholic campaigns in the 1920s and 1930s. John White was a committed Tory and Unionist; at the same time, the Catholics were joining the Labour Party in very considerable numbers, as Tom Devine has noted. While it would be wrong to suggest that, in contemporary Scotland, the

Catholic Church is the Labour Party at prayer, the links between Labour and Catholicism are enormously strong, particularly in west-central Scotland (although the view of Mike Russell MSP, of the Scottish National Party, is that the Labour Party also has a strong Orange support in certain areas).

The modern Kirk has more or less lost its links with the Conservative and Unionist Party. Indeed, David McLetchie MSP, the Edinburgh lawyer and leader of the Tory Party in Scotland, has told me in two separate conversations that he is not particularly impressed by today's Kirk, although all he was prepared to say publicly was that he finds it 'mired in relativism'.

The official opposition party in the Scottish Parliament is, of course, the SNP. Its former leader, Alex Salmond MP, asked Mike Russell MSP, a few years ago, to convene a small *ad hoc* group to examine how the party might appeal more to Catholic voters. The conclusion of this exercise was that the SNP vote was, in religious terms, pretty well proportionate, even though some elements in the party had been associated with strong Protestantism in the 1950s and 1960s. 'I'd say we are the most secular of the Scottish parties and, to be frank, a party with no great enthusiasm for religion', said Russell, himself an Episcopalian. Having said that, he then surprised me by saying that the late Cardinal Winning had been a great supporter of the SNP behind the scenes.

The Church of Scotland played a positive role in the postwar campaigns for a Scottish Parliament, and in Prof. Will Storrar it has a leading figure who is personally determined to continue to be at the cutting edge of public debate in Scotland. But it needs many more like him. Paradoxically, now that the Parliament has been delivered, some observers feel that the secular influence of both the General Assembly itself and the flagship Church and Nation Committee will inevitably be further diminished, although I am not convinced by this theory. On the contrary, I see the Parliament as a new opportunity for the Kirk. In this context, I was most interested in the views of the Rev. Gordon Kennedy, a member of the *Without Walls* team. When I chatted with him in his manse in Stranraer, he told me with some vehemence: 'The Church of Scotland is right to raise a Christian voice on *all* issues affecting the life of our nation. Indeed, it is not a right; it is a responsibility.

The need may well be even greater because of our new Parliament. For the Church to talk to MSPs regularly is an absolute necessity. We must make sure that our voice is well heard by the new Parliament.'

A key figure in this context is an experienced minister, the Rev. Dr Graham Blount, who was appointed the Kirk's parliamentary officer in 1998, well in advance of the first Scottish General Election. He told me: 'On the issue of the General Assembly formerly being the nearest thing we had to a Parliament, the creation of the Parliament liberates the Assembly from being something that it never was. We are now seeing a major change of dynamic in civic Scotland; and, while the Church of Scotland may well have filled a vacuum in the past, it now has greater opportunities to contribute to the policy-making process than it has had for many years.' So far, so good. Dr Blount is employed by the Kirk, but his remit is to establish and develop an ecumenical parliamentary office for the Scottish churches. As an individual, his line manager is Finlay Macdonald (who played a leading role in creating the post of parliamentary officer), but an ecumenical advisory group oversees his office. Still, so far, so good. But, significantly, the Catholic Church has appointed its own parliamentary officer who, in Graham's words, 'is very much a hands-on lobbyist, whereas I see myself as more of an enabler'.

I wondered if the Graham Walkers of the world might be a touch suspicious at this point; was this an example of the Catholic Church pulling a fast one on the Kirk, and ensuring that its voice was heard more loudly than the Kirk's in a key public and political forum? I'd say the jury is out on that one. In any event, Dr Blount is convinced that his job is going well – that he is, for example, helping more and more Kirk individuals and boards to contact MSPs and to give evidence to parliamentary committees.

Meanwhile, I must, with a weary heart, return to the discussion of residual sectarianism in Scotland. And, much as I would like to, I cannot avoid discussing the Old Firm, namely Celtic and Rangers football clubs. I might have been expected to be a Rangers supporter, having been born in Glasgow into a Protestant family of Glaswegians; but we moved to Aberdeen when I was very young, and I am happy to say that I became early on, and have remained ever since, a loyal Aberdeen supporter. My father, of whom I was very fond indeed, was totally uninterested in football, preferring to spend his Saturday afternoons on the golf course – but I did notice that, in the nineteen years he was based in Aberdeen, he only attended Pittodrie about five times, and it just happened that every time, as far as I can recall, Rangers were the visitors. The only relevance of this personal history in this particular context is that it has given me a perspective on the Old Firm, shared I am sure by very many Scots, which could be summed up as 'a plague on both your houses'.

The annual visits of Celtic and Rangers to Aberdeen in the 1950s and 1960s were big (and bad) events. Their supporters did not behave well, and there was always special pleasure throughout the city when the Dons beat them, as they frequently did, I am glad to recall. But the Celtic and Rangers fans were certainly noticed. They made an impact, albeit a negative one. The supporters of other teams, such as Hibs and Hearts, crept into town and crept away again, almost unnoticed. And so it continues. Old Firm derbies in Glasgow are particularly noxious occasions, and I would not advise anyone to have an accident in Glasgow in the twelve hours after such clashes; the city's A&E receiving stations are emphatically not good places to be at such times. The games are always attended by considerable chaos and mayhem, and the anarchy is not benign.

Indeed, I think that most Scots who live and work beyond the west-central area have only a limited idea of what might be called the unfortunate sociological potency of the Old Firm. I know that in most areas of Scotland there are Rangers and Celtic supporters' clubs, and that football-related sectarian excess can be visited on neighbourhoods many miles from Glasgow. But, in the West, it is rooted in a folk consciousness of religious division which is much, much stronger than it is in most other parts of Scotland. One tiny example is that, when I worked for a decade on *The Scotsman* in Edinburgh, I never had the faintest idea – with just one or two exceptions – which of my colleagues were Catholics and which were Protestants. Yet, when I went to work in Glasgow, I was somehow, insidiously and without really realising it, made aware of which of my colleagues were Protestants and which were Catholics, within weeks of arriving. And it also became generally known, without my telling anyone, that I was a Protestant. This is the soil in which other things take root.

It has to be said that many of us, including so many working in the media, tolerate the Old Firm, and some people who should know better (though I absolve myself in this instance) even celebrate them. I suppose the one justification for allowing the Old Firm to continue at all is that their visceral sectarian rivalry acts a conduit, a release, a sort of safety valve, for tensions and bitterness which might otherwise explode in much more unpleasant Ulster-style sustained violence. Some people are sceptical about this theory; but I, reluctantly, accept it. I must also say, in fairness to both clubs, that they have made efforts to stamp out the worst manifestations of sectarianism within their organisations. Things have improved in the last decade or so.

The most successful recent Scottish football figure, by a country mile, is Sir Alex Ferguson. He played for Rangers in the 1960s, and, when he achieved spectacular success as the manager of Aberdeen in the early 1980s, it was inevitable that Rangers would join the many other big clubs that would try to tempt him away from Pittodrie. In the event, he resisted all blandishments until he left for Manchester United, potentially the biggest club in the world (and he made it so) at the end of 1986. Rangers had, in fact, approached him twice; and one reason he turned them down was the position of his wife, who is a Catholic. In his autobiography (*Managing My Life*, 1999), he writes: 'The truth is that I was already reluctant to entertain exposing my family to the risk of a recurrence of the bigotry I had encountered at Ibrox in my playing days ... Cathy's religion would probably have been enough in itself to convince me that returning to Rangers was not a good idea' (reproduced by permission of Hodder and Stoughton Ltd).

Ferguson is a searingly honest man and is not given to mincing his words, even on such sensitive topics. Earlier in the auto-biography, he describes the 'poisonous hostility' that was directed towards him in his playing days at Ibrox by Willie Allison, the club's PR man, who Ferguson believes had an 'alarming influence on the club's then chairman, John Lawrence'. He writes: 'Allison was a religious bigot of the deepest dye. I had a thoroughly Protestant upbringing but, of course, Cathy is Catholic and so were my mother's family. Such facts were sure to count for much in the twisted mind of Allison and, as an intriguer behind the scenes at Ibrox, he was as dangerous as he was despicable.'

Much has changed since those days, and for the better. Rangers have employed many high-profile Catholic players (to be fair to Celtic, they had employed Protestant players for many years). In commercial terms, they are both very big clubs and they have made efforts to become modern and even enlightened institutions, although there was an unfortunate incident, at the very heart of the Rangers club, in 1999. The vice-chairman, the eminent advocate Donald Findlay QC, was filmed singing sectarian songs at a private function. He promptly resigned, amid a welter of media disapproval. He was then disciplined by the Faculty of Advocates, and St Andrews University withdrew its offer of an honorary degree.

When the progressive aspirations of the modernising tendency and the more backward-looking aspirations of the residual sectarians collide, the results can be almost comic. Such a moment was beautifully caught by Graham Spiers in *The Herald* when he described the scene as Rangers' new manager Alex McLeish was being presented to the media in December 2001. I quote: 'Here was David Murray, the modern football club chairman, sitting in the Blue Room like a captain of industry. Murray prides himself on his modern, progressive style, as well he might. He often refers to Rangers being a modern business with modern ideas, and he was at it again the other night while unveiling McLeish to the media. The only problem was that someone had left a window open in the Blue Room. Outside, on Copland Road, alas, some not so modern Rangers fans, the type that Murray himself has called an embarrassment, were gathered almost in vigil. So, just as all this modern baloney was being spouted inside, up chimed the choristers: *With heart and hand and sword and shield we'll guard those Derry walls / Altogether now, the cry was no surrender . . .* Before any Pope of Rome could be mentioned, a flunky hastily slammed the window shut.' Coincidentally, just two days later, Rangers' captain, Barry Ferguson, was widely reported as saying that he wanted to quit Scottish football because he and his family had been suffering sectarian abuse.

All this may seem a long way from the Church of Scotland – but I sometimes wonder. If there is one immediate thing it could do in this context, it would be to start disengaging as publicly as possible from any assumptions that Kirk people should automatically be understood to support Rangers. Obviously, this whole business is atavistic and tribal, and no-one could wave a magic wand and order people to drop, or change, allegiances just like that. (Indeed, for people at the bottom of the heap, passionate support for their football team is one of the few things that can give them heart, a sense of belonging and self-belief and self-esteem amid a society that seems to spurn them in so many other ways.)

On the other hand, I think that, were the Church of Scotland to dissociate itself as publicly and as frequently as possible from Rangers FC, that would do no harm at all and might do some good. It would certainly make clear once and for all that what Graham Walker (himself the most articulate and thoughtful Rangers supporter I know) terms the 'Protestant identity' should not simply be a glib alignment with the fortunes of Rangers Football Club. At first, such moves might well confuse and even anger the alienated people Graham was talking about; but, if the Kirk were to take high-profile political, social and cultural initiatives elsewhere, then that could slowly begin to fill the void. And were Glasgow presbytery to form a Celtic Supporters' Club, the ploy might send out useful signals and be a small step in the right direction. I have to admit, however, that when I put this notion to the distinguished religious broadcaster the Rev. Johnston McKay, who has been a good friend to this book, he told me he thought the idea was just plain daft.

I also suggested it to Brian Wilson MP, the senior Labour politician and Energy Minister, who is a Protestant and a noted historian of, and supporter of, Celtic. Brian told me: 'When I was growing up in Dunoon, not then and not now a hotbed of sectarianism, my family was very pro-Celtic. My father was a Church of Scotland elder, but he was very pro united Ireland. From my boyhood, I do not remember a single Celtic supporter apart from myself who was not from a Catholic background, but I think that things changed dramatically in 1967 [when Celtic became the first British team to win the European Cup, doing so with enormous flair]. I think Celtic increasingly did gain some non-Catholic support after that. So, I think the sort of gesture you are suggesting for the Church of Scotland might have been ground-breaking and very valuable say forty years ago, but now I am not really sure if it is needed.' Perhaps not; but the Kirk should be aware that many people assume that the Kirk and Rangers are still somehow linked.

Meanwhile, the veteran Scottish politician and Liberal Democrat MSP Donald Gorrie, who is a Kirk elder in Edinburgh, tried in 2001 to make sectarianism a criminal offence. He was prompted to do so by the Carfin Grotto fiasco. The background to this is that Carfin is a small village a mile or so north of Motherwell where, in the early 1920s, a group of local Catholics, returning from a visit to Lourdes, decided to create a little grotto. The shrine was dedicated to Saint Theresa, the 'little flower', a French Carmelite nun who died of tuberculosis in 1897, aged 24. Miraculous cures connected with the grotto have been reported since 1923. The grotto has grown, and it is now a significant place of pilgrimage. The Irish Taoiseach, Bertie Ahern, was due to visit Carfin to unveil the Irish Famine Memorial, after having watched Celtic at Parkhead. The visit was suddenly cancelled after the MP for Motherwell, Frank Roy, advised that there might be sectarian trouble. This relatively minor incident developed into something of a major diplomatic stushie after adverse comment in both the Scottish and Irish media.

Donald Gorrie's concern, in the aftermath of this fiasco, was that the Scottish Parliament should attempt to legislate against sectarianism. He told me: 'The Carfin affair was very badly handled, and the publicity did Scotland no good whatsoever'. As I write this, at the end of 2001, an all-party Scottish Parliament committee is to examine all aspects of the problem, and Donald is confident that a bill will come before the Parliament sometime in 2002, and that 'aggravation' will be a key component. This means, in essence, that if, say, an assault is found to have a sectarian element, it will be regarded as an aggravated assault and will carry a stiffer sentence. Donald said that religious hatred had been around in Scotland for far too long, and the coming of the Scottish Parliament meant an opportunity for the country to make a fresh start and rid itself once and for all of the scourge of sectarianism. He thought that, as well as legislation, an intensive educational effort would be required.

In his official consultation document, Donald draws attention to various recent incidents, including the 'vice-chairman singing sectarian songs' debacle mentioned above. He notes that the timing of this particular incident 'could not have been worse, as that same evening Thomas McFadden, a Celtic fan aged 16, was murdered on the street by a Rangers supporter'. The document specifically says that both Celtic and Rangers admit that 'they need legislation to help them help themselves'. It also pays tribute to the work of Nil by Mouth, a charity to combat bigotry and sectarianism set up by a young Glaswegian, Cara Henderson, after a friend of hers was murdered in the East End of Glasgow following an Old Firm game at Parkhead in 1995. In his document, Donald Gorrie explains his motivations thus:

> It is my view that sectarianism does still exist in Scotland and that for far too long it has just been accepted as part of our culture and history, a legacy of the past with the immigration of Irish Catholics, which occasionally spills out at football matches. There is little recognition of how deep-seated the prejudice is among certain groups and how dangerous it can be, and indeed how it can be used in a wider context against other religions.

Donald Gorrie's initiative seemed to me thoroughly commendable; but a wise note of caution was struck by Graham Walker, who pointed out to me that it would be dangerous to assume that the perpetrators of sectarianism could somehow be distinguished from their surrounding communities and wider cultural and environmental influences. Graham also thought that the Carfin affair indicated that Protestantism in Scotland had lost the will or the capacity to make itself heard, at such moments of tension or even crisis, beyond the extremist fringe.

Meanwhile, the Kirk itself surely has a duty to try to do something imaginative and pragmatic about sectarianism; and I hope that the Church and Nation subcommittee comes up with some positive proposals. And, as a final reflection in this section, I have to say that if the Kirk is seriously concerned about mission and outreach *at home*, it could do worse than start in the streets and pubs of

Glasgow and its environs on the day (and night) of an Old Firm derby. It would be brave and possibly dangerous to send specially selected and trained outreach teams through Glasgow and the West of Scotland, to talk and mingle with supporters and try to explain to them that religion (and, for that matter, football) should not be about sectarian hatred. Brave and possibly dangerous; but, as I wrote in the Introduction, the Kirk has in the past not been scared to go into bad places. I am happy to record, that when I mentioned this proposal to Donald Gorrie, he thought it was a good idea. If the Kirk in Edinburgh can reach out to the city's clubbers (as it has been trying to do), then surely in Glasgow, and beyond, it can reach out to football bigots. Such mission is all the more important, as so many of the bigots polluting public places think that they are the front-line soldiers of Protestantism.

I think Graham Walker is right when he says there is a large (and largely ignored, or at best patronised) Protestant constituency in Scotland which feels that the Kirk is not punching its weight *vis-à-vis* the Catholic Church. That is no doubt true in the political arena, where the Kirk should undoubtedly have a higher profile (and should also remain aware of its grave errors in the past). Indeed, Graham Walker, a distinguished academic analyst of modern politics, told me bluntly that, when it came to the political arena, the Kirk was 'artless and timid'. But, when it comes to overtly religious matters, I think the Kirk has to move with great care. I do not think that any significant ecumenical initiatives are going to come from the Catholic Church in Scotland in the short or medium term (I hope I am wrong); so, if there are to be any major ecumenical proposals, that implies that they are going to have to come from the Kirk.

I am aware that, in the course of this pretty bleak chapter, I might at times have appeared at bit harsh on the Kirk and a bit soft on the Catholic Church. I admitted that I actually asked a Catholic bishop to tell me what was wrong with today's Kirk. But then, this book is in part about how others see the Kirk – and, again, I am dealing with the Kirk's problems, not those of the Catholic Church. I am convinced, as I have tried to explain, that in the world context the Catholic Church is immensely powerful and a great force for good. To reiterate, it has played a pivotal role in establishing

Christianity as the world's biggest and fastest-growing religion. That is a positive, of course it is; but it is maybe of scant consolation to the Kirk as it struggles on at home. So let me try to be positive in the context of Scotland; let me put forward one big idea, and a smaller one, even if the omens for serious ecumenism are not propitious.

I wish to propose that the Church of Scotland should promote a great revival of Easter as *the* Christian festival. This would obviously start in Scotland, but it might take off around Britain, around Europe, even beyond. If so, the Church of Scotland could yet manage to do global Christianity a great service. I thought of this when I read the words of the eloquent existentialist theologian Paul Tillich: 'Each year when Good Friday and Easter Sunday approach us, our thoughts turn towards the great drama of redemption, culminating in the pictures of the Cross and Resurrection'. I am not sure if most people's thoughts do turn thus, but the sentence did serve to remind me of the centrality of redemption in the Christian religion; and that, in turn, led me to the almost throwaway thought which one of my interviewees gave me: 'If Christ had simply lived, and then died on the cross, there would be no Christianity. It is because He rose from the dead that we have Christianity.' In a way, I think these are the most important words in this book. In a spirit of humility, I am really asking the Church of Scotland to consider reinventing Easter.

I write these words in the approach to Christmas. I am now going to play a short season as Ebenezer Scrooge. As usual, commercialism is rampant; the great (but not the greatest) Christian festival has been consumed by capitalism at its most sickening, slushy and tawdry. This is the stuff of cliché – but, like so many clichés, it is true. The real spirit of Christmas is still there, but it is ever harder to find. Those who are close to children at Christmas time can still catch the palpable sense of excitement and wonder, which can also occasionally hit even the most world-weary and cynical of souls as the waft of a distant, ardently sung carol drifts from afar across the cold city air; and some watchnight services can still provide an almost tangible delivery of good news.

Yet even the religious side of Christmas, so horribly subsumed in bloated and grotesque secular indulgence, is insignificant compared to that of Easter. And Easter, expressing the very essence of the Christian message, passes by with hardly anybody in the secular world noticing. It is without doubt a festival ripe for revival – and revival as an unashamed religious celebration. 'It is because He rose from the dead that we have Christianity.' This is what it is all about: the defeat of death. To quote, for the second time in this book, from 'Vastness', the greatest poem by the greatest Victorian poet, Tennyson: 'The dead are not dead but alive'.

How would the Church of Scotland go about a great evangelical project such as this? I don't really know; I don't know how strong the evangelical impulse is, though it is certainly there. I certainly hesitate to suggest, as a critic of bureaucracy and of the current multiplicity of committees, boards, panels and departments, the setting-up of a new committee 'anent the revival of Easter'. But the Kirk still has great talent and great energy; and somehow, with a will, the mechanism could be found to harness this latent strength in a good and simple and straightforward Christian cause. As to the form that the beginning of the revival might take, one way might be to organise several spectacular open-air services across Scotland. (Sir Timothy Clifford, the ebullient and ecumenically Episcopalian director-general of the National Galleries of Scotland, believes that huge, well-publicised services are probably the most effective single method of connecting with people, particularly young people, who do not go to church any more.)

I have not forgotten that I am writing here about ecumenism. If the Church of Scotland could find the will, the energy and the spirit to launch this project, surely it would be fitting to invite the other Christian churches in Scotland – in particular the Catholic Church – to join in. The planning of massive outdoor ecumenical Easter services might just be what is needed to galvanise the churches to work together in other ways too. Or am I ingenuous?

And, at the risk of being thought even more ingenuous or, indeed, of exposing myself to ridicule, let me present another, lesser, idea. I believe that Scotland is still, despite everything, a Christian country. But the public monuments and physical evidence of this were mostly created in earlier times, whether we are talking about our few great cathedrals or the wonderful spires of our Victorian churches (the most beautiful of which, I reckon, is that of Lansdowne Church in

Glasgow's Great Western Road – the most perfect spire I have looked up to anywhere in the UK). Maybe the time has come, in Scotland, to create a magnificent and assertive new Christian monument.

There are plenty of precedents elsewhere. If you travel at all in Catholic countries, you are invariably going to come across the kind of monument I have in mind. I recall the excitement with which I approached the colossal, modern, marble statue of Christ, the *Redentore* (Redeemer), on Monte San Biagio in the deep south of Italy, near the small coastal town of Maratea. (This is about 150 miles south of Naples, and well to the south of the fleshpots of Sorrento, Amalfi and Positano, so it is not an area in which you find many Brits; and it is also, to throw in a literary reference, quite a bit south of where *Christ Stopped at Eboli*.) The statue is about 25 metres high; and, as it stands at the top of a mountain that rises 650 metres directly above the Tyrrhenian Sea, you can imagine how spectacular its situation is. But it is not the drama of its physical position that impressed me as much as its symbolic and spiritual power, no doubt crude but undoubtedly there. One of the fascinating things about this *Redentore* is that the huge white Christ, with his arms out-stretched, is facing inland, to the bleak mountains of Basilicata, and his back is pointedly to the glittering sea behind him.

A less dramatic but equally interesting modern public monument is Gormley's huge *Angel of the North*, just south of Gateshead on Tyneside, and easily seen from both the A1 and the east-coast main railway line. If this kind of thing can be done in relatively obscure places like Maratea or Gateshead, why on earth can it not be done in Scotland's capital city? Have the Scots lost all notion of creative risk-taking, of grand, physical, public art? Let me propose, at the risk of inviting more mockery (I have already had some from my ever-sceptical wife, with whom I canvass some of my notions), that the Christian churches in Scotland, in particular the Kirk and the Catholic Church, get together to commission a great celebratory monument of modern Christian art, to be placed at the top of Arthur's Seat in Holyrood Park, Edinburgh. I originally had in mind a statue of Christ, which could be dramatically floodlit at night; but, when I discussed my idea with Sir Timothy Clifford (who was happily disposed to take the idea seriously), he came up with the concept of a great, metallic holy rude sprouting from the peak of that kenspeckle volcanic plug.

And yes, I know there would be problems. Where is the money to come from? Well, I have ideas about that (see Chapter 9). Holyrood Park is royal land; it belongs to the Queen. So, I'm sure a future moderator could persuade the monarch, and Prince Charles, on one of the moderatorial visits to Balmoral. And would it offend multicultural sensibilities? Surely not. And so on. Naysayers would have a field day. But, apart from the ecumenical possibilities, the completed art might become an international symbol for our capital city, as well kent and as universally potent as Rio's Christ or the Eiffel Tower of Paris. And, again, the planning, the politicking and the execution would all evince ecumenism in action. Future generations might even be grateful.

Most of this chapter is about the lack of ecumenical progress with the Catholic Church. Matters are much brighter when we come to the other reformed churches; but so they should be, for movement is, in this more limited context, much easier (if we keep Anglican bishops out of the equation, that is). All sorts of initiatives are taking place in Scotland, such as the work of SCIFU (the Scottish Church Initiative for Union). The Kirk, inevitably, has a Committee on Ecumenical Relations, consisting of twenty-seven members, including one permanent corresponding member from the Catholic Church. I really hope I am wrong; but I suspect that its work may be somewhat bogged down in bureaucracy, with a tendency to talking-shop discussion rather than practical work in the field and in the streets. The Committee has a long and eight-point remit, at once detailed and vague; to give a flavour of this, I shall just quote in full the first two points:

> One. The Committee will be the body through which the World Council of Churches, Action of Churches Together in Scotland, Churches Together in Britain and Ireland and, as appropriate, the other Ecumenical Instruments in Britain and Ireland, relate.
>
> Two. The Committee will call together for planning, briefing and the exchanging of information, the Church of Scotland's representatives on WCC, ACTS (Central Council, Commissions and

Committees), CTBI (The Assembly and the Church Representatives' Meetings) and the like.

(Somehow I enjoyed those last three words, 'and the like'.) This is
one of the times when I felt like saying 'Thank God for the Neilson
Commission' (*Without Walls*) and its emphasis on initiative and
progress at a local rather than centralised level.

I hope I have been right to concentrate on relations, however problematic under the surface, with the Catholic Church, for I believe
that that is the one area that matters profoundly. Maybe I must
guard against a slight tendency to dismiss the other churches in
Scotland, apart from the Kirk and the Catholic Church, as minor
and insignificant (I have detected the merest hint of some Catholics
treating *all* Protestant churches in this way; there is great friendliness, and absolutely no message of triumphalism, but just a tiny
whiff of 'do you really matter that much?'). Even if ongoing
moves to union with smaller reformed churches are a potential
positive, there are dangers here too. For example, Principal Andrew
McGowan of the Highland Theological College told me that he
would be most concerned about any moves that might lead to the
Church of Scotland endangering any part of its Presbyterian heritage.
He said, with great vehemence, that its doctrinal and confessional
position was of absolutely paramount importance to people such as
himself. This is, apart from anything else, a most useful warning,
because I reckon that any conclusive moves to unity would then be
followed by splits, as night follows day. I am only too aware of the
chronic and fissile Protestant tendency for split, breakaway and
counter-division in Scotland. History is not with those working for
unity, even in a limited sense.

That said, there are good things happening all over the country,
at local level. When I was in Carluke, Lanarkshire, the Rev. Iain
Cunningham told me: 'Here, we have a Baptist church, a United
Reform Church, three kirks and a Catholic church. We have a joint
youth project; but, in a way, what is more important even than that
is the way the ministers all make a real effort to get together. We
meet once a month for a meal, along with the youth workers. We
work at keeping in touch. When I was at Duntocher, I was very

much on my own, and I had nothing like this shared support. In some ways it is almost easy here, for this is a self-enclosed town of about 16,000 people, surrounded by green belt. We are all in it together, if you see what I mean. Each of the congregations has members from all over town; about the only thing that is done on a parish basis is funerals. And the churches make an effort to get on with each other in all sorts of ways.'

And when I was in Orkney, I was fascinated to learn of what had been going on at St Magnus Cathedral. The former associate minister there was Eleanor Morson, an Episcopalian who was actually ordained in the cathedral by the Bishop of Aberdeen. There were also joint services conducted with the above-mentioned Jesuit, Father Ken Nugent. Ron Ferguson told me: 'We also had a Baptist organist and a Quaker choirmaster. And one of the elders is an Episcopalian. In other words, ecumenism in action. We have had no unease at all from anyone in the congregation.' Of course, the awesome twelfth-century building, which is Britain's most northerly cathedral and one of the wonders of Scotland, lends itself to all this, with its great ecumenical symbolism. When its 800th anniversary service took place in 1937, the preacher was an archbishop from Norway. 'In the building, we obviously have an ancient Catholic tradition, but we also have other Norwegian and Lutheran traditions', Ron told me.

At the time I spoke to Ron, he had long previously intimated his intention to demit from the ministry of the cathedral, and was still smarting from the absurdly long-drawn-out vacancy process, which had included a visitation to Orkney by no fewer than four members of the Board of National Mission Parish Reappraisal Subcommittee. Ron, normally the most gentle of men, said to me somewhat tartly: 'It would surely have been much better for 121 to have sent four people up here to study practical ecumenism in action than indulging in this bureaucratic interference'. And I am sure many in the Kirk would say 'Amen to that'.

7

THE PRINCESS
AND THE PIONEER

❖

FEMALE ELDERS ARE THE GREAT HOPE – A NEW
ELDER'S CREDO – THE EMPOWERING OF THE
ELDERSHIP – SEXISM AND SOLUTIONS

This chapter looks at two related subjects – the role of elders in the Kirk, and the role of women in it. And yes, they are related. Principal David Lyall of New College, one of the most shrewd and compassionate of Kirk insiders, told me that by far the most positive and exciting thing that had happened in the Church of Scotland since the late 1960s or so was the decision to admit female elders. Not female ministers, but female elders.

However, before we examine the potential of female elders, let us look at what has happened since the Church of Scotland admitted female ministers in 1968. The short and cynical answer might be: not much. There were, on 27 April 2001 (for this precision, I am indebted to page 39/5, Appendix R, of the mini-'Blue Book' or, to give it its official title, the *Supplementary Reports to the General Assembly 2001*), 1,101 ministers in charges, of whom 166 were female. (There were 169 vacant charges.) So, the proportion is 935 males to 166 females – not very impressive, after more than thirty years, and not very indicative of any positive will to achieve gender balance. It is also exceedingly disturbing to note that there are actually more vacant charges than charges served by a female minister.

To compound matters, many female (and some male) ministers will tell you that female ministers tend to be in the lesser and smaller charges rather than big, prestigious ones, and that they have little real influence in the key courts of the Kirk. And, most notoriously of all, there has not yet been a female moderator. Mary Cranfield, the minister of Culsalmond and Rayne linked with Daviot in Gordon, told me emphatically: 'As far as I'm concerned, feminism is not part of the Christian gospel'. Yet, at the same time, she said: 'It is very important that women are treated equally in the Church, and I do think that it is hurtful that there has not yet been a woman moderator'.

This last is, without doubt, a big issue for many people, including many in the media – yet I'm not personally sure that it is too significant. The lack of a female moderator up until now does serve as a symbol of a wider problem; but it has become a debilitating issue in itself, diverting the Kirk from more serious ones. When Finlay Macdonald was elected moderator-designate in the autumn of 2001, most media attention focused on the fact that the two female candidates on the short list of four had not succeeded, rather than on Finlay's indubitable merits. I accept that this is the way things are going to be until we get the first female moderator (in my opinion, it would be good if we could get two for the price of one – the first moderator who is both an elder and a woman). And, as for Finlay himself, he has stated that the moderator's role is largely ambassadorial. The real power within the Kirk lies elsewhere.

The Rev. Lezley Kennedy, minister of Downfield South in Dundee, was quoted as asking: 'Why do moderators have to be high-profile people who have worked the system? It would be good to hear of a moderator announced and you could say "Who?" Someone who was just Joe Bloggs, who has tirelessly worked for years and isn't known, or even someone young and starting out.' There are a lot of points in that one quote. I think that, if we look *outside* the Kirk, her remarks are slightly naïve – for, every year when the next moderator is appointed, most people in Scotland, if they pay any attention at all, will ask 'Who?' (even if the appointee is someone senior and very well known *within* the Kirk). There are, of course, a lot of exceptional, meritorious and unsung people within the Kirk; but I'm not sure if suddenly elevating one of them to a year's moderatorship would achieve anything other than to make a transitory symbolic point.

Indeed, I am far more concerned by the fact that many very hard-working elders (many of them women) can serve the Kirk for twenty or thirty years or more and never even get near its supreme court, the General Assembly, despite the fact that the Assembly meets every year and has hundreds of commissioners in attendance. Anyway, I now wish to make it as clear as I can that I do think there is at least some residual sexism in the Kirk, and that it will have to be addressed urgently. The cleverly titled report *The Stained Glass Ceiling: (En)Gendering Debate*, which was published by the Board of Practice and Procedure's Gender Attitude Project in September 2001, included evidence that women in rural charges were subject to more acute forms of sexism than their urban counterparts, that ministers and elders who held sexist attitudes often cited the Bible in their defence, and that there were still few women in perceived high-status charges.

The Kirk will have to work pro-actively to deal with the first two problems; and one immediate initiative might be the one suggested in the report, that is, for a 'support group for women ministers to discuss problems and ways of dealing with sexism and/or discrimination, so that they do not feel isolated'. But, of course, as the report acknowledges, advocating separate support groups on the basis of gender does tend to emphasise difference rather than diminish it.

As for the lack of women in high-status charges, I'm sure that they will come, particularly as the older cadre of grandee male ministers gradually fade into the sunset. And, at the same time, the nature of the ministry will slowly but surely be changing. Team ministries will probably replace the old 'one parish, one minister' formula; it could be that Ron Ferguson's idea of specially selected, ultra-creative teams centred on great churches will take off; and, in any event, the ministers' calling will become more collaborative, to use one of the favourite words of the convener of the Board of Ministry. It seems pretty obvious to me, if I may be allowed to make a gender generalisation, that women are better suited to this collaborative approach than men.

And yet, there are dangers for the future of the Kirk in all this. It is hackneyed to note that most congregations have more than their fair share of old people; what is less often observed is that, among these old people, women greatly predominate. As ever, that most acute of sociologists, Prof. Steve Bruce of Aberdeen University, has some stark warnings for the Kirk. He believes that greater recruitment of female ministers, and greater influence for them within the Kirk, will be as likely to hasten decline as to reverse it. He explains his position as follows: 'The gradual reduction in the scope of the clergy role and its concentration on the therapeutic is part of a general process of secularisation in which religion is pushed out of the public arena and concentrated on the private and the domestic. I have repeatedly heard it said of female ministers that they are especially good with children and the elderly, and at visiting the sick. If such "feminine" and domestic roles come to be seen as their main virtue, then it is likely that the current under-representation of men in the pews will continue, and be deepened. If churchgoing is already becoming a leisure activity for women, then a female clergy may strengthen the ties between the officials and the members of the Church, but at the cost of making that membership increasingly female.'

Funnily enough, one area of gender imbalance that has attracted little comment lies in academia, in the divinity faculties. There are four of these in Scotland – Aberdeen, St Andrews, Edinburgh and Glasgow – and, in recent years, it is the last two (which are far bigger than the two more northern ones) that have educated most of the new Church of Scotland ministers. At the University of Edinburgh, the principal of New College is Prof. David Lyall and the dean is Prof. Stewart J. Brown. The vice-dean is also a man, Dr Peter Hayman. New College, with more than 450 students from almost thirty different countries, is the largest school of theology and religion in the UK, and it has no fewer than nine chairs, all of which are held by men. The chair of philosophy of religion is held by the Principal of the University of Edinburgh, Lord Sutherland of Houndwood. At Glasgow University, the dean is the Rev. Prof. David Jasper. In addition, there are seven chairs, each of which is held by a man.

Now, as I write this, I am privileged to hold a visiting fellowship at New College, and I have to say that in no way does it appear to me (as a man) to be a sexist organisation. Although it is recognisably rooted in the Reformed tradition, it is a diverse school with many different religious affiliations and disciplines among its students and staff. Indeed, one of its leading lecturers in Christian Ethics and Practical Theology, Dr Marcella Althaus Reid from Argentina, is a world expert in advanced liberation theology and 'queer theory'. Her book, *Indecent Theology* (Routledge, 2001), explores the connections between sexuality, politics and theology and has been hailed as 'the best feminist theology of the last decade'. Yet, given that New College's most senior and influential academic positions are, without exception, held by males, it could be said to be sending out the wrong signals to those students who are starting out on the road to become ministers.

The *Stained Glass Ceiling* report by the Gender Attitude Project has this to say about training: 'Ministers' recollections about training revealed two salient factors. First, that training colleges were not blind to gender issues, and that there were many gender-aware lecturers. Secondly, they could all name incidents that were blatantly sexist, and people who had justified their attitudes and behaviour largely on theological grounds. This applied to ministers who trained in the 1960s, and every decade thereafter until the present time.'

Let me now quote some most lucid, thoughtful and hopeful comments prepared for me by a young (29-year-old) woman elder.

> Perhaps few Church members are more keenly aware of the 'how others see us' question than those of my generation, 20–30-somethings, at the beginning of the twenty-first century. To be a church member, let alone an ordained elder, certainly sets me apart from the vast majority of friends, colleagues and acquaintances in other walks of life. That is, at best, a challenging place to be.
>
> In practice, it means that how the Church is perceived is of considerable importance to me. Perhaps obviously, I want my church to be seen as relevant, mature, passionate, self- and socially aware, dealing with the world as it is, not as the Church might like it to be; and perhaps above all, not self-satisfied or complacent, and in no doubt at all about its core beliefs and values and how to put these into action.
>
> On a personal level, it means learning how to own a faith which is not always easy to explain in the language I would normally use in everyday life. Perhaps in Scotland we are particularly stunted in our ability to communicate such things with feeling and conviction. Do we need a new language of evangelism for the twenty-first century?

As an elder, with the additional unambiguous commitment that role implies, all of these issues come even more strongly into focus for me as an individual. I don't think I subscribe to the saying that the Church is an institution which exists primarily for the good of those who are not its members – but communicating our mission to non-members in words and deeds is one of our most challenging duties.

Of course, there is always going to be a problem for us as a church, so long as we are seen as being shut up in our buildings; the Church 'out there' (or without walls?) must play a significant part in our view of how we want to be in the future. How do we reconcile that core human desire for the familiar, the safe and the ritualistic (be it in worship or in buildings) with the challenges of embracing the new? Do we expect new members to learn our ways or teach us new ways? Why do modern theories of organisational behaviour and self-examination so rarely seem to get past the church door? Are we afraid of change, and, if so, is that not the most dangerous thing of all? I think that the membership in general and perhaps the eldership in particular will be the key to addressing these issues.

Perhaps one of the problems of our 'otherness' lies in the nature of the ordained ministry and the extent to which it is perceived as so clearly 'set apart' from other members of the community in an almost mystical sense. If others, i.e. non-ministers, are not empowered to be identifiable ambassadors and representatives, then the Church cannot hope to reach the parts that it currently does not reach, those other walks of our lives I referred to earlier.

I think that is a remarkable credo; in its own considered way, it is addressing the need for very radical change, and it also speaks of the personal 'apartness' that younger people committed to today's and tomorrow's Kirk are bound to feel. I think that its essential humility is all the more remarkable as it was written by a high-powered young woman very much in the public eye. Her name is Sarah Davidson and she is the director of the Holyrood Project, the bold new building for the Scottish Parliament, a project which she took over when it was already well over budget and well behind schedule.

That someone who is wrestling daily with such pressing and high-profile public and temporal matters should be able to devote so much time and energy to the service of the Kirk gives me hope that the future is brighter than many would have us believe. Sarah is a member of St Andrew's and St George's in Edinburgh, and she is also a member of the Church and Nation Committee. She gave me those words shortly after she had attended her first kirk session – a meeting she found more demanding than she had expected.

A woman who is slightly older than Sarah Davidson and who has recently decided not to become an elder, at least for the time being, is Liz Manson of Greyfriars, Dumfries. Her decision does not reflect a lack of commitment to the Kirk; quite the opposite, in fact, as she has thought long and hard about it. 'I'm just not ready', she told me, as she explained her vision of eldership. 'Traditionally, elders have been very good at keeping in touch with the members they are responsible for; but I believe that more spiritual leadership is needed from elders. In other words, there must be a real difference between a close family friend popping round and an elder popping round.'

Liz felt that what she called the 'front-of-house stuff in the church' was fine, but where she saw the spiritual leadership by elders really coming into play was in home visiting and in leading small cell-groups. Greyfriars currently has two such groups meeting on Tuesday and Wednesday nights; they pick up themes from the previous Sunday service and develop them. You can take along a friend who has not necessarily decided to go to church but has been flirting with the idea. At the group which meets on Tuesdays, there are quite a few younger people with very young families. After speaking to her, I am convinced that Liz Manson will become an elder before too long. And I think that the future of the Church of Scotland is in the hands of people like her and Sarah Davidson – committed, busy people who are emphatically not in the Kirk for status or social reasons, although both of them are very convivial people.

Indeed, I don't want to give heart attacks to the remaining male supremacists in the Kirk; but I do believe that, as the eldership develops, and women become more and more influential in it, the Church of Scotland will increasingly be dominated by women in leadership as well as membership terms. The men haven't done all that well anyway, have they? So, I think that, in one way, Steve Bruce is right, and maybe his views, quoted above, should be regarded as not so much a warning as an optimistic prognostication.

I think this process will take at least a generation, and meanwhile the male-dominated ministry – for whom I have enormous sympathy – will continue to be all-important. And as so many ministers, even relatively young ones, are weary and embattled, overworked and isolated, I think that the eldership has, at present, a key duty to support them more than at present, not to fight them or make life unnecessarily difficult for them. At the same time, ministers must learn to devolve more tasks to their elders and to unleash the creative potential that is surely there in most congregations, dormant and untapped. Gradually, as the ministry becomes more collaborative, and as team and group ministries supplant the old solo parish ministers, the elders will become exactly what they should always have been – the Kirk's shock troops.

Although he would express it in different words, this is essentially the view of Principal David Lyall. He told me: 'The Church of Scotland now has a growing cadre of women elders who are creative, dedicated and innovative. There may well be tensions between these younger elders, who realise the need for training and even some kind of professionalism, and the older, more traditional elders. Some of the most important work in the Kirk at present is being done by Sheilah Steven, the Board of Parish Education's national adviser, who is developing elder-training programmes in all sorts of imaginative and forward-looking ways.'

I don't like the word 'elder'; I think it sends out all the wrong signals, but I have to admit that it is rooted deep in the Kirk's past. (It might be droll, at this stage, to suggest an alternative designation.) John Knox and his five colleagues who wrote the wonderful *First Book of Discipline* (first published in 1560) formally prescribed elders for the Kirk. 'Men of best knowledge in God's word and cleanest life' were to be nominated; elders were to be chosen *yearly* by common and free election. Their duties included assisting the ministers in all the public affairs of the Kirk. A stipend was not considered necessary, because election was for one year only, although re-election was allowed; and elders were not to be so occupied with the affairs of the Kirk that they could not reasonably attend 'upon their domestic business'.

It was not too long before it was decided that elders should be elected to serve for life – a huge step from one year. Personally, I think this was a wrong decision, although the Kirk clearly does not think so, as elders are still, to this day, chosen for life. I think that elders should be elected for a maximum of ten years, and, if appropriate, then they can be elected for another fixed period. They should also be allowed sabbaticals of, say, six months or a year. I realise that this might make life more rather than less difficult for kirk sessions from the organisational point of view; but the overriding concern should surely be to enable elders to serve the Kirk as effectively and diligently as possible. Many of the best elders are likely to be very busy people anyway. Should elders be paid a mini-stipend? I think so, but I realise that this is a contentious suggestion. Where would the money come from? Well, I shall look at that in Chapter 9.

I also think that elders, who are, after all, ordained servants of the Kirk and, more importantly, of God, should at all times wear some badge, emblem or symbol, not ostentatious but not too discreet either, which would indicate clearly to all people at all times that they are indeed elders. An elder should obviously be operating as an elder constantly – at work and at home, as well as when engaged on specific Kirk duties – and if an elder is worried about ordinary people, strangers and colleagues, knowing that he or she is an elder, then his or her commitment must be questioned.

I have suggested that ministers should wear a similar emblem at all times. I think the Kirk should organise a great national competition, perhaps in conjunction with one of the schools of art or the National Galleries of Scotland, to come up with an appropriate design for an elder's, as well as a minister's, emblem. Ideally, the design for elders would be similar to but easily differentiated from the one for ministers. Such a national competition could engender useful and positive publicity for the Kirk, could create interest among younger, creative people and could help to revive the Kirk's somewhat moribund reputation in Scotland's wider artistic fraternity.

Ewan Aitken, the minister of St Margaret's, Restalrig South, Edinburgh, believes that elders should be asking themselves not 'how can I survive?' but rather 'how do we grow?' and 'how do we develop?' The Kirk can of course help elders to develop and grow by giving them more responsibilities. Ministers can help by leading, encouraging, involving, training and generally cajoling their elders. This is already happening, with elders taking a greater part in the conduct of worship and, very occasionally, taking funerals. As elders are ordained, I see no reason why, if and when they are properly trained, they should not be allowed to take the sacraments of baptism and communion also. At communion, they already play a key role in handing round the wine and the bread; and, although it would be theologically a major step to allow them actually to administer the sacrament, I don't think it would be such a big spiritual or psychological step.

As I write this, I'm constantly aware of the reformative phrase *priesthood of all believers* echoing in my mind. It seems to me that the very essence of Protestantism is its incredibly exciting emphasis on the direct responsibility of individual believers to communicate and interact directly with their Maker rather than always having to operate through the intercession of a minister or a priest. To reduce it to its bare bones, Protestantism seems to me to imply the eventual redundancy of ministers. On the one hand, it could be argued here that I am trying to make the elder more like a priest or a minister; but, on the other, it could be said that the more elders, who are lay, take on the traditional tasks of ministers and priests, the more the Kirk would be developing logically and bravely along the lines laid out by the founders of the Reformation in the sixteenth century. Has it got the courage to do this?

I'd like elders to be more visible and to have more sense of self-esteem and of their essential worth and significance within the Kirk. I think that there should be a great elders' conference, with only a very few, if any, ministers attending. Some or all of the ideas adumbrated above, and many others, could be discussed. In a way, I am asking for elders to become more militant in fighting for an enhanced role in the Kirk. But – and this is crucial – I do not want this to be seen as an attack on or as a threat to the current ministry. Rather, I'd like to see a cadre of 40,000 or 50,000 elders (at present there are 40,000, but not all are as effective as they could be) eventually leading a great revival of the Kirk. This cadre of younger, more militant and more effective elders – many, perhaps a majority of them women – should mobilise as a progressive and radical force within the Kirk and, indeed, in the wider Scotland. Think about it: a spiritual army of 50,000 committed, energised and driven people, working with gusto and verve in a country of only 5,000,000 people. They could just about move mountains. They certainly could not afford to tolerate complacency, apathy or lethargy.

I'd like elders to have much more say in the running of the Kirk. It is utterly ridiculous and even scandalous that an elder can serve industriously and well for thirty years and never get near the Kirk's supreme body, the supposedly democratic General Assembly, whereas all ministers are guaranteed to get there at least once every four years. There needs to be an urgent constitutional overhaul to give elders a more direct say in the affairs of the church of which they are, potentially, such a vital component. This implies a system of national plebiscites; but this I shall examine in Chapter 10.

And finally, I think that the manner in which elders are nominated and elected needs to be rationalised. Some congregations leave it to the kirk session, which inevitably means that the session will have a tendency to become self-perpetuating; those elected will usually reflect the style and standards of those who have gone before. This encapsulates what David Lyall calls the 'aye been' syndrome, which can be so debilitating for the Kirk. Some congregations elect elders more democratically, from a constituency that includes the congregational membership and not just the session. I think that this is the better model, and I'd have thought that it should be adopted everywhere, although congregations that are heavily dominated by older people do tend to be very conservative.

In the short term, the Kirk must surely address the imbalance in the convenerships of its more important committees and boards; very few are convened by elders as opposed to ministers. A current exception is the Assembly Council, convened by Helen McLeod, a most thoughtful and diplomatic elder from Forfar. However, she and her council, which is in effect the Kirk's great think-tank, more or less stood aside to let the *Without Walls* team complete their report. Indeed, you could argue that the existence of the Assembly Council should have made a 'special commission anent review and reform' unnecessary in the first place.

Meanwhile, to conclude this section on the eldership, here are the thoughts of some experienced and sage (male) ministers. Ron Ferguson in Orkney told me: 'Think of 40,000 active and committed members of a political party in Scotland, and then you begin to understand the potential of the eldership – but our elders too often lack confidence in what they are doing. I think their training needs to be changed, too. They don't need to delve into theology, they just need the basics of faith. I personally do not see why, if they are trained properly and the Church authorises it, they should not be permitted to take the sacraments. But a lot of people would disagree, and I am not sure if the Church is quite ready for this. I certainly do think that elders could take more funerals. If you look at the more remote islands, where you can have ministerial vacancies for many years, a minister can go to an island where he doesn't know anyone at all in order to take a funeral. A local elder could do it much better.'

Iain Cunningham in Carluke told me: 'Without doubt, our elders need to be better resourced, and they need to be encouraged and developed. We now have a system here whereby every other session meeting does not deal with routine business; we just discuss, informally, anything that comes up. And this has made me realise what a huge amount of leeway and freedom we have at local level in the Church of Scotland. Elders, and ministers, should be using this freedom to think and act much more creatively.'

Gordon Kennedy in Stranraer told me: 'In our congregations, we have tremendously gifted people who could be serving the Church more effectively. Many of them could be trained by the minister to lead worship, to preach and so on. People would not need to go to conferences or training courses all the time; a lot of this could be done locally. The minister will become more of a team leader, and we are going to have to rethink the whole relationship between the minister, the elders and the congregation.'

John Munro in Kinross told me: 'Some elders, in fact, could be more skilled in leading worship and/or pastoral work than the minister. We are going to have to let the minister be more involved in training and enabling the elders.'

John Cairns in Gullane told me: 'What we have not done with so many of our elders is let them know that we want to use their talents and their wisdom and their creativity much more. They are rooted in the neighbourhood and the community in a way the minister sometimes isn't; yet a lot of elders think that their real work is done at meetings. From the 1930s onwards, the Church became more and more minister-dominated, and slowly but surely we are going to have to turn this round if the Church is to be really effective again.'

Norman Shanks, leader of the Iona Community, sounded a note of warning when he told me: 'There is a danger of people who have not made it in life, who are maybe unfulfilled in their career or their marriage or their relationship, compensating for that by dominating kirk sessions. Meanwhile, younger, creative people may well decide that they could do more to build up the Kingdom of God by working for a charity or an environmental group or whatever. As the Church is presently organised, it might be better for committed young people to be involved outside the Church rather than in it. So, we have to change things.'

And finally, Johnston McKay, Scotland's pre-eminent religious broadcaster, told me: 'At present, most elders think their duties are as follows: to visit with communion cards, to be on duty on a Sunday, and to attend kirk sessions. If the minister is working well and hard, then, as things are at present constituted, *the elders are let off the hook*. Elders should be doing more to support their ministers – but then how are elders to know exactly what the minister is supposed to do?'

What we are seeing here is a varied group of experienced and thoughtful male ministers, none of them particularly young, and some of them quite old, all wanting to unleash, in their different ways, the creativity and potential inherent in the eldership, and realising that the process, however it develops, is bound to involve a completely new relationship between the minister and the elders.

To conclude this chapter, I return to the role of women in the Kirk. Although they have increasingly dominated the membership, very few women directly connected with the Kirk have, over the years, made their mark in leadership terms or as national figures. I played a little game with some of my interviewees: I would ask them to name the principal female figures in the Kirk's long story. Otherwise fluent people would promptly dry up. But I was able, eventually, to come up with the following, painfully exiguous, list.

We start with the legendary 'Princess of the Tron Adventurers', the feisty Jenny Geddes, who was outraged by the introduction of Archbishop William Laud's Anglican liturgy to Scottish Presbyterian worship. She reputedly yelled: 'Daur ye say mass at my lug?' and then flung a stool at the Dean of St Giles, James Hannay, during a service in the High Kirk of Edinburgh in July 1637. What actually triggered the events that followed has possibly been mythologised, but there was certainly a riot in the kirk that commenced when stools, stones and Bibles were flung at the hapless Hannay; and Jenny does seem to have thrown the first missile. (The fact that stones were among the missiles would appear to suggest an element of premeditation, for presumably loose stones were not lying around inside the kirk.)

When the Bishop of Edinburgh bravely took to the pulpit to remonstrate with Jenny and her friends, he too was driven down under a formidable barrage of stools, stones and Bibles. The 'princess' and her enraged colleagues were at last forcibly ejected from the kirk. They did not scatter, but remained outside, consumed with Presbyterian fury, screaming and hammering at the doors and throwing stones at the venerable windows of St Giles. This was a very colourful incident but maybe not quite as edifying an episode as that involving my next heroine, the splendid Mrs Christian Granger, who saved the Scottish crown jewels in 1651.

I remember several times as a child, as we visited Dunnottar Castle just south of Stonehaven, or drove along the coast road between the castle and the hamlet of Kinneff, hearing the tale of the intrepid Mrs Granger. The Scottish regalia had been removed to the fastness of Dunnottar. The resourceful Christian, wife of the minister of Kinneff, James Granger, on the pretext of a visit to the wife of the governor of the castle, managed somehow to secure the jewels. She is supposed to have concealed the crown and sceptre under her own clothes. The other regalia were hidden in flax and then lowered by rope over the high cliff by the castle, to be retrieved by a waiting accomplice, a young girl who was supposedly gathering seaweed by the shore of the North Sea. The Honours were then hidden under the Grangers' bed in Kinneff manse before being moved into the church, at dead of night, and buried under a large slab by the front pew. A year later, Dunnottar Castle was systematically ransacked by Cromwell's troops, but no trace of the regalia was found. After the restoration of Charles II, the regalia were taken in triumph from Kinneff Kirk to Edinburgh Castle, but they were never again to be used in a Scottish coronation.

Jenny Geddes and Christian Granger were clearly redoubtable women with a starring role in Scottish Protestant folklore, but I can now move on to one or two others who made a more orthodox contribution to the Kirk's development. Willielma Campbell was an eighteenth-century evangelist who was way ahead of her time. She organised ecumenical services in Edinburgh and was a notable patroness of many leading evangelical ministers. Lady Grisell Baillie was an acclaimed Presbyterian poetess in the early eighteenth century, and a second Lady Grisell Baillie was the first Kirk deaconess, being appointed at a service in Roxburgh in 1888. Two dauntless missionaries were Mary Slessor, who served in Nigeria, and Annie Small, who worked in India and later founded the Women's Missionary Training Institute in Edinburgh (although most of her career was in the Free Church). Letitia Bernard was the first female doctor appointed by the Kirk to work abroad (in Poona in 1884).

Mary Lamond served a long stint as national president of the Women's Guild between the First and Second World Wars, and she also played a leading role in the negotiations leading to the Union of 1929. She was, amazingly, the only female speaker at the great Union Assembly in 1929. (I wonder whether, if women had been more prominent in the Kirk at that time, it would have been permitted to embark on its hateful anti-Irish racist campaign.) The woman who did more than any other to build up the Guild was Katharine Davidson: when she started her work, it had fewer than 2,000 members; by the time she died in 1925, there were well over 50,000.

And Lady Frances Balfour was the leading Kirk activist for women's suffrage.

In more recent years, the outstanding female figure has been without doubt Mary Levison, a deaconess who petitioned the General Assembly in 1963 on the grounds that her appointment as a chaplain at Edinburgh University in effect constituted a call to the ordained ministry. A very clever and charismatic woman, who had gained a first in PPE (philosophy, politics and economics) at Oxford and then studied systematic theology at New College and gone on to further study in Switzerland and Germany, she was eminently suited to blaze this most important of trails. It led to the eventual ordination of female ministers from 1968 onwards, although Mary herself was not ordained until 1978. She served as moderator of Edinburgh presbytery in 1988; and, when she was associate minister of St Andrew's and St George's in Edinburgh, she pioneered that church's mission to local businesses, offices and department stores.

Ann Allen was a formidable and high-profile convener of the Board of Social Responsibility in the 1990s; Dr Alison Elliot was an equally high-profile convener of the Church and Nation Committee, with a more consensual style than some of her male predecessors in the 1980s; and, of all the female ministers in the Kirk, the one who seems to me to have made most of a mark is probably the Rev. Margaret Forrester of St Michael's, Slateford, Edinburgh, a notably humane and liberal minister. She has twice made the short list for moderator, but sadly on neither occasion was she elected. As I said, it is a shamefully exiguous list, given that we have been reviewing a period of more than 400 years.

One thing is certain: many more women will rise to real prominence in the Kirk. One who is going to do so very shortly is Marjory MacLean, who will be acting principal clerk during Finlay Macdonald's year as moderator. Indeed, before too long, I suspect that women will be dominating all aspects of the Church of Scotland. But the key scandal at present is not the continuing absence of a female moderator so much as the lack of women in prominent positions in the Kirk's boards and departments.

The annual *Year Book* of the Church of Scotland lists twenty-seven Assembly boards and committees. Of the pivotal positions in these, very few are held by women. The Rev. Jean Montgomerie is convener of the Board of Communication; the aforementioned Helen McLeod is convener of the Assembly Council; the Law Department is run by the Kirk's solicitor, Mrs Janette Wilson; and the Guild is convened by Mrs Elspeth Kerr. And that's it. I think that this situation represents more of an immediate challenge for the Kirk than just about anything else apart from the crisis in ministry recruitment and retention.

Presumably, part of the blame lies with the Nomination Committee, which has a male majority but not an overwhelming one. Of its forty-four members, eighteen are women. It is surely about time that these eighteen women really asserted themselves and made waves; at the very least, they should be doing their best to ensure that articulate, feisty and forceful women are appointed to many more vital positions in the courts of the Kirk.

8

MINE EYES HAVE SEEN, MINE EARS HAVE HEARD

❖

This is a small chapter about a big subject – preaching. I'd like to start with a diversion to the USA, where the man who was, in my opinion, the greatest preacher and indeed the greatest speaker of the twentieth century managed to do more for the exploited, suppressed and degraded black people of America in a mere twelve years than all their other leaders had achieved in 200. Quite simply, he gained for them their civil rights. Even more amazing was the fact that he totally and absolutely rejected violence, at a time when many other charismatic black leaders were advocating seriously violent protest. He suffered violence himself: his house was bombed, he was thrown into prison and put into solitary confinement, and he was under attack by thuggish sheriffs and evil, hate-frenzied white mobs and even other black leaders who did not accept his constant emphasis on the need for *peaceful* change.

This man, probably the greatest Christian leader of recent times, and certainly the greatest Christian orator, was of course the Baptist, Dr Martin Luther King junior. And if you ask how he achieved so much in such a short space of time, I'd answer: by preaching. That is, of course, simplistic; but Martin Luther King's success, the key to his gargantuan political reach, lay in his inspirational Christian preaching. His most celebrated sermon – his greatest speech – was the 'I have a dream' oration before a crowd of 300,000 at the climax of the memorable March on Washington in August 1963. It contained a sentence that was to resonate throughout America: 'I have a dream that my four little children will one day live in a nation where they will not be judged by the colour of their skin but by the content of their character'.

Within a year of that most moving and utterly spellbinding of sermons (thank goodness it was recorded for posterity on television), the Civil Rights Bill was signed into law after more than eighty days of Senate debate, and the next year ended with Dr King receiving both the Kennedy Peace Prize and the Nobel Peace Prize. Martin Luther King was a deeply cerebral man, a sophisticated political thinker – but everything he said was rooted in his Christianity. The Christianity came first; the politics was an add-on. He preached a social gospel; for him, faith was not just about the individual soul, but also about securing God's peace and justice in our wounded and torn world. He despised the notion that any democratic society could tolerate poverty. 'The poor can stop being poor if the rich are willing to become even richer at a slower rate', he was given to saying. He also insisted that any religion that professed to be concerned only with people's souls and not also 'with the slums that damn them, the economic conditions that strangle them and the social conditions that cripple them' was a no-good religion.

Dr King died, aged 38, when James Earl Ray shot him as he stood on the balcony of the Lorraine Motel in Memphis, Tennessee on 4 April 1968, shortly before he was to lead a small march of local sanitation workers who were on strike. The previous night, he had preached what was to be his last sermon – and I'd like to quote the final sentences of this, his final address to a public audience.

And then I got into Memphis. And some began to say the threats, or talk about the threats that were out. What would happen to me from some of our sick white brothers?

Well, I don't know what will happen now. We've got some difficult days ahead. But it doesn't matter with me now. Because I've been to the mountain top. And I don't mind. Like anybody, I would like to live a long life. Longevity has its place.

But I'm not concerned about that now. *I just want to do God's will. And he's allowed me to go up to the mountain. And I've looked over. And I've seen the Promised Land.*

> I may not get there with you. But I want you to know tonight
> that we, as a people, will get to the Promised Land. And I'm happy
> tonight. I'm not worried about anything. I'm not fearing any man.
> *Mine eyes have seen the glory of the coming of the Lord.*

We have there a powerful, prophetic and almost perfect fusion of
politics and religion.

The point of this extended preamble is not to say that the Church
of Scotland should be producing preachers like Dr King. Although
there is social injustice in Scotland, there is no mighty cause like
the civil-rights movement. And preachers of the calibre of Dr King
don't come along that often, anyway. No, the point is rather that, at
a time when so many people in the West, if not elsewhere, are
questioning the relevance of Christianity and its ability to engage
people in an aggressively secular society, the potential power of
the preacher should never be underestimated.

I have talked to several people in today's Kirk who frankly doubt
if there is much point in preaching at all. I think, personally, that a
church service without a sermon is a bit like an ocean without water;
but I do understand that many modern ministers think they have
more important things to attend to, and they also have genuine
concerns about their own ability to preach well and to hold a
congregation's attention for more than five minutes or so. I have
sympathy with them; and, when the Kirk has devolved so much
concerning the conduct of worship to the local level, it would be
impertinent and silly of me to suggest that every service should be
built round a sermon. But, where the minister is good at preaching
and where he or she wishes to devote time and energy to a weekly
homily (or homilies, in many cases), then I think that minister
deserves every encouragement. In other words, I'd like preaching
to become fashionable again.

I also think that, in terms of outreach, the Kirk should be considering deploying the talents of its world-class preachers (there is
maybe not a Dr King around, but there are some quite exceptional
preachers operating in Scotland today) in the context of much bigger
audiences than are to be found in most kirks on a Sunday morning.
I'd love to see the Church of Scotland planning some really big
outdoor services, possibly but not necessarily on an ecumenical

basis, and especially at Easter time. The key point is that the Kirk would be *taking the lead.* If other churches, particularly the Catholic Church, wanted to join in, then all well and good, and that would be a significant ecumenical development. But this would be a Kirk initiative, and would be seen as such.

To hear a Sinclair Ferguson or an Andrew McLellan or a Peter Neilson preaching before a crowd of many thousands in some great open-air venue would be, without any doubt whatsoever, inspirational. These are three magnificent preachers I have recently had the privilege to hear, as I described in Chapter 3. But I am sure there are other powerful preachers in the Kirk who could seize the opportunity of mass worship to embolden the faint-hearted, to challenge the complacent and generally to give spiritual succour and hope, and also to try to answer the question that so many of us are asking. Yes, so many people, of all ages and backgrounds, Christians as well as non-believers, in Scotland today are asking a very simple question (they ask in different ways, but it is essentially the same question): *What is life for?* Where better to start to give the answer, the Christian answer, than before thousands in Holyrood Park or Glasgow Green on Easter Sunday?

Why not, for heaven's sake? Why on earth leave this kind of thing to the Pope or to Billy Graham, once in a generation, if that? And, dare I say it, the Kirk might even do it better than the Pope or Billy Graham. This is where I wish the Church of Scotland would wake up and *use* the immense talents and energy it still has, if only it could learn to deploy these attributes. This is where I would plead with the Kirk to get out there and speak, speak to the people of Scotland. Nothing else really matters. That is what the Kirk, ultimately, is for: to tell us what life is for. Many in the Kirk might be surprised; there are so many, many more of us out there who want to hear, who are waiting to hear.

Although Scotland is not racked by the systematic suppression of human rights or any kind of mass social evil, there is a terrible amount of cruelty, alienation, despair and injustice all around us in our supposedly civilised, prosperous, caring and clean society. Preachers must never be scared of the overtly political, which is rooted in the here and now. When a political message is fused with the Christian message, it is just about the most powerful thing in all the world – certainly more powerful than any gun or bomb. Ron Ferguson told me that the Swiss Protestant thinker Karl Barth (whom Pope Pius XII described as the greatest theologian since Saint Thomas Aquinas) had a saying: *The preacher should preach with a Bible in one hand and a newspaper in the other.* Ron developed this notion for me when he said: 'You have to bring politics and the Bible together. You have to link insights from the Bible with what is happening around us in our society, and then you get this crucial tension at the heart of the sermon.'

I was interested to note, when I attended worship in various parts of Scotland, that not one of the sermons I heard was overtly political. But surely politics is far, far too important to be left to the politicians? I'd personally rather listen to the average Church of Scotland minister than to the average MSP. The problem is that the average politician has more confidence than the average minister. And our new Scottish Parliament is much discussed and analysed in a way that the doings of the Kirk sadly aren't. MSPs are encouraged by the world around them to think that they are important and that this world wants to hear what they have to say. But surely Christians, too, must engage in the political world if the Christian message is to be spread effectively?

Funnily enough, if more Christians linked Christianity with politics, there might be a revival in Scottish national politics which, despite the new Parliament, is also facing something of a crisis. To conclude this point, let me quote the thoughts of one of the finest preachers around, Andrew McLellan: 'Anyone with any familiarity with the kind of things Jesus spoke about all his life, like riches and poverty, like war and peace, like race issues and women's issues and the rule of law, would have expected him to be political right from the start. And so he was. Those who bleat about keeping politics out of religion have a hard time with the words of Jesus.'

Some of the ministers I talked with worked enormously hard at sermon preparation – none more so than Derek Morrison in the far north-west, who spent over eight hours preparing each of the three sermons he delivered each week. David Scott in Bearsden told me that he started preparing his main sermon on a Tuesday and spent much of Saturday completing it. Iain Cunningham in Carluke told me that, although he had trained in drama and was confident in the pulpit, the actual preparation of his weekly sermon was still, after twenty years of practice, the most difficult and demanding single thing he had to do.

I think that ministers such as these deserve every support, particularly when there are these silly notions around that people are so inured to the sound-bite culture, and that young people have so lost any powers of concentration on the spoken word, that no-one can pay attention to a sermon that lasts more than a few minutes. I do have sympathy with those ministers who think that they cannot hold an audience's attention for long; but I'd certainly wish to give great encouragement to those ministers who see preaching as absolutely central to their work.

Gordon Kennedy in Stranraer told me: 'It takes me between six and eight hours to prepare a Sunday sermon. I am ordained as a minister of the Word as well as sacrament. Over the last century, there has been a loss of confidence in the gospel and, therefore, in preaching. If you are not convinced that the Bible is God's Word, then your confidence in preaching must decline. In a few situations, I accept that you might have one or two people in a congregation who could not keep the thread of a fifteen-minute talk. But I would say that, if an address of fifteen minutes or so is well prepared and well presented, then a 14-year-old would certainly be able to keep up with it. We must work at making it easy to follow the thread: that is the main thing, and that is where the preparation comes in. The sermon must resonate with people.'

As I say, ministers such as these must be nourished and nurtured by the Kirk. But it should also be encouraging lay preaching. In some respects, I would agree with Marjory MacLean, depute clerk, when she says there is nothing worse than amateur preaching; but there is the potential for good preaching among the laity and particularly the eldership, and I don't see why their talents should be lost to the Kirk in this time of desperate ministerial shortage and overstretch.

When I attended a meeting of St Andrews presbytery, there was a minor stushie because the Readers at national level (Readers are members of the laity, but they are entitled to conduct services and

preach) had objected to a certain elder from the presbytery conducting services and preaching. He was evidently a very good
preacher, and much in demand. The Readers had objected because
he was not licensed to preach. One member of the presbytery
told me: 'It is just the Readers' trade union in action. This elder
does it for free, and the Readers don't want to see their £45 fee
slipping away.' It was an awkward dilemma: the Readers were
technically in the right, but the elder in question was popular and
much respected locally, and a lot of eloquent words were spoken
on his behalf. Eventually, the meeting decided to take the classic
bureaucratic way out of such an impasse: the presbytery's business
convener, the Rev. John Hegarty of Cupar, was instructed to seek
clarification about the complaint and then report back to the next
meeting.

I am aware that there are dangers in getting too excited about the
importance of preaching. For one thing, some great preachers do
seem to have feet of clay; it is the old *Don't do as I do, but do as I
say* syndrome. The great Dr King was a womaniser. Another outstanding modern preacher was Allan Boesak, whose superb sermons in
the 1980s did as much as anything to pave the way for the ending of
apartheid in South Africa. This inspirational church leader from
Kakamas became President of the World Alliance of Reformed
Churches. Unfortunately, his personal life was by no means
exemplary. Yet, I do feel that preachers of genius like King and
Boesak should be readily forgiven their sins, just as ordinary people
are.

And it is easy to mock certain styles of preaching, whether it be
the lugubrious 'I. M. Jolly' mode or the oily, inflated, Chadband
type of rhetoric. I must admit that I always smile to myself when a
preacher stands up and commences his address (often at a funeral)
with the words: 'My dear friends . . .' The splendidly greasy Rev.
Chadband is my favourite comic character from Dickens. Here is
an example of his preaching style (from *Bleak House*): 'My friends,
why do I wish for peace? What is peace? Is it war? No. Is it strife?
No. Is it lovely, and gentle, and beautiful, and pleasant, and serene,
and joyful? Oh yes!' Or again: 'I say this brother present here among
us is devoid of parents, devoid of relations, devoid of flocks and

herds, devoid of gold, of silver and of precious stones, because he is devoid of the light that shines in upon some of us. What is that light? What is it? I ask you what is that light? . . . It is the ray of rays, the sun of suns, the moon of moons, the star of stars. It is the light of Terewth . . . Of Terewth. Say not to me it is not the lamp of lamps. I say to you, it is. I say to you, a million times over, it is! It is! I say to you that I will proclaim it to you, whether you like it or not; nay, that the less you like it, the more I will proclaim it to you. With a speaking trumpet! I say to you that if you rear yourself against it you shall fall, you shall be bruised, you shall be battered, you shall be flawed, you shall be smashed.'

That is Charles Dickens at his magnificent, satirical best. It is very funny, but there are disturbing echoes there of sermons I have heard delivered in all seriousness. It is easy to mock preachers; but to present a strong sermon that does not at times teeter on the ridiculous is not necessarily an easy thing to do. I think that to preach well requires a certain amount of risk-taking and quite a lot of courage.

It also requires considerable intellectual resource. The Church of Scotland can still deploy intellectuals of the highest calibre. I was privileged to hear, in New College, two public lectures of patent merit. Both were delivered in a crowded hall; indeed, on both occasions, more seats had to be brought in, and even then it was a case of 'standing room only' well before the doors were closed. Many of the audience, on both occasions, were members of New College, staff and students; but there were also many members of the public present. Each lecture lasted more than an hour; each speaker spoke with notes he rarely referred to; each address was fluent, thought-provoking, eclectic in reference, wide-ranging in allusion and pungent in conclusion. Each was delivered by a minister of the Church of Scotland.

I have heard many mutterings to the effect that the Kirk does not have the brainpower it had fifty years ago. That may or may not be true, but there is clearly still plenty of brainpower around. But even more important than the quality of the lectures was the nature of the audiences. Each audience contained many young people who listened with rapt attention. I know that a public lecture is not quite the same as a sermon, but the point I am making here is that there are plenty of people around, including young people, who want to hear ethical and religious issues discussed at the very highest level. In other words, the serious intellectual tradition of the Kirk, and the need for it, are not dead yet. The first lecture was Will Storrar's inaugural address as professor of Practical Theology and Christian Ethics at New College. The other was the Baillie Lecture, by his predecessor, Prof. Duncan Forrester.

One of the most important qualities of a good sermon is that it can provoke new avenues of thought as well as positive action. Early on in my researches, it was suggested to me that I should have a look at the theology of Paul Tillich, the great Protestant existentialist. (Tillich was a Prussian who studied at various German universities. After serving as a chaplain with the German forces during the First World War, he became professor of philosophy at Frankfurt University. As a virulent critic of Nazism, he had to flee Germany. It is to his enormous credit that he was the first non-Jewish academic driven out of Germany at that dark time. He eventually became professor of philosophical theology at Union Theological Seminary in the USA.)

I confess that I soon decided that his three-volume *Systematic Theology* was well beyond me; but, on the other hand, I found a collection of his finest sermons, *The Shaking of the Foundations* (SCM Press, 1949), to be accessible, stimulating and even exciting. Tillich himself wrote: 'Many of my friends have told me of the difficulty they have met in trying to penetrate my theological thought. They believe that through my sermons the practical, or more exactly, the existential implications of my theology are more clearly manifest.'

Tillich's most famous sermon is simply called: 'You Are Accepted'. Let me quote from it: 'Grace strikes us when we are in great pain and restlessness. It strikes us when we walk through the dark valley of a meaningless and empty life ... Sometimes at that moment a wave of light breaks into our darkness and it is as though a voice were saying, *You are accepted. You are accepted.*' I would say that Tillich's sermons could be extraordinarily helpful to those who do not wish to take the entire text of the Bible absolutely literally but who still believe firmly in the fundamentals of Christianity, for example the Resurrection.

He was also an early and passionate environmentalist. His sermon *Nature Also Mourns for a Lost Good* is as noble an environmental manifesto as I have ever come across, and should be required reading for all who are affronted by our devastation of the natural world, whether they are Christians or not (and, more to the point, those who are *not* affronted by it). Indeed, I'd say that this short but profound meditation on the necessity of living with rather than against nature could be a starting point to bring many young people to religion; but then, all great sermons have inherent in them such capacity for outreach.

I offer two final thoughts on preaching. Sermons do not require to be delivered from pulpits, obviously enough; the broadcasting media and even the new media present potent opportunities for good preaching. The Kirk's Johnston McKay is a superb professional religious broadcaster; and various other ministers, and even the odd lay person, have mastered the discipline of the tight broadcast sermonette. And then, of course, there is the medium of the press. I have already referred to the weekly columns by Ron Ferguson (in *The Herald* and the *Press & Journal*) and by Stewart Lamont (first in *The Herald*, now in *The Scotsman*). Both of these ministers are consummate communicators, and both of them have marvellous ways of making a religious point with cunning subterfuge, of letting it creep up on you unawares, as it were. A very different communicator is the more crusty Canon Edward Norman, Chancellor of York Minster, whose magisterial meditations in Britain's best-selling daily broadsheet, the *Daily Telegraph*, certainly contrive, without fail, to make me reflect long and hard.

The second concluding point is that there is a sadness in this chapter, and that is that no woman has been mentioned. For some reason, women do not appear to have made their mark as preachers. Maybe it requires a certain kind of essentially masculine arrogance to stand in a pulpit and hold forth confidently (though, as I've suggested, it also requires an ability to take risks, and considerable courage).

So, let me be mischievous and cite one unlikely female preacher. The most famous sermon delivered by a woman in Scotland in recent times was Margaret Thatcher's so-called 'Sermon on the

Mound' at the General Assembly of 1988, when the Kirk did not receive its guest with any great grace or dignity. I realise very well that many in the Kirk believed then, and believe to this day, that Margaret Thatcher was not the friend of social justice but its enemy. As a public speaker, however, she was robust, challenging, clear, and a scourge of soft thinking and complacency; and these are among the qualities that I for one would look for in a great preacher. Anyway, I see no reason why power preaching should be a male preserve. That is another challenge for the Kirk's women.

9

THANK GOD FOR MONEY

❖

This is another chapter examining several issues. First, I want to look at the most vexed subject of all – money. Leon Marshall, who runs his own accountancy business in Glasgow and was until recently convener of the Board of Stewardship and Finance, stated categorically at the 2001 General Assembly: 'Thank God for money. Money means freedom for you and me to produce what we need and where we will. Money means freedom for the Church to be equipped for her tasks in this country and throughout the world. Thank God for money, so powerful a servant of Jesus Christ when he is our master.' He acknowledged that he was quoting from a speech by a former moderator, Fraser McLuskey; but, as he said, the sentiments remained constantly relevant.

The Kirk has a huge problem with money: it does not have enough. Yet, it is a wealthy organisation. It has total assets of over £300 million. But there we hit the first big problem; that money is held by different boards and committees in about 4,000 – yes, 4,000 – separate funds. Almost all of these funds are subject to donor restrictions or to General Assembly restrictions. The Assembly is the Kirk's supreme body and, whether we like it or not, if it decides that a certain fund must be restricted or disbursed in a particular way, nobody can do anything about it, at least not until the next General Assembly. You will probably already be saying that this is no way to run a business, and you would be right. But here we hit another problem. In my opinion, there are far too many people in the Kirk who refuse to think of it as a business; who think that, because this money is being used for God's work, contemporary professional business practice need not apply. I personally have contempt for this attitude; but it is around, and it is powerful.

The man wrestling with these and related difficulties is one of the Kirk's finest servants, a chartered accountant who has worked for the Church of Scotland for more than thirty years and who has been its general treasurer since 1995. He is Donald Ross, and I am particularly indebted to him because, at the end of 2001, when he was working overtime to get the Kirk's annual financial statements completed, he took time, over two separate sessions, to go over the Kirk's complicated accounts with me. Now, I do have some sympathy with those out in the field who resent 121 George Street, and who regard it as an incubus. But they must always remember that, deep in the heart of 121, there are dedicated professionals like Donald, committed Christians who are giving their all to this most complex and cumbersome of structures. I am particularly happy to give Donald a big build-up here because, as will shortly become apparent, he and I had a very serious disagreement, and I want to make it clear that that disagreement in no way colours my admiration for the stalwart work he does for the Kirk.

The Church of Scotland, notoriously, lacks a chief executive or indeed any kind of modern management structure. Donald Ross has what I would regard as an almost impossible working brief. He has to deal with the heads of more than twenty executive departments who are responsible to their own boards and committees which, in turn, are responsible to the General Assembly. This atomised system militates against efficiency and maybe even encourages overlap, slackness, incompetence and sloth. It undoubtedly makes life more stressful than it need be for those who are attempting to bring a little order and spirit – or smeddum, to use a good Scots word – into the Kirk's affairs. And, anyway, if you are responsible to the General Assembly, to whom exactly are you responsible? A body which meets annually with hundreds of *different* voting members each year may have its merits, but it is surely not the right body to make long-term executive decisions. Sooner or later, the Kirk is going to have to wake up and sort this out.

Let me take a very quick look at where the most pressing specific financial problems lie. First comes the ministry. There are ministry funds of more than £50 million, but these are absurdly inadequate to pay any kind of reasonable stipend to the Kirk's ministers (its elite troops, as I call them) and to provide reasonable assistance to the many congregations who cannot afford the full costs of supporting a minister. Second, there is World Mission. Here, the budget, currently at about £40 million, has been heavily reduced in recent years; and so, more than ever, it is inadequate to sustain the work the Kirk wishes to undertake abroad. I have no hesitation whatsoever in saying that this foreign mission should be cut back in a swingeing, even draconian, manner; the Kirk has plenty of urgent mission work at home. It is failing in Scotland, so I am afraid that sustaining work abroad must be regarded as a secondary priority.

Third, and perhaps most controversially, we come to the consolidated stipend fund, which is the most covetously eyed of the big funds. It has around £60 million. All the annual income is used to help the stipend needs of congregations. However, while some of the capital could undoubtedly be released to assist individual congregations, this would obviously result in far less income being available to increase stipends at the very time when stipend enhancement is an undoubted necessity.

There are many other separate funds, but the above three are the biggest. Thus, the Kirk faces that most classic of dilemmas: it can either raise more money, or it can spend less. Spending less, funnily enough, is the more difficult option. I have suggested above that the World Mission budget should be cut drastically; but this is a most contentious proposal. And, even if the budget were to be cut by, say, 33 per cent, the Kirk would still be facing colossal problems.

If we look at raising more money, someone has to come up with radical solutions. The members of the Kirk should be giving more. It is not that they have been mean; they have, in fact, been generous. In the year 2000, average offerings per member actually increased by 7 per cent, which is very creditable. However, that figure becomes less impressive when you realise that the average member contributes less than £2 per week. I suspect that a significant minority of members is being very generous indeed. Some are, without doubt, tithing – that is, giving 10 per cent of their income. (I believe that this practice is commonplace in the 'gathered' conservative evangelical congregations.) But others are giving hardly anything at all.

Donald Ross, who knows far more about this than anyone else in the Kirk, told me bluntly: 'If every member gave 10 per cent, it would solve all our money worries overnight'. Donald is personally saddened by the consistent failure of the Kirk, through its Board of Stewardship and Finance, to promote tithing. He describes the average giving as 'shamefully low' and reckons that the Kirk has opted for an 'undemanding' rather than a 'sacrificial' standard of giving. He says starkly: 'We do not honour God in our giving, and this is an indication of the low level of commitment of many of our members'. These are alarming words, coming as they do from such a sedulous and knowledgeable Kirk insider.

One thing I have become convinced of, having looked at the Kirk intensively over a period of six months, is that its greatest resource is the very large number of good and decent people it has among its members. I reckon that many of them could be persuaded to tithe, if the Kirk went about the campaign of persuasion in the right way. So, here I agree with Donald: tithing should be promoted forthwith.

Now I come to my own proposal for raising money. Quite simply, I believe that every manse should be sold, over a period of three to five years. But, before I go into the details, I have to report that both Donald Ross and Alan Cowe, another veteran servant of the Kirk, thought this simply could not be done. I listened carefully to their cavils and shall come to them shortly.

Meanwhile, I remain convinced that the manses are a menace. Most ministers seem to dislike them; some dislike them intensely and regard them as a serious psychological and physical hindrance in their work. Principal Lyall of New College told me that, when he and his wife could at last give up their manse, he felt a stronger sense of freedom than he had ever experienced before or since. When I spoke to three trainee ministers at New College, they were all dreading – and I use the word advisedly – having to live in manses. Altogether, I think it is pretty clear that the majority of people who are living in them (that is, not just the ministers, but their families too) do not like them.

And here is the exciting part: to sell them would raise a minimum of £300 million and maybe even as much as £500 million. The income (even if it were, conservatively, as little as £20 million a year, though it would almost certainly be far more than that) from that capital sum could provide a very generous annual stipend supplement for every minister, to be spent on personal property requirements. In addition, there would be enough income left over to support the appointment of a youth worker to most congregations and also to support various other artistic and creative projects. The capital itself could be ring-fenced.

I came up with the figure of between £300 and £500 million, not by calculating creatively on the back of an envelope, but by chatting with some Scottish property experts. I emphasise that these were casual rather than detailed discussions and that I have no explicit professional backing for the figures quoted above. Also, the experts were not particularly impressed with the proposal; they thought it could seriously distort Scotland's property market. But that should be the least of the Kirk's worries.

Anyway, this is where I had my serious disagreement with Donald, who insisted that the idea was a non-starter. He told me that his predecessor had come up with the same idea but had discarded it after he had looked at the mechanics of the mass sale. Further, he said that the Board of Ministry had also set up a working party to examine a significant sale of manses. But, once again, the conclusion was that such a project was not feasible. Donald then patiently took me through the main reasons why he felt the idea could not work; and, in fairness to him, I shall now rehearse them.

1. In prosperous, upmarket purlieus such as, for example, Cramond in Edinburgh, no minister could afford to live in the parish, and possibly not even near it.

2. In really remote rural parishes, there would be no suitable houses available.

3. Manses had certain minimum requirements, for example a guest bedroom, a study and so on. Would ministers, particularly those starting out, always be able to find or afford houses of a sufficient size?

4. There would be other practical difficulties for ministers at the start of their careers. What would happen if a minister kept bidding for houses in the parish but simply could not get one?

5. There would be all sorts of tax difficulties, not just for individual ministers, but also for the Kirk itself.

Well, I accept that this is a formidable catalogue of difficulties; but I am not sure that, were the will there, they could not be surmounted, although I do not have the expertise to deal with tax complications. (The current Chancellor of the Exchequer, as a son of the manse, might be persuaded to help out; or is that ingenuous?) I am certainly not convinced that it is essential for the minister to live within the parish. It is obviously preferable to live not too far away; but most congregations maintain some kind of office, whether in a hall near the church or in the church itself. And ministers in rural parishes soon learn the necessity of travelling vast distances anyway. Also, stipulations about the requirements for specific rooms and so on within manses could easily be amended or scrapped altogether.

What became clear was that Donald and I were never going to agree on this one. And he had solid support from another redoubtable Kirk servant, the long-serving secretary and clerk to the General Trustees, Alan Cowe. When I put the idea to Alan, he simply grinned at me and said: 'People from outside quite often think this is a good idea; you are by no means the first! It actually came up two or three times between the 1960s and the 1980s, and we did look at it seriously. But I am certain that the present system cannot be over-turned, if only because of the tax position.'

I sincerely hesitate to disagree with two such sage and diligent servants of the Kirk, but I think the two potential prizes are so vast that I would like to remain committed to this as one of my principal proposals. I reiterate: ministers do not like their manses, and minis-terial morale would be given an enormous boost if the Kirk got rid of them. I appreciate that there would be specific problems with ministers in particularly big and prestigious manses, and with ministers embarking on their careers; but these could be resolved. And the financial prize to be grasped is colossal.

Indeed, if the Kirk could raise, say, £400 million by selling its manses, and if it could also persuade its members to commit to tithing, then it could do much more good than it has dreamed of for many generations. A new era of meaningful mission would indeed be upon us. Its financial worries would be over forever, and it would have a most exciting opportunity to galvanise its exertions and its efforts in a way that currently looks utterly unlikely, given present restraints.

Before I leave Donald Ross, I'd like to mention three other points. First, Donald suggested to me that he was sometimes close to despair at the Kirk's inability to cut back, or to shed, what are obviously redundant operations. He believed that there was no structure in place to carry out what he termed 'major surgery' such as closing down whole operations and areas of work, and then transferring the saved resources to other more needy areas. He cited the protracted fiasco (and I emphasise that fiasco is my word, not his) of the St Ninian's Training Centre, Crieff, as an example. But I'm sure there are a myriad others.

Let me throw in just one example of my own. Why in God's name does the Church of Scotland find it necessary to maintain ministers in Amsterdam, Brussels, Budapest, the Costa del Sol linked with Gibraltar (where next? Ibiza linked with Alicante?), Geneva, Jerusalem, Lausanne, Lisbon, Malta, Paris, Rome, Rotterdam, Jersey, Guernsey, Bermuda and the Bahamas? I can *just* about see the need for maintaining a minister at Brussels, the centre of the European Union; and at Rome, the headquarters of the greatest Christian church; and in Jerusalem, for obvious reasons; and indeed in Geneva, which is the diplomatic centre of Europe and also where the World Alliance of Reformed Churches is headquartered (and where, incidentally, there is a massive public statue of the Kirk's greatest figure, John Knox). But Lausanne, or Jersey, or Rotterdam, or Budapest, or the Costa del Sol? What a grotesque waste of hard-earned and hard-given cash.

Let me ask two simple questions. First, how many of the Kirk's 600,000 members, very many of whom do indeed give generously every week, know that their Kirk has ministers operating, if that is the appropriate word, in, say, the Costa del Sol or Guernsey? And, second, what on earth do these ministers do, and whom do they answer to? If the answer to the first point is that they have to minister to a handful of rich expatriate idlers at a time when *there are 169 vacant charges in Scotland* – well, if that is the answer, I just cannot take the Kirk seriously. I mentioned above that there have been big cutbacks in the budget of World Mission and that I'd want to cut it even more. But World Mission, at its most purposive, is concerned with alleviating 'desperate situations' (to use another of Donald's phrases). These are situations of famine, persecution and pandemic. I'm not aware of much famine, persecution and pandemic in the Costa del Sol and Guernsey. Obviously, many other agencies, some of them better organised and equipped than the Church of Scotland, are involved in famine relief and dealing with the AIDS pandemic and so on. Yet, everything helps – and, if it comes to priority, I'd far rather have money spent in Africa *and indeed in Scotland* than in Bermuda or Guernsey or the Costa del Sol. I'm getting on my high horse here, but perhaps a little indignation about how the Kirk wastes its money does not come amiss.

The second point that Donald raised with me was his firm belief that tenure for ministers should be ended as soon as possible. He told me: 'Vacancies don't always occur at the right place at the right time'. He believed strongly that it would be most helpful to the Kirk if it could move ministers around as it saw fit (and, of course, this idea ties in to some extent with Ron Ferguson's notion of creating centres of creative excellence, with several ministers, around the church's greatest buildings). Donald admitted to me that his idea would imply more rather than less centralisation, as it would remove one of a congregation's most precious powers. His plan was to introduce a vastly increased stipend, keeping the manse but abolishing tenure. The Board of Ministry would then be able to move ministers around as appropriate. This system would apply immediately to all new ministers, but existing ministers could either volunteer for abolished tenure or retain their existing conditions. I should mention here that the two classic historical reasons for tenure rarely apply nowadays. The first was to prevent interference by local patrons, such as rural lairds; the second was to protect ministers whose preaching or politics (or whatever) did not please their congregations.

And now I come to Donald's third point, which has to do not with money but rather with *The Way We Live Now*, to use the always up-to-date title of Anthony Trollope's greatest novel. Donald believes that Scotland is 'increasingly sick with crime, pornography, permissiveness, materialism and occultism'. He says that its 'pagan atmosphere' is all too obvious. He also says, in a concomitant point, that the Kirk's members are not receiving the spiritual nourishment that they need.

Taking his comments as a starting point, let me now go back a few years to the words of the Very Rev. Prof. Tom Torrance, one of the Kirk's more distinguished theologians of recent times (and yet another former minister of Beechgrove, Aberdeen). He wrote in 'Crisis in the Kirk', *St Andrews Rock: The State of the Church in Scotland* (Bellew Publishing, 1992), of an 'unprecedented crisis in morality', and continued: 'It is no answer to blame governments and their policies in daily life and especially in education. There has been a disastrous slump in the impact of Christian teaching upon the human conscience allied to an abject failure of the Church to uphold Christian moral standards.' These are strong words. And they were echoed a decade on, when Donald Ross told me that, in the Church of Scotland today, there was considerable activity concerning just about everything other than the Holy Spirit. 'New buildings, new hymn books, new services, new reports, new stipend structures, new reunion schemes, new organisations, when nothing else but the Holy Spirit's revival will save the Church from increasing ineffectiveness and decline.'

It is pretty obvious that Britain is indeed beset by a rotten, creeping sickness, evinced by – among many other things – an almost universal decline in personal discipline, increasing disrespect for our old, a reckless tendency for drug- as well as drink-driving, growing crime and yobbishness, a crass ignorance of our history, a pervasive philistinism, a tolerance of squalor and, perhaps worst of all, enormous parental irresponsibility, particularly on the part of men. There is unremitting consumerism and a glib prosperity (glib in the sense that it has been earned not by sustained hard work, but rather by the efforts and sacrifices of previous generations). You do wonder sometimes if the sacrifices of these generations have been in vain; and you also wonder if other cultures, particularly those in the Far East, with their emphasis on stoicism and their disapproval of indulgence, have not far more to offer than our secular culture.

(There is a wonderful Korean saying which I often quote: *After the mountains, are mountains.*)

Now, there are plenty of people around who are concerned about this social sickness (Donald Ross is obviously one of them), but they are not always the most likely people. Although I am no longer a journalist, I remain an interested consumer of newspapers, and in 2001 I was interested to note that the most eloquent writing in the papers about 'the way we live now' came not from religious commentators or leader-writers but from, of all people, sportswriters. Much of this writing was inspired, if that is the appropriate word, by the disgustingly yobbish behaviour of senior English football players, who were and are paid many thousands of pounds *per week*. Among the incidents that were widely reported were an all-day drinking spree by four Chelsea players which culminated in them insulting a group of American tourists less than forty-eight hours after the 11 September attacks, and a West Ham player urinating publicly in front of guests at party in a London nightclub. The most notorious case involved two Leeds United players who, after a highly publicised trial, were found not guilty of attacking and severely injuring a British Asian student after a night out in Leeds. But one of them was found guilty of affray. He admitted that he had drunk, on the night in question, eight pints of a vodka-based drink.

The example of morally concerned writing I am going to quote comes not from a football writer but from the *Daily Telegraph*'s redoubtable cricket correspondent, Michael Henderson, describing the city of Leeds on a summer Friday night:

> It offered a microcosm of a society that had lost its soul. When you had picked your way past the drunks in the streets near the ground [Headingley], you could visit one of several bars in the middle of the city, all amplified noise and tat, each with its own heavily muscled doormen. Awash with money, and yet ugly beyond belief, our towns present the landscape of modern England, and things are getting worse. How can any person who truly cares about this land not be disturbed by the vulgarity and unthinking hedonism of our young people, who are without argument the most feckless, the most aggressive, the most stupid in Europe? What is more, they wear their ignorance as a badge of honour . . . everything

is trivial and disposable and available for the people with their diminished expectations. Those people have money, pots of it, but there is no spiritual dimension in their lives. They have been neutered by junk television, junk newspapers, junk food, junk beer, junk pop music, junk advertising, junk films. A kind of affluent poverty exists, in which nobody feels anything except a permanent boredom. (*Daily Telegraph*, 20 August 2001)

That is a magnificent polemic, and I think it redounds enormously to the credit of the *Telegraph* that it publishes such writing on its *sports* pages. And I know that the passage is about modern England – but who among us could say that it does not apply to Scotland also? The crucial thing here is that we have a *cricket* writer complaining most eloquently about the lack of a spiritual dimension in young people's lives. This points to a failure by other journalists, and then to a much wider failure – and, I have to say, it is a failure of the clergy.

Henderson was polite enough not to add a 'junk church' to his catalogue; but surely no church worthy of the name could tolerate the mess he describes for very long. It is almost getting to the stage where we could do with a new Girolamo Savonarola – a new Bonfire of the Vanities. (If such a figure does emerge, I reckon he or she will emerge from the Catholic Church rather than the Reformed Churches. And, indeed, the late Cardinal Winning, while he was no Savonarola, was always prepared to speak out strongly on issues of morality, public and private. The way we live now, to use that phrase again, mattered enormously to him, and part of his efficacy as a church leader was based on his frequently expressed discontent with the bad way we are living.)

As I travelled around Scotland talking to ministers and others in the Kirk, I had many fascinating conversations, and people were unfailingly helpful and kind to me. But, as I look back on these chats, I become aware of a kind of void; few people seemed particularly concerned about *the failure of the Kirk to uphold moral standards.* (Maybe I did not specifically ask about this, but I would often ask people at the end of our chats if there was anything we had not covered that they would like to raise.) In fairness, I must record that there were a few excellent and honourable exceptions. Some of the evangelical conservatives I talked with were particularly concerned about homosexuality; but it is promiscuity that seems the problem to me, and heterosexual promiscuity I would regard as just as reprehensible as homosexual promiscuity.

I think that the clergy and the eldership must, as a matter of urgency, become more concerned with this matter of the way we live now. There is nothing mysterious or difficult here; the problem is all around us, day in, day out. It has been eloquently described by an eminent Anglican clergyman, Chancellor Edward Norman: 'The decline of organised religion, the pervasive philosophical incoherence within the ruling and the influential elites, and the scramble to happiness, have produced a generation of spiritual nihilists – forever substituting aesthetic or emotional pleasure for authentic human purpose . . . Modern people own so much; so many material possessions. What they own becomes linked to how they use time. If you buy a yacht or a comic book, time is mortgaged to enjoy them. We are becoming – we have already become – the victims of our own possessiveness.'

Too many people, even in the Kirk, think that it is up to politicians to get us to live and behave more responsibly. Too many parents think it is up to schoolteachers to get their children to behave better and more responsibly. These are both tragic cop-outs. A word I have often heard in the Kirk is 'outreach'. I am well aware that there is superb and compassionate practical *reactive* work being done, in helping to mop up the consequences of our social problems; but these problems have already happened. There should surely be more of an emphasis on preventing them from happening in the first place. A lot of our society's difficulties are caused by a lack of social responsibility. It is in many ways an amazing society: great wealth lives side by side with real poverty, although thankfully there is not that much serious economic poverty; whereas poverty of the spirit is commonplace.

I find it slightly worrying that Donald Ross, who is, after all, an accountant and not a minister, seems to be more concerned about such matters than many ministers apparently are. It was Donald who got me thinking about the Kirk and morality; we had been talking in detail about the Kirk's finances, and then Donald articulated his worries about wider issues. I think he did me a service; and, having thought about it, I believe that the Kirk should be making much more of an impact here. So, outreach should surely include the mission of impressing on people that their current selfish behaviour is irresponsible and will lead to ill, hurt and unhappiness. I have suggested in Chapter 6 that the Kirk should try to do something about the mayhem that takes place in Glasgow and its environs in the aftermath of Old Firm matches. This is just one tiny specific example of what could become the most important mission of all – to the people of secular Scotland. So many of them, just like the young people described in the cricket report, have no spiritual dimension in their lives.

I don't want to go too far here; Donald Ross is a compassionate man, and I hope that I, too, am not devoid of this quality. I am aware that Jesus Christ preached compassion above everything else, and that sometimes those who tilt eloquently against the ills of our times – our possessiveness, our materialism, our selfishness, our hedonism, our emptiness – can seem to be somewhat bereft of compassion. I remember the Rev. Jane Barron, in Dundee, saying to me simply yet magnificently: 'My understanding of the Christian faith is that it is one, above all, of compassion. My understanding of Jesus Christ is of a figure who was inordinately compassionate.'

And I am not sure that I would agree with Tom Torrance that the Kirk has *abjectly* failed to uphold moral standards. But there is, without doubt, a case to be made that its ministry and its eldership, and indeed its ordinary members, could be doing much more to uphold moral standards than they are. There is an element in all this of 'physician, heal thyself'.

10

THE KIRK'S
GREAT MONSTER

❖

This chapter deals with the Kirk's greatest mess – its bureaucracy. Towards the end of 2001, the Kirk's national youth adviser, Steve Mallon, was quoted as saying: 'The Church has to change, or it is going to have massive problems in the future'. How often did I hear that very sentiment, more or less word for word, as I moved around Scotland! The need for change is more or less universally accepted, and I have made plenty of my own suggestions, some of them quite radical and no doubt controversial. But one of the great difficulties for the Kirk as it contemplates change, whether radical or cautious, concerns how that change is to be pushed through the General Assembly. The Assembly is the Kirk's supreme body, its sovereign court, with both administrative and legislative responsibilities; it is also, to be candid, a bit of a monster, and a distinct impediment to progress. I understand that writing those words will offend, for the General Assembly is viewed by many Kirk people with an almost mystical veneration. (Unfortunately, it is hardly noticed by most people outside the Kirk.)

Throughout this book, I have tried very hard not to be gratuitously offensive. Examining the Kirk intensively for a few months, as I have done, does make you frustrated, for it has so much talent and such potential that are going to waste; but I have tried hard not to let this frustration seep into irritability or unpleasantness. But I do believe that I must be candid to the point of impudence here, for I am utterly convinced that the Assembly needs to be reformed drastically, and soon. The first point to make about it is that it is not properly democratic. The Church of Scotland is not a hierarchical or authoritarian church, and in many ways it is actually too democratic for its own good; but the Assembly is manifestly not a democratic body. It is not democratic because it is not truly representative. It is not congregations who decide which elder will represent them at the Assembly. I reiterate the point that it is a scandal that an elder who gives long and dedicated service to the Kirk may well never get near the Assembly. And, if we move on to ministers – well, at least they do get the chance to attend every fourth year; but that begs the question of what happens in the other three years. Assemblies appear to be a bit like waves breaking on a shore (which reminds me, incidentally, of what I feel is the greatest religious poem of recent times, R. S. Thomas's wonderful 'The Other'). I mean that the big one only comes along every seventh time, as it were. The big Assembly may come along a little more often or a little less often, but the point is that a minister with a lot to contribute could easily attend six or seven Assemblies in a lifetime and yet never get to one of the ones that turn out really to matter.

Let us divert to politics, for a moment, and wind back to the great agitation of the 1830s and 1840s in Britain, when the country was nearer than it has ever been to a cataclysmic and bloody revolution. There were three main reasons why that revolution never transpired. First, Britain was at last blessed with a genuinely reforming government – that of Sir Robert Peel, in the early 1840s – which passed a great deal of progressive legislation. Second, there was the powerful influence of Protestant religion in general and Methodism in particular, which – rightly or wrongly – helped to prevent brutal and riotous protest. And, third, and most importantly, there was the responsible concern of so many of the workers' groups to operate non-violently, despite social and working conditions that from the perspective of this day and age are almost beyond belief. Most of the leaders of these groups insisted on trying to use what was then an absurdly undemocratic and inadequate political process as the vehicle for their aspirations.

Many of the groups agreed to merge their demands into the great National Charter; and the Chartists, as they became known, held huge rallies in pursuance of their six specific ends. Five of these demands eventually came to pass in parliamentary legislation:

universal suffrage, voting by secret ballot, equitable electoral districts, no property qualifications for MPs, and the payment of MPs. But the sixth never made it onto the statute book because, frankly, it was nonsensical. It was for annual parliaments. Slowly but surely, it became obvious that annual parliaments would militate *against* democracy.

But the Church of Scotland did not learn from this or from any other examples. To this day, it has a supreme decision-making body that meets annually with a completely different membership each year. This is preposterous, and it is no wonder that from time to time the Assembly takes a decision one year, overturns it the next and overturns the overturn the following year. That is no way to run anything, let alone a great national church.

Let me now recount the views of a perceptive Assembly-watcher, the *Herald* journalist Lynne Robertson. Although she is still a young woman, Lynne has already covered nine Assemblies for a newspaper which, I am happy to say, attempts to take the Church of Scotland seriously. She has some very pertinent comments to make. 'The first thing I would say is that its procedures are quite arcane. It took me two or three years to understand exactly what was going on. At my first Assembly in particular, I found it very hard to get to grips with how the decisions were being taken, and on what basis. The commissioners, let alone the journalists, must get confused. I have sometimes had the impression that rank-and-file commissioners attending do not agree with what is going on but either don't know how to intervene, or are just too inhibited to do so. Maybe they are slightly afraid. I'm sure that the Assembly can be quite intimidating, especially for someone attending it for the first time. It is also cumbersome, and I do not think that it's representative. The elders who attend seem largely to be people who are not in work. They are mainly retired people, and a few housewives. I am not being derogatory, but are these people representative? They are clearly not representative of the country at large, but are they even representative of the Kirk? The Youth Assembly does now send representatives to the main Assembly, but it is more people in the age range 25 to 45 that I am concerned about. There are very few of them in evidence; but surely they are the very people that the Church desperately needs? I get the impression that there is quite a lot of change and innovation coming in at parish or congregation level, but that this is not reflected at the Assembly at all. And sometimes there is a debate about a smallish or trivial matter that just seems to go on and on and on.'

Writing in 1934, the much-loved Scottish author Lewis Grassic Gibbon was scathing about the Assembly. He wrote: 'There is still the yearly Assembly of the Kirk in Edinburgh: the strangest of functions, with the High Commissioner some vague politician generally discreetly unintelligible and inevitably discreetly unintelligent ... Nor does the yearly General Assembly resemble (as once) the Sanhedrin of the Jews. To a large extent it is the excuse and the occasion for much tea-drinking and the exchange of views on theological scholarship, rose-growing and the meaner scandals. Its public speeches have an unexciting monotone of supplication and regret: the young are leaving the Kirk, how may they be reclaimed? The tides of irreligion and paganism are flooding in upon us: how may they be stayed? A similar tidal problem once confronted King Canute.'

The young are leaving; how can they be reclaimed? *Plus ça change*, as they say. There is a conspiracy theory abroad among some Kirk-watchers, to the effect that the mandarins and satraps of the Kirk actually like it this way. The cosiness, the hand-wringing, the built-in inertia – all of these militate against radical change, and that is the way the high heid yins want it, or so the theory goes. Norman Shanks, leader of the Iona Community, intervened in the 2001 Assembly 'debate' on *Without Walls* to point out that other major reports calling for serious reform – the Hugh Anderson report, the Committee of Forty reports – had quietly been shunted aside and forgotten.

I personally don't subscribe to the view that there is a concrete conspiracy to frustrate change; after all, the Assembly has managed the occasional significant reform in the past fifty years or so, such as the introduction of female elders and female ministers. But those two particular changes owed much to the determination of one brave, determined and altogether outstanding individual, Mary Levison. I think that the *nature* of the Assembly manages to frustrate those who genuinely want to change the Kirk (and I reckon that is a majority of its members). And the truth is, so many of those who are frustrated by the supreme body do not know how to reform it, and you have to reform it if you are to reform anything else. Nonetheless, I shall offer some modest proposals which might help. But, before I do so, let me cite the views of two terrifically committed servants of today's Kirk.

Ann Allen has served the Board of Social Responsibility for seventeen years, including a distinguished recent stint as convener. Her husband, Martin, is the long-serving minister of Chryston, near Glasgow. Ann told me: 'The trouble with the Assembly is that it is so cumbersome. We need to have more of a conference Assembly where we can genuinely debate things; and we should keep specific-ally legal matters separate. At present, the average commissioner is confused and restricted by legal formulas, and these work against free debate. I do think that we need to thrash through issues where there is division, and we are not doing that in the Assembly these days. As it is constituted, it is not helpful to the people in the pews. It's fine for the people who have been going for years, like the former moderators who know their way around it; but it is daunting for people going for the first time, and it does not facilitate either debate or fellowship.'

Her husband told me: 'We don't seem to get big debates of quality any more in the Assembly. But, in any case, what is said there is often ignored; not too many ministers take much notice of the debates, and certainly most members don't take much notice at all. More and more people in the Kirk are just doing their own thing locally. They ignore the Assembly.' I cannot prove it, but I suspect that the Allens speak for vast numbers of people in the Church of Scotland. And, if it is indeed true that most grass-roots members just ignore it, that it has no relevance for them and their life in the Kirk, then something has clearly gone very significantly wrong. This disconnection between the supreme decision-making body and the ordinary members bodes ill.

My impressions of the 2001 Assembly are described in Chapter 1 and will not be reiterated here; but I did, without doubt, sense an absence of real debate, for example on *Without Walls*. For *big* decisions, I think that the Assembly is the wrong forum, simply because it is not democratic, for the reasons outlined above. For really important decisions, there could be a plebiscite; not of all members, but certainly of all ministers and elders. As the elders outnumber the ministers by almost forty to one, this mechanism would immediately decrease ministerial influence, which is not something that I wish to do at this stage. On the other hand, plebiscites would be democratic, they would help to involve the eldership much more in decision-making, and they would create great interest beyond the Kirk – all of which are highly desirable outcomes.

Indeed, a plebiscite of the entire membership might be no bad thing; but at present the membership records are too slackly maintained. (The true as opposed to the claimed membership is, I reckon, well under 600,000.) You could argue, however, that a plebiscite of all the membership would act as a discipline to enforce more accurate roll-keeping. The other main flaw in this plebiscite proposal is: who would decide what was a big decision? Obviously, the system would be abused if *routine* decisions were put to an electorate of over 500,000.

Lynne Robertson, having thought hard about the flaws in the Assembly as presently structured, believes that there could be two or three Weekend Assemblies each year. That way, the membership would be more democratically representative and there would be more of a 'conference' atmosphere (something which Ann Allen also wants). Another bonus would be that it would be easier for the Assembly to become peripatetic. Major administrative or legal matters could be dealt with separately, possibly at a biennial or even a triennial Assembly.

The Very Rev. John Cairns believes that Assemblies would be improved greatly if the conveners of boards and committees were not allowed to speak. Instead, they, and department heads, would be grilled elsewhere, by a small number of selected commissioners, who would quiz them publicly about their annual reports, their financial competence and so on. This would create something similar to the parliamentary select committee system at Westminster, where ministers and senior civil servants are cross-examined, sometimes very aggressively, by all-party select committees of backbench MPs. I think this is a first-class idea. It would subject the presentation of annual reports to more rigorous scrutiny than is customary at present, and it would prevent well-established conveners from dominating the actual proceedings of the Assembly. In other words, it would help to give the ordinary commissioner more of a chance to make his or her mark. The difficulty, inevitably, would lie in the selection of the commissioners to conduct the cross-examinations.

A serious problem associated with the Assembly is the widespread distrust and resentment of 121 George Street that I have heard expressed so often. Not everybody in the Kirk seems to appreciate just how closely 121 and the Assembly are intertwined: there is real animus against 121, but less anger focused on the Assembly. Yet, when you have a system of centralised boards and departments and committees based at 121 which are responsible to the Assembly and the Assembly only, the nature of the relationship should be obvious enough. I write there 'responsible to the Assembly and the Assembly only'; but, as that most astringent observer of the Kirk, the Rev. Johnston McKay, told me, 'If you are accountable to the Assembly, you are *not* accountable'. While the implications of that devastating truth sink in, I shall alarm everybody by raising the prospect of Prof. Steve Bruce as the Kirk's first chief executive. Well, perhaps not; but I mention Steve here because he insists that there are far too many centralised boards and committees (and also that some of them are far too big). He told me that, if he were in charge of the Kirk, he would soon have the present plethora of Assembly committees and boards whittled down to four or five at the most.

One clear manifestation of what has gone wrong is the absurdity of demarcations. For example, the Board of National Mission is responsible for animal cloning, but the Board of Social Responsibility is responsible for human cloning. I could point out such anomalies all day. It is easy to go through the various remits listed at the beginning of the *Year Book* and to note how many of them clash and overlap. Another instance of the confusion at the Kirk's centre is that, when reform is in the air, as with the proposal for superpresbyteries, the Kirk has to set up an 'interboard group' to handle the matter. And, of course, the members of the interboard group are not always disinterestedly seeking consensus; some see their role as the fighting the corner of their own particular department or board, and its vested interests and viewpoints.

Let me quote from the Presbyteries Boundaries Group leaflet *Tomorrow's Presbyteries*: 'The 2000 Assembly established an Inter-Board Group, which consists of representatives from the Boards of Practice and Procedure, Ministry, National Mission, Parish Education, and the Director of Stewardship. The Inter-Board Group presented to the 2001 Assembly a report prepared in consultation with representatives of the Special Commission on Review and Reform, the Assembly Council, the Committee on Ecumenical Relations, and McKinsey Management Consultants.' That means that the group started off with representatives of four separate boards, plus the director of stewardship; then there was consultation with the special commission, with outside consultants, and with another council and another committee. This process had started early in 1999, when the Assembly of that year instructed the Board of Practice and Procedure to review presbytery boundaries. As I write this, more than two and a half years later, we are not much further on (at least, that was the impression I strongly received when the matter was debated at a meeting of Edinburgh presbytery in November 2001).

But one side-effect of the debate, such as it has been, is to heighten ministers' concerns regarding centralised bureaucracy. I am indebted for this insight to the Rev. John Ferguson, minister of Peterculter, who edits the monthly newsletter *Ministers' Forum*, now nearing its 250th edition. The *Forum* regularly features robust contributions from ministers in the field; and, as its editor, John Ferguson is obviously well qualified to comment on what is particularly exercising ministers at any time.

John told me: 'The debate about reforming presbyteries has galvanised ministers to look at the whole question of bureaucracy. The biggest issues for quite some time have been those of ministerial isolation, stress and overload, but more recently there has been growing concern about bureaucracy. There are concerns about 121, the great expense of running it and the large number of people who work there, and these concerns have been heightened because of the proposals for bigger presbyteries. The idea may have been for devolution, but many ministers felt that bigger presbyteries would just mirror what goes on at 121, rather than lead to any diminishing of the centralised bureaucracy. There is a belief that the centre lacks sensitivity and that, if you create bigger and more centralised presbyteries, you might end up losing the sensitivity that some presbyteries do presently show to the needs and concerns of their ministers.'

I can echo John Ferguson's remarks; as I moved round the country, I found a great deal of dissatisfaction with 121, much of it a generalised resentment rather than focused criticism. And some of the ministers who had their doubts about the performance of 121 tried hard to be fair – none more so than Martin Allen of Chryston, who told me: 'When you go into the ministry, it is almost as if you inherit this sense that 121 is not on your side. I think it is exaggerated, for much fine work is done at the centre; but there is an increasing tendency to centralisation that is not healthy. I do think that those in the corridors of power are out of touch, and many of them have a liberal agenda which is out of step with what local congregations want. And yes, there is a danger that bigger presbyteries would simply mean a series of lesser 121s dotted round the country. In the Church, we *must* have less paperwork, not more; and the ministry needs to be set free for action at local level. Revival will come locally, and I cannot understand how people can do much good work at congregational level if they are spending their time in 121 or in a big presbytery.' Of course, these remarks reflect the thrust of *Without Walls*, which is very much away from the centre towards the local effort.

Maybe all this is getting too pessimistic. There is a case that bigger presbyteries would inevitably remove at least some power from 121 and its 'old-boy networks', as one minister described them to me. I am convinced that, if you asked a genuinely tough-minded outsider, a Steve Bruce or a Colin McClatchie, to work out what functions should remain at 121 and what should be transferred to, say, seven new superpresbyteries, they would wish to devolve many, and probably most, of the functions currently centralised at headquarters. They would also, surely, seize the opportunity to slash the number of boards and committees.

Having done that, the challenge would be to prevent the super-presbyteries in turn from becoming bloated bureaucracies. This would be a special danger in the biggest, which, on the seven-presbytery model I have seen, would be centred on Glasgow and would have 323 charges, 145,520 members and an annual income of over £19 million. (Currently, Glasgow is the biggest of the forty-six Scottish presbyteries, but it covers only 153 charges. Its total income in 2000 was just over £12 million. That indicates the boldness of the proposal under discussion: what is already by far the biggest presbytery could more than double in size.)

Before I leave the issue of superpresbyteries, I have to record that one or two of my interviewees detected in the proposals what might be termed a dark ecumenical conspiracy: in other words, they pointed out that the proposed superpresbyteries would be remarkably similar to dioceses, and that the whole thing was just a back-door plot to bring in bishops. I doubt it very much; but, in the Church of Scotland, you never know.

The final point I'd make on the question of bureaucracy would be that, even if the current multiplicity of boards and committees were left untouched (although it shouldn't be), at the very least the number of members of most of the boards and committees should be subject to swingeing cuts. It is a simple enough rule that the bigger the committee, the less effective it is. Let us take two examples. The Board of Parish Education currently has fifty members, including a convener and a vice-convener, plus a director and a deputy director, plus one representative from the Church of Scotland Guild (who might be just slightly overwhelmed), plus seventeen other staff. The board meets twice annually, and its various committees meet four or five times a year. Then there is the Board of National Mission. It is much more significant and has a much bigger budget than the Board of Parish Education (over £6 million compared to £1.3 million), but has only thirty-four members, although some of its constituent committees are bigger, for example its committee of parish reappraisal, which has no fewer than fifty-two members. Now, I am not saying that these various boards and committees are not doing good work; Bishop Joe Devine of Motherwell specifically told me that the Church of Scotland has been far bolder and more effective in attending to parish reappraisal than the Catholic Church. Having conceded that, is it really necessary for the fifty-two-strong committee of parish reappraisal to meet eight times a year?

There is a sadness here. Over many years, the Kirk has been careless and slack. It is difficult to be condemnatory, for there has been no specific failure (in this respect, the Kirk is a most elusive target). The problem has been one of weakness rather than badness or gross incompetence, although some of the individual boards have clearly been incompetently run. But how could it be otherwise, given the nebulous nature of executive structure? People in a bureaucracy work best if they know exactly who they are reporting to, and if their work is rigorously and constantly assessed. Too many of the people at 121 have no understanding whatsoever of basic management techniques. You may well ask: as people of God, why should they?

As I write, the latest available figures show the Kirk's annual support and administration costs at almost £7 million, which is an increase of 9 per cent from 1999. Staff salaries amounted to £4.7 million and committee expenses to £300,000. The Kirk is Scotland's biggest charity; and, in common with many other charities, its costs have been increasing faster than earnings or inflation. This process has not been helped, in the Kirk's case, by the creation in recent years of new offices for the Committee on Artistic Matters and the Church and Nation Committee.

Meanwhile, I would defy anyone to spend more than five minutes in the company of the senior staff at 121 – say the principal clerk, the depute clerk, the general treasurer and the clerk to the general trustees – without being greatly impressed by their diligence and their industrious commitment to the Kirk. The professional servicing of the Assembly and the various Boards is, for example, quite superb. But the difficulty for this quartet (and other senior figures) is that they do not have enough power; they cannot, even in quite small things, tell the various boards and committees what they should be doing.

This makes for a vacuum at the very heart of 121. It also makes for an atomised structure, with various more or less autonomous bodies and boards operating alongside each other. This in turn makes for an incoherent and confused organisation which is not operating anything like as efficiently as it should be. I think that the Kirk should be proud of its distinguished, long-standing servants such as Donald Ross and Alan Cowe; but, instead, such committed people are often seen as being part of the malaise at 121. They are able people, working very hard for an organisation which denies them the power and influence they would have in most other comparable organisations. That is not to say that they should not be accountable; of course they should be. Rather, it is to say that they should be empowered and enfranchised.

Over the years, the Kirk has all too often gone for the easy option. The behemoth of boards and committees has just grown relent-lessly, and nobody – and certainly not the General Assembly, itself cumbersome and inert – has had the inclination or the guts to call a halt. And, as Donald Ross says, the Kirk seems incapable of getting rid of things. The unfortunate truth is that, when the surgery for this great, bloated, obese and costive creature comes, as sooner or later it will, it is going to be all the more painful.

And now I come to a brief discussion of the bureaucratic language of the Kirk. I write as an unabashed champion and lover of the Authorised Version (AV) of the Bible, which is, in my view beyond any doubt, the greatest single Christian achievement in the history of the British Isles. (It also gives the lie to the theory that nothing worthwhile can be produced by a committee. The AV was actually produced by six committees: two met in London, two in Oxford and two in Cambridge. When they had completed their work, it was reviewed by a super-committee of twelve; and then Bishop Bilson of Winchester and Dr Miles Smith, two of the greatest heroes in the long story of English-speaking Christianity, refined and reviewed the whole and added the finishing touches.)

I am embarrassed by the inadequacies of the language of the New English Bible – and I am particularly embarrassed, as a Scot, to note that the impetus for this flawed project came from the Kirk's General Assembly in 1946. There are, of course, many good modern versions of the Bible; it is unfortunate that the New English Bible is not one of them. And funnily enough, although many Scots have traditionally prided themselves on their way with words – we are a very literary nation – we have never managed to produce a Tyndale or a Cranmer. Over its long history, the Church of Scotland has been notably poor at producing literature, either directly or indirectly.

One of the very finest and most eloquent of Scottish novels, *Gillespie*, was written by a Church of Scotland minister, John MacDougall Hay; and two wonderfully written novels, *Adam Blair* by J. G. Lockhart and *Ringan Gilhaize* by John Galt, are in part about the Kirk. Indeed, *Ringan Gilhaize* is a literary masterpiece, and by far the finest fictive treatment of Presbyterianism that I have come across; but there is nothing particularly religious and certainly nothing pro-Kirk about the works of our three most powerful and celebrated (if not greatest) authors – Scott, Burns and McDiarmid. Indeed, the latter two were not very keen on the Kirk at all. And another fine and much-loved Scottish author, Lewis Grassic Gibbon, was especially scathing about the Kirk; his withering comments on the General Assembly were quoted on p. 181 above.

This is a roundabout way of coming to my concern, which is that the Kirk's official language is far too archaic. One section of the Kirk seems very keen to embrace modern language at its most modish; a recent example was the decision to 'update' the Lord's Prayer to make it more child-friendly. Thus 'And lead us not into temptation' is replaced by 'Save us from the time of trial'. But, at the same time, the courts of the Kirk remain mired in out-dated and obscure language, which often serves a function that is the precise opposite of communication. I see no point in dismissing the language of the Authorised Version, which is sublime, as being archaic if the Kirk cannot shake off its own rather legalistic and out-of-time habit of mangling the English language.

Without Walls was officially *The Special Commission Anent Review and Reform*. ('Anent' is my least favourite Church of Scotland word; my second-least favourite is 'deliverance', which – alas – means, for the Kirk, not deliverance from evil but rather the deliverance of a proposal or a decision.) Why bother rewriting the Lord's Prayer for children, if grown-ups are going to be treated to English which is constipated and wilfully obscure? Here are two examples of legalistic Kirk gobbledegook, taken at random from, first, the 'big Blue Book' (*Reports to the General Assembly 2001*, p. '3/7'), and then the 'wee Blue Book' (*Supplementary Reports . . . 2001*, p. 45) of 2001.

The General Assembly of 1965 directed that when congregational trustees were disposing of churches which had originated in the former United Free Church they should insert, in the title granted, restrictions against use as licensed premises or for gambling. This was affirmed by the Assembly of 1982 which extended the scope of the earlier direction to the effect that clauses must be inserted on sales by congregational or local trustees of churches vested in them and falling within the ambit of Act XIV 1979 (now Act VII 1995), preventing the subjects from being used as licensed premises, for gambling purposes or for religious or quasi-religious purposes but with power to the General Trustees in any case and after consultation with the Kirk Session and the Financial Court of the congregation concerned and the Presbytery to dispense with, modify or discharge the said conditions in whole or in part.

In the light of the legislation referred to in section 8.1 above the General Trustees propose that the Assembly should withdraw the directions to local or congregational trustees and leave the question of the incorporation of restrictions on future use to local parties operating within the new legislative framework.

There we are. I have just one question: what are quasi-religious purposes?

'Presbyterial Commission' shall mean a body of five persons, three of whom shall be selected from the Presbyterial Panel randomly as provided for in terms of s. 10(2), together with a Convener and Vice-Convener appointed by the General Assembly on the Report of the Nomination Committee, such convenership and vice-convenership being so arranged that one office is held by a minister and the other by an elder qualified to practise as a lawyer. An alternate Convener and Vice-Convener shall be appointed at the same time, but if for any case a further alternate shall be required, the Secretary to the Commission shall consult with the Convener of the Nomination Committee for a further appointment. The Solicitor of the Church shall normally serve as Secretary to Presbyterial Commissions, but may appoint a Depute to act in his or her place in any particular case. The Secretary shall not be a member of the Commission.

These two passages are all too typical of much of the Kirk's bureaucracy. It has got bogged down in legalese. I understand that it's well-nigh impossible to avoid legalistic language when dealing with legal (or quasi-legal!) matters; but the Kirk would be doing us all a huge favour if it could make more of an effort to undertake its business in language that is direct and accessible. No religious organisation should have recourse to clumsy and evasive phraseology. Religion, supremely, is about communication. Obfuscation serves the true interests of no-one, and certainly not God.

And there is a grave danger, if the Kirk operates in the centre as a bureaucracy and in the field as a church of mission, that the first function will choke the latter one. If that happens, the legalistic language will start to filter into the work of the Kirk where it really matters, and clog things up. It would be good and useful, then, if the senior servants of the Kirk could make a determined effort to encourage those who draft its papers to keep them as simple and non-legalistic and understandable as is practically possible.

Finally, on a more positive note, I would like to commend those who prepare the Kirk's many papers for the speed with which they are produced, particularly at Assembly time. It is easy to mock bureaucrats, and in many ways the Kirk's bureaucracy serves it well. It could, and should of course, be streamlined – but that will take time. Meanwhile, just make the language a little more lucid, please. And a brief word to those in the Kirk who don't like the Authorised Version: watch your own language.

To end this chapter, I'd like to present brief impressions of the two presbytery meetings and the one kirk session I attended. The meetings of Edinburgh presbytery are held in Palmerston Place Church, an impressive Victorian building which is, nonetheless, dwarfed by the massive, Gothic, Episcopal Cathedral of St Mary, almost directly across the road from it.

I was given a warm welcome by the presbytery clerk, the Rev. Peter Graham, who entertained me to tea in the church refectory before the meeting. Also present were the presbytery moderator and two ministers who had been ordained fifty years earlier, the Rev. John Craig and the Rev. Gordon McGillivray. Their long and distinguished ministries were to be recognised during the meeting later on. At another table, there were various international students attending as guests of the presbytery, and there was a general atmosphere of convivial friendship.

Unfortunately, the meeting itself, which was attended by just over 200, including the observers in the gallery, was none too convivial. It oscillated uneasily between the tedious and the slightly unpleasant. This was no reflection on the moderating of the Rev. Tom Gordon, who got through the business as briskly as he possibly could, in a fair and businesslike manner. Most of those present were quite elderly, particularly the elders, and I sensed an under-current of chippiness which I had not been aware of during other Kirk occasions. We were considerably over one hour into the meet-ing when the first intervention from the floor occurred. Eventually, things livened up just a little as a rather rambling and discursive debate on the plans for superpresbyteries took place. It was felt that the proposals were not sufficiently specific and had not been fully thought through. The discussion was somewhat inconclusive, and I found this depressing, given that the whole exercise had commenced two and a half years earlier at the 1999 Assembly.

Far more time was spent, however, on the issue of the manse in a parish in southern Edinburgh. The discussion was overtly about whether or not the minister should be allowed to live in a house other than the official manse, an issue that had first been raised eighteen months previously. There was an animated if rather nit-picking debate which suggested a considerable degree of unease about the state of the parish. Some of the comments were quite cross and indeed verged on the bitter, and I was very surprised that the minister, who was present, chose not to put his own case.

There seemed to be something of an animus against the con-gregation building up, and eventually the elder representing the congregation stood up to complain about a lack of pastoral care in the debate. When, at long last, the vote came, there was an over-whelming decision that there were no exceptional circumstances to prevent the minister from living in the parish in the manse provided. After this protracted discussion, I was left with a faintly nasty aftertaste; a whiff of restrained unpleasantness was hanging in the air. I attach no blame whatsoever to the clerk, Peter Graham, or the moderator, Tom Gordon, who conducted the proceedings in a civilised, enlightened and proper manner. But, on the floor, there seemed to be a lack of Christian goodwill.

The other aspect which depressed me was that, looking down from the gallery, I could see various senior ministers such as Marjory MacLean, Andrew McLellan and Will Storrar. I wondered whether it was the best use of their time for them to be sitting through such a long and unedifying discussion about one very local problem. No doubt, democrats will say that's the Kirk at its best; but I wonder. I'd like to see the eldership play a bigger and more positive role in the affairs of the Kirk; but the eldership did not seem to be at their best on this particular night.

Now on to Cupar in Fife, and a meeting of St Andrews presbytery on a bitterly cold December evening. Before it, I was entertained to tea by the Rev. Peter Meager, the presbytery clerk. Peter told me that he had been an army chaplain for sixteen years, which included several years in the Far East and four tours in Northern Ireland. He said that, when he had come back to Scotland to be parish minister in Elie, he had expected to find that a great deal had changed – but hardly anything had. He was now convinced that change was more necessary than ever. In particular, he thought that administrative procedures needed to be streamlined and that presbyteries needed more powers and responsibility. He thought there were far too many different agencies to be dealt with before any property matters could be resolved. As for worship, he thought it needed to be changed so that it appealed more to the heart and the emotions; it was still too cerebral.

The presbytery meeting was held in the handsome church of St John's in the town centre of Cupar. The main discussions centred on changes to the hymnary; there was a recondite discussion about the pitch of hymn music, although eventually someone made a remark I could certainly agree with, to the effect that the actual tunes were more important than anything else. There was then the matter of the Readers' complaint about a local elder conducting services, which I mentioned in Chapter 8. There were about seventy-five people present, and the atmosphere seemed much more relaxed and informal than it had been in Edinburgh. After the business was concluded, the moderator, the Rev. Rosemary Frew, conducted a brief and very pleasant advent service. It was very much a service for the committed, and the hymns were sung with great gusto. Then we adjourned for tea and mince pies. There was a real spirit of good fellowship and pre-Christmas cheer. It did occur to me that, if superpresbyteries are created, then something will almost certainly be lost, namely the friendliness and informality that are much more likely to characterise the meetings of smaller presbyteries.

Finally, we move back to Edinburgh, to a meeting of the kirk session of St Michael's parish church in Slateford. St Michael's is a big church, and I did not do too well at the start. Two middle-aged women entered the church building ahead of me, and I followed them upstairs; but it turned out that they were going to the midweek ladies' keep-fit class, which was already in full swing. I hastily beat a retreat back downstairs and then found myself in a large room, surrounded by noisy Brownies.

Eventually, I found my way into the church itself, where the kirk session meeting was just beginning at the back of the nave. I was asked to step back out while the meeting voted on whether or not I could attend. I reflected on all the activity that was going on in the church during this winter Wednesday night, and reminded myself how much of this congregational activity is so far removed from the concerns of many of those who attend presbyteries and General Assemblies.

Then I was welcomed into the session meeting. Nineteen people were taking part; twelve women and seven men. Most of the elders were middle-aged to elderly. There was quite a long discussion about the arrangements for a conservation exhibition which the local council wanted to hold in the church hall; but the main item of business concerned how the elders were going to improve the pastoral care they provided. Individual elders had traditionally been allocated a specific district within the parish, but this had inhibited the provision of pastoral care where it was really needed. If elders were to concentrate on new members, potential members, older teenagers, the elderly and the housebound, this implied dismantling the traditional structure of districts, although that would cause administrative difficulties; and, as was pointed out, 'districts had been built into the psyche' of the kirk session. In essence, the proposal was for elders to become leaders as opposed to visitors, and to handle a portfolio of responsibilities rather than a specific district of households.

The minister, the Rev. Margaret Forrester, allowed the discussion to flow back and forth for quite a long time. What came over was an understanding of the necessity for change, but a reluctance to commit to it. Eventually, Mrs Forrester brought the discussion quite firmly to a conclusion. A working party was appointed with a strict timetable; they had to come up with hard proposals, and a final decision would be made within two months. 'We are going to make this work', said Mrs Forrester; and I'm sure they will. But once again, I sensed that what David Lyall calls the 'aye been' tendency would not give up without something of a struggle.

11

YET ANOTHER SCHISM?

TENSIONS IN THE NORTH

Is the Church of Scotland going to have to brace itself for yet another schism? Probably not, but the possibility cannot be dismissed. There is a festering resentment among some members of the conservative evangelical wing of the Kirk at what they regard as a takeover by the liberal wing. They feel that their voice is not being heard, and maybe all they need is a leader. Were they to find that leader, they might well assert themselves and force a crisis that the Kirk, in its present state of decline, would be ill-equipped to handle. The main reason that this possibility, however remote, must be given credibility is historical. Presbyterianism in Scotland has been racked by secession and counter-secession. There is a fissile tendency in the Kirk. It has always been there, and I suspect that it always will be. The Kirk should surely by now be mature enough to contain it.

By far the most depressing page in the *Collins Encyclopaedia of Scotland* (HarperCollins, 1994) is page 995. Simply titled 'Presbyterian Churches of Scotland Post-1700', the page consists of a chart that illustrates in graphic form the tendency of our Presbyterian churches to split and split again. It is the most direct presentation I know of a simple truth: presbyterianism in Scotland is not cohesive. I was appalled, when I was in the parish of Gairloch in Wester Ross, to find five separate Presbyterian churches practising in one parish. This is a nonsense, and indeed it makes Protestantism in Scotland a laughing stock.

I think that yet another secession from the Kirk would be a disaster, and I sincerely hope that it does not happen. And all that is required, I think, is for members of the conservative evangelical wing to be listened to a little more, and to be given more of a voice in an organisation which prides itself on being democratic and which is, by any standards, a broad and inclusive church. The paradox here is that what so many people object to in the conservative evangelicals is their apparent exclusivity: they think they are being excluded, yet that is the charge that is most often made against them by liberals. In other words, conservative evangelicals are perceived by others as being narrow-minded and more prone to turn those they regard as sinners away than to welcome them into the Kirk. The danger signals are there, and they should not – they must not – be ignored.

If I were to nominate a leader-in-waiting for the conservative evangelicals, it would be the Rev. Dr Andrew McGowan. A strong and very clever man, he is at a cusp in his career. He has spent eight years of his life setting up the non-denominational Highland Theological College, which was very much his idea. It is now in good physical shape, in solid premises on the high street of the douce Highland town of Dingwall; more to the point, it has quickly established its academic credentials. The teaching is 'from an evangelical and Reformed perspective'. The college has, in its short existence already made itself the most impressive academic component of the new University of the Highlands and Islands, and the first to offer validated postgraduate courses. As Dr McGowan showed me round the college, of which he is the first principal, his pride was palpable but well justified. Few individuals have the drive to turn a dream into such established and successful reality in so short a space of time.

When we went for a pint and a chat in the excellent Mallard pub across the road from the college, Dr McGowan was choosing his words very carefully indeed. I emphasise once again that it is I who am casting him in the role of the possible leader of a putative breakaway. He said nothing that implied disloyalty to the Kirk; rather, he expressed vehement unease and unhappiness at its current leadership and direction. 'Unless the Church of Scotland recovers its roots – the Bible and reformed theology – then it's going nowhere,' he said. 'If we evangelicals are going to make any impact, then we are going to have to make much more effort to get our position heard. We do need to get organised. We do need to set out clear objectives and then work to achieve those objectives within the courts of the Church.'

He continued: 'We must take the Church back to its roots. My position is that the historical and theological position of the Church has changed. I have not moved.' He demurred at any suggestion that he was living in the past. 'Not at all. I have helped to create this new college, and, as its principal, I read and indeed I teach modern theology. I am well aware of what is going on around me. The Church of Scotland is in danger of abandoning its Presbyterian heritage. I want to stay in this church. It's my church. But I say again: it is the Church that has changed, not me.' I pressed him on whether, now that the college was up and running, he was prepared to spend his time leading the evangelical wing. 'I'm happy to promote the evangelical position within the Church of Scotland. Leaders have to lead. That is all I will say now.'

Andrew McGowan is 48. He was born in Uddingston, and holds two degrees from Aberdeen University and a further one from the Union Theological Seminary in New York. He served as a Church of Scotland minister in Mallaig. In April 1993, he convened a meeting of ministers and businessmen, drawn from several denominations, in Inverness. All those attending received a document he had prepared, outlining his plan for a new theological college in the Highlands. A steering group and an executive committee were formed. A year later, a second crucial meeting was held, this time with the chairman of the academic advisory committee of the proposed new University of the Highlands.

That second meeting was also positive. The first two members of staff were appointed, and they began work in a hut in Elgin. Now the college, relocated in Dingwall, has six academic staff and a library of more than 30,000 books. It offers a BA in theological studies and a Doctor of Ministry degree, as well as two postgraduate degrees. It also offers evening classes and various short non-certificated courses. 'I have put all my time and energy into creating this organisation. And I have to continue with it. But, yes, I was saying to my wife June, just the other day, that I am getting very, very impatient with the Church of Scotland. My 15-year-old son goes to the local Baptist church. That's where his friends go too. He has had a renewal of his faith there. I have to say that, in so many Church of Scotland congregations, people have lost heart.' He himself has most certainly not lost heart. I was left with the sense of a man, very much in the prime of life, who had attended to one great project, with conspicuous success, and was now carefully assessing where next he should direct his energy and his drive. I would advise the Church of Scotland to pay attention to Andrew McGowan.

An older man who would endorse a great deal of what Andrew McGowan says is the Rev. David Searle, warden of Rutherford House in Leith, who gives much support to ministers of the conservative evangelical persuasion. He reckons that there might be as many as 400 of them in the Kirk, many of them younger ministers. 'Yes, they have been marginalised, and yes, a breakaway is possible,' he told me. 'If you look at the history of the Church of Scotland over the last 200 years or so, whenever it has become removed from Scripture, it has become indistinguishable from society. That is the position now. We have to go back to our Biblical roots and show the relevance of Scripture to the here and now. A secession could certainly come.' I asked what might force the matter, and he said either the issue of homosexuality – here echoing the Rev. Ian Watson of Caldercruix (see Chapter 3) – or interfaith worship. He did not think the latter was very likely to loom as an issue after the events of 11 September 2001 in the USA, but he thought that the ordination of openly homosexual clergy in the Church of Scotland could well, if it happened, lead to a division. 'For a start, you would have no Church of Scotland congregations north of Inverness, not one.'

I'm sure most secular observers would think that a modern and mature church should be able to accommodate frankly homosexual clergy without too much difficulty; but, when you have a significant minority of ministers in the Kirk believing that their concerns about such matters are not being taken seriously, then you are, at best, creating a debilitating sense of discontent and, at worst, sowing the seeds of secession. Again, if a body of ministers believes that it is not only being ignored but, worse, deliberately ostracised, then you will get not one but two vitiating outcomes. You are almost certainly going to get serious unpleasantness of one kind or another, for that is the inevitable consequence of smouldering resentment; and, more specifically, you are not going to be able to reach a sensible and inclusive resolution of doctrinal difficulties.

There are two loose groupings within the Kirk which, in recent years, have appealed to those of a conservative evangelical disposition. There is the Crieff Fellowship, which concentrates on prayer and mutual support, and there is Forward Together, a broad conservative grouping. But my understanding is that, for various reasons, neither of these is overtly political and that neither would or could form a focus for discontented evangelicals to take action. I am aware that some of those on the liberal side of the Kirk – the side apparently in the ascendancy at present – would regard the views of the conservative evangelicals on, say, homosexuals as little short of repellent and would take the view 'if that is what they believe, and they want to leave the Church, then good riddance'. I myself don't see homosexuality itself as a problem – as I said at the end of Chapter 9, I think it is promiscuity, homosexual or hetero-sexual, which is the evil – but then my views are not particularly important here. I would rather sum up this section by making three simple points.

1. The Church of Scotland is in no position to lose the services of any group of dedicated and committed ministers.

2. Dialogue is better than stand-off.

3. What I have described above does not yet constitute a core problem for the Kirk. But there is deep unhappiness and unease among a minority of ministers who have much to offer a ministry that is already overstretched. Should a forceful and politically effective leader of the conservative evangelicals emerge, what is at present a chronic difficulty could develop into an acute crisis, and quickly.

12

THE DOOR CREAKS

❖

Religion is booming in most parts of the world. And Christianity is doing particularly well, mainly thanks to the Catholic Church. It is worth reiterating that Christianity is both the world's biggest religion and its fastest-growing one. But here in Britain? Here, Christianity is fading (and failing) fast. Missionaries are now coming *to* Britain – from Chile, from the Czech Republic, from Brazil, from the USA, from many other countries. Recently, the Anglican Archbishop of Brazil issued a clarion call to Brazilian missionaries to go to Britain and 'save London' by returning its godless people to Jesus Christ.

Cardinal Cormac Murphy O'Connor, leader of the Catholic Church in England and Wales, said in Leeds that Christians in Britain now had to adapt to an 'alien culture'. He called for *revolutionary* thinking on how his church could reach lapsed Catholics, non-believers and young folk. 'Christianity as a background to people's lives and moral decisions and to the government and to the social life of Britain has almost been vanquished', he announced. People had turned to consumerism, and to the transient pleasures of alcohol, drugs and recreational sex, rather than to God.

A little before the Cardinal's pronouncement, the Archbishop of York, Dr David Hope, had made an equally gloomy assessment from the perspective of the Church of England. In an exceptionally eloquent sermon at Cambridge University, Dr Hope warned that the spiritual health of England was in jeopardy, no less. He said his church was failing in its duty to help a 'spiritually lost' people. He condemned the mountain of paperwork and the labyrinthine bureaucracy that were stifling his church (sounds familiar?). He said he wanted a less institutionalised organisation, with fewer committees, fewer boards and fewer management structures. He spoke of the danger of institutional arrangements becoming ends in themselves, dictating the nature, shape and function of the church. He said: 'There are deep spiritual yearnings and longings. Large numbers of people say they pray. But they are not into religion.' Later, Dr Hope reiterated his message: 'We need a more dynamic, more flexible and more responsive church'.

In August 2001, a poll by NOP showed that 43 per cent of Christians in Britain thought that the existence of the churches in Britain put more people *off* Christianity than attracted them. Only 40 per cent of those questioned thought that Jesus Christ would go to church if he were alive in Britain today. The position is currently worse in England than in Scotland; but there is absolutely no room for complacency, as the decline in Scotland is faster. And, to be fair to the Church of England, it has in at least one direction confronted the need for change. It has embraced many positive figures from beyond England. Bishop Nazir Ali is from Pakistan; in London, there is an Anglican bishop from Uganda and there are parish priests from Congo, Nigeria, the West Indies and many other countries. A (brave) Ugandan minister even does so-called 'faith slots' between the acts of stand-up comedians in Leeds working men's clubs.

Unfortunately, this ability to take on assistance from elsewhere appears to be lacking in the Church of Scotland (although, as I shall explain later in this chapter, its leading conservative intellectual is an Englishman). One of the more passionate interventions during the 2001 General Assembly came from a foreign delegate who pointed out that hardly any Asians or Africans were Kirk ministers here in Scotland. But this is where they are needed. I simply cannot understand why the Kirk deems it necessary to maintain so many foreign ministries when there are 169 vacant charges in our own backyard.

And I have to say that the Kirk seems to find it easier to talk about mission when it is talking about mission to a foreign land. Mission is desperately needed in Scotland, and now. One of the wisest slogans of the twentieth century (and I wish more people had paid attention to it) was *Think globally, act locally*. That is what the Kirk has to learn to do, and quickly. In Scotland, we are still, just about, a Christian people; but we are well on the way to becoming a godless nation. Time is not on the Kirk's side.

Before I go on to ask what has gone so terribly wrong here at home when Christianity is flourishing in so many other parts of the globe, let me quote, once again, my atheist friend George Rosie. 'I'm totally unimpressed by claims that churches are piling on adherents in places like Africa, Latin America and Asia,' he said in his customary robust manner. 'The poor and the uneducated and the desperate are usually more credulous than the rest of us. And, given the way that Western culture and technology have been rolling across the world in the past fifty years, it's hardly surprising that the winners' religion appears attractive.' Well, there is a good deal of truth in that, although I would say that in some Islamic countries this idea of 'winning' is resented and actually makes Islam stronger; and it is also important to remember that Christianity is booming in the USA, the world's most powerful and prosperous, if by no means its best-educated, nation. This is especially the case in California, the most vibrant state, where the Los Angeles County Board of Supervisors has recently had to impose a moratorium on church-building, as so many new churches have been built in the past few years. One resident of Los Angeles was quoted as saying: 'Nobody is against churches, but there comes a point when they are taking over residential neighbourhoods'.

So, just what has gone wrong here in Britain, and in Scotland in particular? The decline has been alarmingly rapid. I have heard Finlay Macdonald reminiscing, once publicly and once privately, about the time he played the organ as an 18-year-old in a Church Extension kirk in Dundee when there were 600 (yes, 600) in the Sunday school.

I asked Andrew McLellan, who travelled the world as moderator, to give an overview, and he obliged me with a list of reasons for the decline here. The Kirk had completely failed to engage young people and to communicate the gospel to them. That applied to Western Europe generally. Then he made two particular criticisms of the Church of Scotland: it had been on the side of the comfortable, not the weak; and, in worship, it had tolerated the second-rate and the second-best. 'We regard John Bell as remarkable and exceptional –

but we should have fifty John Bells,' he said. 'We have not encouraged creativity.'

The seriousness of the current crisis is grimly indicated in figures I received from Prof. Steve Bruce. In 1980, the percentages of the adult population who were church members or who attended church in parts of Great Britain were as follows: England 13, Wales 23, Scotland 37. So, in comparative terms, twenty years ago we were not doing well, but not doing too badly either. But now look at the percentages for 2000: England 8, Wales 8, Scotland 13. In other words, Scotland is moving fast towards the English nadir.

Steve went on to note that Scotland, when it recently established its Parliament, did not take the opportunity to give a position of 'social honour' to its own distinctive religious tradition, that is, Presbyterianism. Rather, the favoured option was for what he called 'a lowest-common-denominator religious input' that aimed to be as comprehensively inclusive as possible. And that, Steve concluded, 'is important as a factual reminder to Willie Storrar and those who want to argue that the national church has some special role to play as the guarantor of national identity'.

And that leads me neatly on to the question of whether the Church of Scotland is, or should be, a national church. It certainly thinks it is: the *Year Book 2001/2002* (p. 19) has a definitive reference to its being a national church with a responsibility to all the people of Scotland on a territorial basis. I asked Andrew McLellan about this. Would it not help to release energy and creativity within the Kirk if it stopped trying to be a national church? Would it not be set free? Andrew said: 'Well, yes, if you abandon being or aspiring to be the national church, you are freed up. But the price to be paid is that you would then abandon that sense of care that good ministers, sessions and congregations have for *everyone* in their parish. Inevitably, Catholics, Episcopalians, Baptists and others in Scotland see their pastoral responsibility as being to their own folk, whereas we see it as being to everybody, including people who are members of no church at all. Also, if we are a national church, we can engage more easily with the established national structures and ensure that in that way we are contributing to the life of the nation.'

That veteran and most astute of commentators on the Kirk's affairs, Bob Kernohan, former editor of *Life & Work*, author of various books on the Kirk, and long-serving elder at Cramond, told me: 'The essential problem now is that the Church of Scotland does not have the residual strength of a national church or an established church, even if the people in that church don't attend much. Neither does it have the evangelical strength and vigour of a free and independent church.' Bob Kernohan, incidentally, edited a fascinating series of reflections on Presbyterianism and Calvinism in the new Scotland, published by the Handsel Press in 1999 under the title *The Realm of Reform.* The centrepiece essay in the collection was by Professor David F. Wright of New College, a scholarly Englishman who is much more committed to the Kirk than most Scots are (he is an elder at Holyrood Abbey and was not so long ago nominated for the moderatorship). Indeed, he could legitimately be described as the Kirk's leading conservative intellectual. This essay, 'The Kirk: National or Christian?', is cerebral and challenging, and says a great deal in a few pages; but I attempt here a précis, which I have checked with David himself.

He suggests that the Church of Scotland would do well to concentrate on its core mission to the people of Scotland, while shedding any aspirations to be a national institution. In so doing, it could be liberated to tilt more effectively at so much that is wrong in modern Scotland. In other words, the Kirk should be prepared *not* to be a national body, and in some ways even to be anti-Scottish, were that necessary; or at least to be against the prevalent Scottish *mores.* I think that just about serves as a summation of the thrust of this brilliantly argued piece; but let me now quote four specific points from David's essay:

> My concern is with the peculiar temptations that may seduce a church like the present-day Church of Scotland, which remains national in name, and even remains proud of it, when the reality is a thing of the past . . . We lack the stuff that martyrs are made of, and so we will decline to enter the lists against the mocking taunts of the irreverent. If we still hold to any convictions that unbelievers might object to, we will keep them to ourselves. Accommodation is the order of the day . . . There is a real risk that without a realistic reappraisal of its position a national-minority church ends up with the worst of all worlds – with neither the recognition and influence appropriate to national status nor the freedom of action and initiative

indispensable for a minority body ... The Church of Scotland's national network of parish churches offers immense opportunities for a nation-wide ministry of the gospel. Any other national role looks increasingly like dangerous self-delusion. If the national church holds anything in trust for the Scottish people it can only be the faith of Christ crucified and risen, not some all-encompassing consensus redolent of a pre-pluralist Britain.

When I spoke to David in New College, just over two years after he had written this superb essay, he told me: 'My greatest hope is that more people in the Kirk will recover confidence in the gospel. I want to see the Church becoming explicitly missionary again, here in Scotland. This includes evangelism and outreach. I'd like a church that is vibrant in its Christian ministry and its distinctiveness. This might seem provocative or insensitive in our multicultural world; but Christianity made its way in such a world, seeking converts.'

And what about the national nature of the Kirk? 'I am not averse to the Church of Scotland seeking to maintain its ministry to all the people in every parish, but I am very much afraid that increasingly this will be seen as a social ministry, not a ministry of faith. Too many ministers suffer from a lack of confidence and a loss of nerve. And the elders are even worse. They have been bowled over by the strong forces of secularism. Far too many of our ministers are driven by sentiment rather than doctrine.'

I'd like to develop this theme that too many of the key people in the Kirk have lost their nerve and have been bowled over (if not knocked out) by the strong, and often bad, forces of the secular world around us. As I said at the start of this book, the situation of the Kirk is dire. It is dire not so much because of the huge decline in members and ministers – that merely represents the *immediate* crisis – but because the utter indifference of the secular world out there has destroyed its self-confidence. I don't think there is much actual hostility – which is a pity, in a way, for the Kirk is at its best when it is fighting obvious and dangerous enemies. Indifference is a more dangerous and insidious enemy.

It is as if a tiny prayer meeting is going on outside the big top. Inside the huge tent, the circus is in full swing, with music and clowning and laughter and thrills, and no thought of tomorrow; outside, the handful of Christians are ignored as the people have their fun. But the circus has to end. Some people will stop and listen to the Christians before they drift off into the night. The circus moves on; its values and its delights are transitory. The Christians must be there, always.

And so, while the situation is indeed desperate, for committed Christians that should represent a challenge and an opportunity. Indeed, this should be an exciting rather than a grim time for the Kirk. As Peter Neilson says, the Church of Scotland is on a cusp. 'This is exactly the time that we can move forward, from demoralisation to hope', he told me. I agree. Times are bad; but this is the very time for renewal to commence. The fightback should – must – start now; and what the Kirk needs more than any other quality is confidence. It has lost confidence, partly because it has succumbed to a world that has lost spirituality. The Kirk needs to give people their spiritual life back; and, to do that, it needs to recover its own self-confidence, in abundance.

But before confidence can surge back into the Kirk, it needs to sort out some pressing problems (and, to a large extent, that is what this book is about). One problem which is evident in the above discussion about whether or not it is a national church is the confusion about its role. Prof. Bruce, the academic outsider, dismisses the notion that it is still connected with our national identity; Prof. Wright, the academic insider from the conservative evangelical wing, wants it to set itself free by not being a national institution except as an agent of national mission, of proclaiming the gospel in every parish; while Dr McLellan, from the liberal wing, wishes it to retain a more comprehensive national role, including engaging with other national structures.

If we come back to this key issue of confidence, I think the Kirk must retain (or rather regain) a high national profile. That could come partly through a confidence-inspiring ability to organise mass outdoor worship, particularly at Easter, with inspirational preaching to the people, plus a Church of Scotland mass choir and goodness knows what else. As I said in Chapter 8, I don't see why this kind of mission should be left to the likes of the Pope or Dr Billy Graham (who are not in Scotland that often anyway). The Kirk might not be able to gather as many people as the Pope, but it might be surprised if it really tried. And, as Sir Timothy

Clifford says, this type of event can be really exciting, and it appeals to the young.

At the same time, I agree completely with Andrew McLellan that the Kirk needs to keep engaging with the other, secular, national structures. Elizabeth Holt, one of the most perceptive and sympathetic members of Edinburgh's diplomatic corps (she is Head of Representation for the European Commission in Scotland), told me she thought that the Church of Scotland was impressively good at organising ceremonies at the time of the Assembly, and big services at St Giles. 'It is good at that sort of thing, but this is a world that is closed to many people in Scotland. It does not seem to be involved that much elsewhere in public life. I know that some of its committees have visited Brussels; but it does not, for example, seem to be involved much in the development of social policy. I mean by this that, in the new Scotland, new conduits of influence are opening up, and the Church of Scotland does not seem to be making use of them.' Most senior diplomats have to send regular despatches back to headquarters, reporting on what is going on in the country where they are based – and Elizabeth is no exception. I pressed her as to how often the Kirk featured in her reports. 'Well, to be honest, hardly at all', she said. She added: 'I'm not sure who takes the strategic view in the Church of Scotland, the view of where it is going and what it is trying to do in the wider world'.

Part of this is about communication; and, as I said in Chapter 4, it is high time that the Kirk appointed a high-profile principal spokesperson. I know that these matters are far removed from the core mission of proclaiming the good news about Jesus Christ in the parishes; but they are important when it comes to this issue of confidence and self-belief. The Kirk's founding fathers were well aware of the interconnection between their spiritual mission and the political realities of the day. They also understood that to engage in the secular structures of the day need not involve kow-towing to the secular powers that be, or grovelling to the forces of the state.

Indeed, it would be nothing short of disastrous if the Kirk ever got itself into the perilous position of the Church of England. Its senior archbishop, who is also the Primate of All England and President of the Anglican Communion, has to give official advice to the government (a government that in turn, through the prime minister, can veto appointments in that church's hierarchy). No, the Kirk must remain a free church and not become part of the Establishment. It must simply be true to its roots – and its roots were political, in the most dynamic sense, as well as spiritual. And that takes me back into history.

It is a consistent theme of this book that far too many people in the Kirk are abysmally ignorant of its history. I am certain that, were there more knowledge of, and pride in, the Kirk's past, that too would help to create the necessary renewal of confidence and self-belief. I have been quite tough on the Kirk's performance in the 1920s and 1930s – the grim, dark days when it embraced racism – but this long and grisly episode was thankfully not typical. And, anyway, I would never argue that the Kirk should only look to the many glories of its past and ignore the dark and bad times. Winston Churchill once said, wisely: 'If we open a quarrel between the past and the present, we shall find that we have lost the future'. To help itself to gain the future, the Kirk must have more confidence in its past.

What the Kirk must surely learn to do is to understand and glory in the Scottish Reformation. My obsession with the sixteenth century might seem eccentric to some people; but I am convinced that, if today's Kirk had more knowledge of the heroism and zest of that era, it would be greatly strengthened to face the myriad tasks ahead. In this context, I believe that the Kirk, as well as learning to be proud of its greatest figure, John Knox, should become more aware of the significance of Martin Luther. Some people in the Kirk seem to want to dissociate themselves from any connection with Luther at all, while other more enlightened people still appear faintly embarrassed when his name is mentioned. I recall that Andrew McLellan gave a little involuntary shudder of distaste when I told him of my admiration for Luther. I know that the Kirk is a Calvinist and not a Lutheran church; but Luther had an immense influence on its founders. And, without Luther, what could Calvin or indeed Knox have done? Let us be more grateful to the greatest reformer of them all. Let us remember his profound influence on some of the most heroic Scots who have ever lived.

How many Scots have heard of Patrick Hamilton? How many members of the Kirk have heard of Patrick Hamilton? This ardent and valiant man was the first Scot known to have embraced Luther's doctrines, and the first Scot to produce significant Protestant theology. Hamilton was Commendator of the Abbey of Fearn (near Bonar Bridge in Easter Ross) at a very early age before going to study in Paris and Louvain. He returned to Scotland, and advocated reformed theology at St Andrews until he was forced to flee in 1527. He went to Germany, where he was privileged to meet Martin Luther. Returning to St Andrews, he bravely taught Lutheran ideas not just to the university students but also to the ordinary people of the town. He was tried for heresy, refused to recant, and was burned to death at the gate of St Salvator's College in February 1528, thereby becoming the first Protestant martyr of Scotland. A gentle but determined scholar, he said just before he died that he was 'content that my body burn in this fire for confessing my faith in Christ'. His long agony (it lasted six hours) was watched by Cardinal James Beaton, the man responsible for his arrest and condemnation. A noble and numinous life had ended; but something bigger had begun.

It was a time of martyrs across Europe; but, even among them, Hamilton stands out, for he apparently faced his horrible death with exceptionally serene bravery. From then on, Lutheranism began to take a shaky hold in various parts of Scotland. It was persecuted by the church authorities, and it was not strong; but it did flicker into life up and down the east coast, notably in St Andrews, where people were inspired both by Hamilton's teachings and by his personal courage, and also in other towns such as Montrose and Leith, ports where the Lutheran message was beginning to filter in from the continent. Henry Forrest, much influenced by Luther, was dean of an abbey on the Isle of May, in the Forth estuary. He proclaimed that Patrick Hamilton was not a heretic but a teacher of God's truth. He, too, was executed.

The work of Lutherans such as Hamilton, Forrest and others, like Alexander Alesius (who later tried to mediate between Lutherans and Calvinists), undoubtedly paved the way for the momentous work of George Wishart and John Knox. (Wishart, mild in persona but apparently a wonderful preacher, was also martyred, in St Andrews in 1546.) It is true that Knox was far more influenced by Calvin than by Luther; but he did acknowledge a debt to the latter.

I would never argue that the Kirk should be ashamed of its Calvinist traditions; but, when Calvinism has become something of a byword for meanness of the spirit, it might be no bad thing if the Church of Scotland were to rediscover its Lutheran roots. I am not saying that it should embrace Lutheran doctrines – of course not – but rather that it should acknowledge, with pride, the Lutheran influence on its beginnings.

I also want to make it clear that I do not wish the early Scottish Lutheran martyrs to be celebrated in any spirit of pernicious anti-Catholicism. Far from it. I just wish that many more Scots, and particularly Scots in the Church of Scotland, were aware of them, of their nobility and their valour. They were truly inspirational figures. It is true that the Scottish Reformation, when it really got going in the 1560s, was notably less bloody than reformations elsewhere. But we should never forget our early Scottish martyrs, those who lit up the trail. I should mention also that the greatness and vision of the Kirk was not confined to its early years. Prof. Tom Devine told me, for example, of a little-known period in its history, when it was notably compassionate and helpful to the very first wave of Irish immigrants in the early nineteenth century. Things obviously changed much later in the 1920s and 1930s, but I think it is indubitable that the Kirk has been, overall, a force for good in Scotland.

I asked Paul Scott CMG, president of the Saltire Society, and a leading Scottish historian, to comment on the Kirk's past and its relevance to the present. 'First, let me quote someone else and say that I may be an atheist, but I am a Presbyterian atheist!' he joked. 'I most definitely do not believe in the doctrines of the Christian religion; but my values, my ideas about how to live my life, have come at least in part from the Church of Scotland. Furthermore, I would say with confidence that its achievements and efforts have been prodigious over several centuries. It has maybe never been democratic as such; but it was, and perhaps still is, a great semi-democratic institution. I think it lost its national status after the Disruption of 1843, but its influence stays with us to this day. That influence is on the wane, yet we have never found another institution to replace it. We haven't found any kind of substitute for it. I wish that it could recover some of its authority. These days, it sometimes seems to lack courage, the courage to stand up and say what it thinks.'

I asked Paul to sum up its national influence, and its influence on him as an individual. 'The Church set very high standards. It emphasised the moral obligations we all have. Right from the start, it set great value on the importance of education, and that was very beneficial. It also emphasised the importance of public service. As for me personally, I do believe that I have taken some of my values from the Church. I mean, for example, its understanding that showing off, pomp and circumstance, and ostentation are bad things. Its teaching that life is not supposed to be easy. Its emphasis on the work ethic. These have helped to give me my own personal values.'

It is fascinating that such a splendid encomium comes from someone who is not just a historian but very much a man of the wider world. Before he returned to his native Edinburgh in 1980, Paul Scott had served with distinction as a career diplomat in places as diverse as La Paz, Havana, Montreal, Vienna and Milan. He got to know, among many others, Fidel Castro and the late Che Guevara, the Argentinian revolutionary. Since he returned to Scotland, he has thrown himself into the nation's cultural and intellectual life. He has written thirteen books on many aspects of Scottish history and literature. His high praise for the Kirk's legacy should be taken very seriously indeed.

In Chapter 6, I quoted George Rosie, another writer and atheist, warmly praising the Scottish Reformation. If outsiders and atheists can be so impressed, why on earth can't the Kirk itself take a bit of pride in its past, in its vast contribution? I am writing here in the context of the regaining of confidence. I'd like renewed confidence to sweep through the Church of Scotland like a bush fire. Confidence would surge back into the Kirk if it became less inhibited by its bureaucracy and its debilitating structure of more or less autonomous committees and boards (not to mention the interboard groups and the Central Co-ordinating Committee). *When in doubt, set up an another committee; but never get rid of an existing one* seems to be the reaction.

Rightly or wrongly, there is a lack of trust in 121 George Street, which cannot be helping the Kirk in its mission and which certainly militates against confidence. As Marjory MacLean, the first full-time depute clerk and a key insider who should know what she is talking about, told me: 'There is, unfortunately, a very wide diversity of ability among the Church's professional servants. Even worse, there is a wide diversity of graciousness. Institutional problems are holding us up, and we do have a lot of people who manufacture problems.'

Yet, I do not wish to focus overmuch on 121; there are more significant problems. One of them concerns the supreme body, the General Assembly itself. As presently constituted, it simply will not do. I think it oppresses the Kirk. I'd love to make it more relevant to ordinary people, inside the Kirk and without. I'd love to smash the hallowed veneration with which it is regarded by so many important people in the Kirk. But this will not be easy. Even such an enlightened and liberal figure as the Rev. Alan McDonald, convener of the Kirk's most outward-looking body, the Church and Nation Committee, told me: 'We as a committee are accountable to the Assembly, and we are passionate about our responsibility to it'.

Confidence would surge back into the Kirk if it had more money. It would surge back into it if it could find a renewed ability to speak to the people of Scotland. It would surge back into it if it could make more of an impact on the secular, postmodern, licentious age in which we are living, an age in which spirituality has been lost yet is still desperately sought. It would recover its confidence if it were less dreary in its affairs, if it could work better with the artistic and creative people who are all around, if it became more joyous and more adventurous. (I am not sure if I agree with Andrew McLellan about how bad worship is; having toured Scotland, sampling Sunday services at a variety of venues, I'd say that the main need is not so much to improve what is on offer as to get more far more people to experience it.) The Kirk would have more confidence if it would listen more to its great preachers (and it still has them). And confidence would surge back if it could find ways of getting those preachers to speak to bigger audiences.

Confidence would also be renewed if more congregations became more vibrant (this is what *Without Walls* is largely about; I hope it succeeds). The Kirk's single biggest immediate difficulty is its inability to recruit and retain a sufficient number of ministers. But, as Johnston McKay told me, the Kirk does not lose ministers – congregations do. Congregations must learn to realise how important their ministers are. They should be supporting them, never fighting them. They should also be asking just how many in their midst have the potential to be good and creative elders, *and also ministers*. The 1,000-plus ministers in the field need to be empowered, enfranchised and invigorated. It is imperative that their congregations understand this. That implies that the current 'one minister one congregation' system should remain. I certainly think it could for the time being, to get revival under way. As I have said, the ministers should be the elite troops, and the elders the shock troops. But, in due course, a more collaborative ministry, with teams and specialisms and creative centres, is going to become the norm. This change is not going to come overnight; but, as it gradually happens, it should be welcomed and facilitated.

Confidence would also surge back if the Kirk rediscovered leadership. And leadership is not incompatible with Presbyterianism or indeed with democracy. One of the outsiders I spoke to was the eminent Scottish Nationalist MSP Mike Russell. Mike is an Episcopalian. He told me: 'I've been brought up in a church that, whatever its faults, has form, substance and hierarchy. I'm not saying that the Church of Scotland should become hierarchical; but it has lost it shape. It is also joyless and confused. It needs leadership. It needs a John the Baptist figure, giving it a vision of where it is going and what it wants to achieve. I know that it is doing good work in terms of its practical social mission, to the elderly and so on – but what about the spirit?'

The theme of leadership, or the lack of it, was also stressed by Lord Sutherland of Houndwood, who – once, when he was younger – considered going into the Church of Scotland ministry. He is Principal of the University of Edinburgh, a member of its divinity faculty, and professor of the philosophy of religion at New College. He is, of course, also well known for the radical and visionary commission he chaired on the long-term care of Britain's elderly. Although not a member of the Kirk, he remains deeply sympathetic to it. He told me: 'I do miss the days when the Church of Scotland seemed to matter so much. There are still issues around that I am sure that the Church could debate much better than our new

Parliament could. But who is listening? The Church of Scotland cannot turn time back if our society has moved on. But it must not respond by falling prey to every fashion. If relativism and materialism are all around us, people are going to be looking for a degree of comfort, consolation and certainty – all sorts of things. The Church can provide these, but it desperately needs leadership.'

Neither Lord Sutherland nor Mike Russell said so, but there is an undercurrent of suspicion among many outsiders that, these days, the Kirk does not like leaders and it wants to bring them down to size. Presbyterianism has been mocked as the governance of the few by the many, but there is a sad element of truth in that pastiche. There are visionary, vigorous individuals around in the Kirk; these are the people who can be inspirational, and they need to be nurtured and encouraged, not cabined and confined. People often confuse effective communication with leadership. They are not the same thing; but confidence would surge back into the Kirk if more people could hear its message coming across loud and clear. Confidence would return if the Kirk had a more effective overall communication strategy. A principal spokesperson (to be called the Kirk's Speaker?) would not only raise the Kirk's profile but would also allow others within the Kirk to speak out without fearing that they were going to be somehow interpreted as official spokespersons for the whole Kirk. In sum, the Church of Scotland still has so very much to offer Scotland, if only it could recover its confidence.

I have been writing about what I (and others) think should happen. What will happen? I am not that good at predictions, let alone prophecy; but let me essay a few thoughts. I suspect that, in the short term, the Kirk will continue to shed members fast, unless a very radical series of actions is taken. As it is unlikely that they will be taken, the terrible danger is that the Kirk will eventually reduce to what might be called a core level, from where it cannot reduce much further. This process would certainly help to free up ministers, who would then be dealing with much smaller, committed congregations instead of bigger ones with plenty of non-committed hangers-on.

But I suspect that the ministry would in any case be moving away from the dwindling congregations and into chaplaincies and team centres. Regular worship might actually start taking place in very small groups, in people's homes. Some ministers would be dedicated and enthusiastic chaplains serving where they are clearly needed and wanted, in prisons and hospitals. I am not saying for a moment that it is easy to be a chaplain in such contexts; but at least there is sustenance in the knowledge that you are needed. It is possibly less easy to be a chaplain where there is indifference, for example in a secondary school or a factory. Anyway, such a church – smaller, harder and inevitably even more inward-looking – would have a higher proportion of really dedicated members. But I would worry if the seemingly inexorable decline to such a diminished church could be spun as any kind of positive. There would certainly be fewer passengers; but it would be an embattled 'us against the world' church.

Would it show compassion, and would it be at all effective at outreach? Would it even be interested in outreach? Would it want to do anything but preach to the converted? Would it be able to speak to the people of Scotland (so many of whom, I am convinced, want to hear what the Kirk has to say)? I doubt it. I'd hate to see defeatism masquerading as realism – a belief that decline is inevitable, that nothing and nobody can halt it, and that anyway there are gains and strengths in being a tiny, cellular organisation. But such a body would become introspective, self-obsessed, perhaps bitterly so, and hardened against the outside world. It would lose any notion of risk-taking, and it would forget how to be compassionate to outsiders, to the lost sheep and the prodigal sons. It would not be Christian in the best and most beautiful sense of the term. Although its members might not realise it, it would be a demoralised church because it had accepted failure and – worse – pretended that failure was some kind of success. I have a terrible fear that certain people in the Kirk almost want this to happen.

If I may paraphrase the Rev. Peter Neilson (and I hope he will forgive me), we have come to a fork. We can continue to move down the path of demoralisation and decline. Or we can start renewal and revival, now. I hope, most earnestly, that the Church of Scotland takes the latter course. It is the more difficult, the more risky course. It is also the brave course and the right one.

I had thought of calling this concluding chapter 'Towering Beneath Us'. The phrase suddenly came to me when I was considering the Kirk's dilemma. It is still a big organisation with so many good and dedicated people working for it, a great edifice of decency and commitment, and yet somehow not showing above ground where it can be easily seen. Not that I would like a gargantuan, overweening Kirk that would loom over the people and scare them and bully them. But I would like a Kirk that is more visible and is heard much more.

As I reach the end of this book, I realise that I have been confused. When I was a journalist, I was used to looking at what might be called targets. This was wrong; that was wrong. This had to be done; that had to be done. The Church of Scotland is so infuriatingly elusive; it is not a meaningful target at all. It has much wrong with it, yet the paradox is that its component parts and its servants are for the most part overwhelmingly good. If I compare it to some other component parts of the Scottish anatomy – the law, the media, education, the finance sector, even the worlds of medicine and science – it is in a different class. It may not be as loud or as efficient or as well managed or as obviously relevant or as successful, in temporal terms; but it is better. *Yet it is nothing like as good as it should be.* I wish that it could cohere more as a godly body, and gather its constituent strengths more effectively.

I am conscious that I have been assisted by so many kind people; I wish them well, and wish them strength for the struggles to come. I have been supported in particular by Finlay Macdonald and Andrew McLellan, both of whom I wish to quote as I near the close. Finlay told me: 'We do need to celebrate and proclaim Jesus Christ simply and effectively. And we must not allow our Presbyterian and reformed traditions to be sold short. Our church affirms participation and the value of *everyone*. I do think that it is intensely democratic. But you are not bound to agree with what the majority decides. We recognise conscience. But we have a lot to turn round. I think you are right to emphasise the importance of the ministry. Part, a very important part, of the minister's function is to harness the goodwill and talent of people outside the Church. And we must not be overly judgemental. We must get people to come along, to look and to listen. We must challenge them, but we must also include them.'

These words echo some of the themes of a fine sermon Andrew preached during his year as moderator. Let me quote from it: 'Jesus' central message was the unlimited, unconditional grace of God. Not just to the hard-working, not just to the religious, not just to men, not just to the healthy, not just to the covenanted people of God; but God's unlimited, unconditional free grace. There is no place where God's grace stops. There is no person who must remain outside. It was that message that Jesus preached from the start. It was that message he lived from first to last. It was for that theology that they tried to throw him over a cliff. And it was for that theology that he was crucified. For that theology stands in judgement on all ownership of God. Whenever people think God is ours, the gospel of Jesus says: No. Wherever people think they have special rights, special privileges, special claims on the grace of God, Jesus says: No.'

To live the Church of Scotland more or less night and day for six months is a peculiar and, on the whole, very rewarding experience, although some of my friends tell me I have become a terrible Holy Willie, or even a Holy Harry. I know I should have spoken to more people in the Kirk; but I ran out of time. And I am also aware that the more I knew, the less I knew. The Church of Scotland is a perplexing, elusive and complex organisation. Anyway, as I wrestled with its problems and its potential, I became aware of a fantasy, a strange imagining. It was a kind of recurring daydream that was nagging at me. Sometimes it would disappear for days, then it would suddenly return as I was driving to yet another manse – or even, dare I say it, as I was listening to yet another sermon. It would come and go. Let me relate it in the form of a little story.

There is a small rural kirk. The beadle walks in with the Bible. The minister enters and climbs into the pulpit and starts the service.

The only problem is: the church is empty. Even the beadle has gone.

Does the minister continue? Yes, the minister continues. The minister is defiant; the minister speaks with that sublime, compassionate defiance which is Christianity at its best. Not bigotry, nor fanaticism, nor mania, nor any of the other distortions of the message of Christ – just a defiant, persistent compassion.

The minister continues to speak with compassion to the people who are not there.

And then the door creaks. Someone comes in. And then someone else. And then someone else.

13

ENVOI

A WARM NIGHT IN MADEIRA STREET

It is Friday, 4 January 2002, and we are building up to the first weekend of the New Year. Edinburgh's young revellers, some of whom appear to have been partying non-stop for five days, are carousing noisily in the city centre's overflowing pubs, warming up for a night of excess and clubbing. Meanwhile, a mile or so to the north, in a dark street in Leith, a group of church people is working flat out in a small, hot kitchen. The kitchen is adjacent to North Leith Church hall, and a team from the Kirk, comprising five women and two men, is preparing a substantial meal for the city's homeless, some of whom will be spending the night in the church hall. The Kirk team doesn't know how many are coming; it could be as few as ten, but they are preparing for as many as fifty.

This is a collaborative effort with the Bethany Christian Trust, an ecumenical organisation that does first-class work with the unfortunates who find themselves on the extreme margins of the boom city. I am to witness the serving of the meal and the general preparations for what should be a period of respite, comfort and warmth on a bitterly cold night. I am allowed to be present on the strict understanding that no camera and not even a notebook will be produced. The Bethany team of three is led by Iain, a tall, shaven-headed and quite tough-looking young Baptist. His colleagues are a young Indian minister and an older woman from the Free Church. The North Leith Church team is led by Juana Molina, an elder who originally hailed from Chile. This is only the second time they have used their hall (and their kitchen) for this work, and I sense a very slight apprehension on Juana's part as she explains to me what is about to happen. I am keen to make myself useful; and, when the van arrives in Madeira Street with the sleeping kit (blankets and thin mattresses), I help to unload it, and then I join in setting up the six big tables. (I stay well away from the kitchen, for reasons that my family will understand.)

Just before the first of the homeless people are brought down from the city centre in vans, Iain gives a low-key briefing. He and his two colleagues are experienced in dealing with the homeless and will be on hand throughout the night, should there be any trouble or difficulty. He warns us not to expect any gratitude; we may be called 'fucking Christian bastards' as we serve the hot meals. And then Iain, as he stands in the kitchen, takes a little service. There is not room for all eleven people in the kitchen, so two or three of us stand outside by the serving hatch. Iain gives a brief reading from Matthew's gospel, reminds us that Jesus Christ is very much with the people we are about to welcome, and then – to my great surprise – asks us, later on that night, to pray. He says that the most helpful thing we can do is to pray for the homeless. Indeed, he beseeches us: please, later on, pray for them.

I say to my great surprise, because all around us is the practical evidence of utilitarian assistance: bubbling urns, the rich smell of heating food, the black sacks full of bedding. This is pragmatic and direct help for the poor and the outcast; yet, in the midst of it, Iain tells us that the most helpful thing we can do is to pray. And then the guests start arriving. All ages, and mainly men, though there are one or two women. They seem quite cheerful. Most of them start preparing their 'beds' with a dignified intensity; one or two lie down and try to get to sleep by the walls of the warm hall straight away. Soon a few are sitting at the tables, ready for the meal. (Big helpings of mince, plus potatoes and veg; and lots of white and brown bread. Plenty of hot tea and coffee, and fruit juice also.)

The younger guests seem quite dour, but some of the older people are talkative, even garrulous. I chat with Davie, a very small man with twinkling eyes, and he shows me his proudest possession, his mouth organ. He was brought up in Belfast, had served in the Pioneer Corps, and had then spent some time in Greenock. He asks me if I know any pubs in Greenock, and I mention the Melrose. This seems to please him enormously, and I feel my credibility going up a notch. Sitting beside Davie is Delia, a Jamaican woman of indeterminate age. She tells me she finds Edinburgh too cold, and she is going to move to Plymouth, though she is not sure how she will get there. I ask why Plymouth; she says it will be warmer there, and there are a lot of sailors, and they are good people. I say there are sailors in Leith, and she seems surprised. I notice that both Davie and Delia are eating a lot of bread, though they don't finish their mince. Another woman, Betty, tells Davie to stop talking and eat up his mince.

The minister of North Leith, Alistair McGregor, arrives, although he is on holiday. He spends an hour or so moving round, working the hall – but not working as a politician would, with ostentation. Alistair is quiet and self-effacing. I notice that he takes care to speak to just about everyone in the hall. More guests arrive, taking the numbers up to about twenty. I am told that, on Friday nights, some homeless people are reluctant to leave the streets, as this is the night when the clubbers and carousers tend to be generous. There is no unpleasantness at all, though after the puddings are served a couple of men rather aggressively demand more mince, which they get.

Davie tells me: 'We're fair getting the VIP treatment tonight'. He gets his moothie out and starts playing loudly. Betty does a little impromptu dance with one of the men from the church. Most of those who are already in their 'beds', trying to sleep, make no objection to the noise, though one does, loudly, thus raising the volume further. A few more guests arrive. One man, Bob, who has terrible eczema, proudly shows me a new tube of cream he had got from the medical mission in the Cowgate that morning. Another man is reading a week-old newspaper with great concentration.

I am thinking about how far removed all this is from the stuff about presbytery restructuring and the like, with which I had been grappling. That seems irrelevant. Then I am surprised for the second time in the night. I fall into conversation with the Indian minister. I ask him which denomination he belongs to, but he refuses to tell me, saying it does not matter. Then he tells me he had been seconded to 121 George Street for a period. He actually asks me if I think there is enough connection between 121 and the rest of the

Kirk. I say I had just been wondering whether such issues were important at all. Oh yes, he says; they are important all right.

It is approaching 11:30, time for lights out. Juana and her team in the kitchen are clearing up. They will be back, sharpish, in the morning to tidy and clean the hall for its next activity. Iain explains that those who cannot – or do not want to – sleep (and Davie, for one, certainly seems to fall into this category) can move to the lobby, where there are seats and the lights will stay on. He and his two colleagues will be there all night.

I say my goodbyes; and, as I slip out into the street, I sense someone behind me. It's Iain. 'I'd like you to put in your book that we are very grateful to the Church of Scotland,' he says. 'For all the support they give us. They are really good people to work with.'

I wish him well. As I walk down the street, is it my imagination, or do I hear the faint sound of Davie's mouth organ wafting through the cold night air? I think so: a wee epiphany in Madeira Street.

And an hour or so later, for the third time on this night, I am surprised. I remember to pray.

READING LIST

❖

Unfortunately, most books about the Church of Scotland are dreary and jejune. This also applies to a lot of books about Christianity in general. What follows is a brief and selective guide, not just to those books I have found useful, but also to books that I can recommend with genuine enthusiasm. First, there are two indispensable reference works.

Scottish football has its 'Wee Red Book'; the Kirk has its 'Big Red Book', better known as *The Church of Scotland Year Book* (issued annually by Saint Andrew Press). The amount of information crammed into its 400 pages almost defies belief – and it is clearly presented, too. I gather there is a small fraternity of Kirk anoraks whose main aim in life is to find errors in the *Year Book* – an exceptionally difficult task. I have spotted one, so I suppose I am now a member of that sad club. I have consulted the book several times every day for the past six months. It has become my Bible, if I can be forgiven the joke. I'd like to congratulate its editor, the Rev. Ronald Blakey.

The other book I found invaluable was the utterly magnificent *Dictionary of Scottish Church History and Theology*. Again, an extraordinary amount of information (and interpretation) is packed into one volume (a very big volume in this case: more than 900 pages). It was published by T&T Clark in 1993 after ten years of preparation. There were more than 250 contributors, from all over the world. The senior general editor was Prof. David F. Wright of New College, to whom I am greatly indebted.

A much slimmer volume is R. D. Kernohan's *Our Church* (Saint Andrew Press, 1985), the best general guide to the Church of Scotland. Bob Kernohan also edited *The Realm of Reform* (Handsel Press, 1999), a stimulating series of essays on Protestantism in the new Scotland. This volume includes notable contributions from Bob Kernohan himself, Prof. Will Storrar, Johnston McKay, Stewart Lamont and Russell Barr, as well as a quite brilliant essay by Prof. David F. Wright.

There are also some fascinating essays in *Scottish Christianity in the Modern World* (T&T Clark, 2000). This book, edited by Prof. Stewart J. Brown and Prof. George Newlands, was prepared in honour of Prof. A. C. Cheyne of New College. Some of the material in it is recondite; some of it is pleasingly eccentric, while Prof. Brown's own essay on 'Presbyterians and Catholics in Twentieth-Century Scotland' is masterful.

The most inspirational book about any aspect of the Church of Scotland in the last century is Ron Ferguson's authorised biography of *George MacLeod* (Collins, 1990). I do not have the appropriate superlatives for this book. It captures graphically the turbulent and teeming life of the Kirk's greatest modern figure. I arranged for the pre-publication serialisation of this exceptional book in *The Herald*; I was fan of it then and am even more of a fan of it now.

A constant theme of the present book has been that the Kirk needs to regain some pride in, and some knowledge of, its past, and the Reformation period in particular. The key figure was, of course, John Knox. I believe that if you don't understand John Knox, you don't understand the Church of Scotland. There are many biographies; and, as I write this, yet another one is about to hit the bookshops. The plethora of books about Knox makes it all the more remarkable that so many people in Scotland seem to know so little about this extraordinary man. Opportunist and visionary, rabble-rouser and prophet, demagogue and political thinker – he was all of these. He was not just the Kirk's greatest figure, but Scotland's greatest figure.

I think the best introduction to Knox's life is Stewart Lamont's *The Swordbearer* (Hodder & Stoughton, 1991). This is a short book, but all the essentials are there; and it is written with tremendous gusto, a quality that its subject had in abundance. A longer, less accessible and more reflective book is Lord Eustace Percy's *John Knox* (Hodder & Stoughton, 1938). I sought out this book after noting that it was recommended by Prof. James McEwen. Prof. McEwen delivered the Croall Lectures at New College in 1960, and they were published in book form by the Lutterworth Press in 1961 under the title *The Faith of John Knox*. McEwen makes it clear that Knox was not a mere undeviating disciple of Calvin, but a man who developed his own considerable political thought and his own theology.

McEwen counsels people not to read Edwin Muir's biography of Knox. 'Not so much a biography as a sustained sneer', he says. I would concur with this advice. Silly nastiness of this kind should be avoided at all costs. At the time this book was published in 1929, it was fashionable to deride Knox; McEwen, writing in 1960, sadly felt that, thirty years later, Muir's book still had a considerable vogue with those 'who confuse historical criticism with mere malice'. A useful reassessment of Knox's tempestuous career came out in 1998. *John Knox and the British Reformations*, edited by Roger Mason (Ashgate Publishing), contains thirteen reappraising essays. Particularly rewarding are those by James Kirk, Carol Edington, David F. Wright and Jenny Wormald.

Readers will note that I have shied away from, rather than engaged in, theology. But I have learned enough to know that one of the most influential Protestant theologians of the last century has been the existentialist Paul Tillich. I have admitted frankly that his *Systematic Theology* is beyond me; but his sermons are more readily understandable. I reckon that they are very sustaining to people who cannot take every single word in the Bible literally, but who want to have the fundamentals of the Christian faith developed and explained. This seems to me to be exceptionally important and helpful. His finest sermons were collected as *The Shaking of the Foundations* (SCM Press, 1949).

The principal sermons and speeches of Andrew McLellan's moderatorial year were collected as *Gentle and Passionate* (Saint Andrew Press, 2001). This is a lively and delightful book. As with Tillich, these sermons can be read for both comfort and challenge.

Two distinguished academics at Aberdeen University have written books that I can thoroughly recommend. Prof. Tom Devine's

The Scottish Nation 1700–2000 (Allen Lane: The Penguin Press, 1999) is beyond doubt the best general history of modern Scotland, and a worthy bestseller. Prof. Steve Bruce's *Religion in the Modern World* (Oxford University Press, 1996) examines the place of churches in our postmodern times from a strongly secular yet not wholly unsympathetic viewpoint.

Moving on to fiction, it is both sad and surprising that the Kirk has produced so very little outstanding literature. The best novel by a Church of Scotland minister is John MacDougall Hay's *Gillespie* (1914), an exuberant, hugely ambitious, over-the-top and altogether splendid exercise in what might be termed, if I may invent a phrase, Scottish Christian Gothic. Set in and around Tarbert, Loch Fyne, it has a stronger sense of place than any other Scottish novel I have read. It is very strong meat, not for the faint-hearted. The same can be said of the best novel about Presbyterianism in Scotland, which is John Galt's heroic *Ringan Gilhaize* (1823). This is, quite simply, a masterpiece. Both of these novels were recently reprinted by the Canongate Classics imprint.

John Buchan, a son of the manse, served as Lord High Commissioner and would have been an outstanding Kirk minister, had he so chosen. His best historical novel, *Witch Wood* (1927), is set in his favourite country, around Broughton and Tweedsmuir; it is about a young minister, David Sempill, and it presents a surprisingly hostile view of the seventeenth-century Kirk. Various editions of this very readable novel are currently available. J. G. Lockhart's *Adam Blair* (1822) is also about a minister (and about adultery). This was a novel ahead of its time. Edinburgh University Press produced an edition with a thoughtful introduction by David Craig in 1963.

In 2000, Saint Andrew Press published a fine anthology of *Scottish Religious Poetry*, edited by Meg Bateman, Robert Crawford and James McGonigal. This is the kind of book that becomes a friend.

Finally, it goes without saying that the Bible is the most important book of all. I won't stir the hornet's nest of which modern translation is the best. If we look at the best Christian writing *beyond* the Bible, a wonderful primer is *The Christian Testament Since the Bible*

(Penguin, 1986). This anthology has become a most stimulating resource for me. It contains extracts from masterpieces by a great variety of Christian writers, including Saint Augustine, Saint Francis of Assisi, Saint Teresa of Avila, Martin Luther, John Calvin, Saint Ignatius Loyola, Saint John of the Cross, Thomas Cranmer, John Bunyan, John Wesley, C. S. Lewis, Karl Barth, Mother Teresa, Dr Martin Luther King and Dr Billy Graham. In other words, it is a treasury.

ACKNOWLEDGEMENTS

—————— ❖ ——————

I have been helped by many people. Some of the assistance I received was relatively minor, yet still important to me; other people gave me a great deal of that most precious of commodities, time, and that has been much appreciated. I wish to thank the following:

Rev. Ewan Aitken, Ann Allen, Rev. Martin Allen, Richard Allen, Peter Andrews, Muriel Armstrong, Rev. Jane Barron, Katharine Beaven, Rev. John Bell, Rev. Shirley Blair, Rev. Graham Blount, Prof. Steve Bruce, Rev. Tony Bryer, Very Rev. John Cairns, Rev. Donald Campbell, 'Celia', Rev. John Chalmers, Rev. John Chambers, Sir Timothy Clifford, Alan Cowe, Rev. Mary Cranfield, Ann Crawford, Rev. Iain Cunningham, Sarah Davidson, Bishop Joe Devine, Prof. Tom Devine, Joanne Evans-Boiten, Cristine Ferguson, Rev. John Ferguson, Rev. Ron Ferguson, Rev. Sinclair Ferguson, Rev. Margaret Forrester, Alasdair Gibbons, Giles Gordon, Rosemary Goring, Donald Gorrie MSP, Rev. Peter Graham, Robin Hill, Pat Holdgate, Head of Representation Elizabeth Holt, Rev. Jack Holt, Lucy Holt, Fiona Hutchison, Rev. Gordon Kennedy, Bob Kernohan, Rev. Stewart Lamont, Helen Lennox, Colin McClatchie, Rev. Alan McDonald, Rt Rev. Finlay Macdonald, Brian McGlynn, Principal Andrew McGowan, Rev. Alistair McGregor, Rev. Johnston McKay, Rev. Marjory MacLean, Very Rev. Andrew McLellan, Helen McLeod, David McLetchie MSP, Liz Manson, Leon Marshall, Rev. Ian Maxwell, Rev. Peter Meager, Juana Molina, Rev. Derek

Morrison, Rev. John Munro, Rev. Peter Neilson, Ivor Normand, Father Ken Nugent, Rev. Fergus Robertson, Lynne Robertson, George Rosie, Donald F. Ross, Rev. John Russell, Mike Russell MSP, Rev. David Scott, Paul H. Scott CMG, Rev. Norman Shanks, Donald Smith, Ramsay Smith, Lord Sutherland of Houndwood, Stuart Trotter, Dr Graham Walker, Rev. Ian Watson, Rt Hon. Brian Wilson MP, Conrad Wilson and the Rev. Alastair Younger.

I also wish to thank the members of the Faculty of Divinity at the University of Edinburgh for electing me as a visiting fellow, and I owe particular thanks to the following members of the faculty: Dean Stewart J. Brown, Prof. Duncan Forrester, Principal David Lyall, Prof. Will Storrar and Prof. David F. Wright.

I wish to thank the Bethany Christian Trust; Duggie Cleeton, who has performed the minor miracle of rendering me about 10 per cent computer literate; and a man I've never met, the Rev. Ron Blakey, who edits the wonderful *Year Book*. I'd like also to thank my wife Julie and my daughter Catherine for their forbearance with 'Holy Harry'.

And, last but not least, the author most gratefully records the offer and acceptance of assistance from the Baird Trust during the preparation of this book.

APOLOGY

❖

I am aware that this book is perhaps too focused on Edinburgh. I said in Chapter 1 that Edinburgh is becoming a boom city and that, in the new Scotland, more and more – far too much, in fact – has been sucked into it. I believe that, because of this, Edinburgh will be more and more resented elsewhere in Scotland. The Kirk, as Scotland's second-greatest institution, could do Scotland a favour by devolving more and more; in my opinion, the General Assembly should definitely be peripatetic, and there is no reason whatever why the Kirk's headquarters should be in the capital city. Indeed, it should be moved in due course to either Stirling or Perth, which are both more centrally positioned. This would send a signal to the rest of Scotland that the Kirk was indeed concerned about equity, democracy and devolution. On the outskirts of these towns, suitable office accommodation could be rented at a very reasonable price. The building at 121 George Street could then be sold, and the Kirk would have made a great deal of money. (Edinburgh's property boom is such that many of the ministers and others who work at 121 simply cannot afford to live in Edinburgh anyway; they commute every day.) I am not proposing that 121 should be sold in the immediate future; this is a proposal that could be implemented in a few years' time.

Meanwhile, I confess that Edinburgh probably dominates this book disproportionately. I am based in the capital, as also are the superb research facilities which I have been using. In addition, the Kirk itself is very strongly rooted in Edinburgh; so much of its activity and work is concentrated in 121 George Street. As I pursued my researches, I did travel round Scotland quite a lot (to do so was not a chore but a glorious privilege) – but I am conscious that I could and should have spent more of the six months outwith Edinburgh. For this, I apologise.

INDEX OF PEOPLE

INDEX OF PLACES

INDEX OF SUBJECTS